MAKE NOISE

MAKE NOISE

A CREATOR'S GUIDE TO
PODCASTING
AND GREAT AUDIO STORYTELLING

Eric Nuzum

Workman Publishing
New York

Library of Congress Cataloging-in-Publication Data is available.

ISBN 978-1-5235-0455-8

Design by Becky Terhune

Photo credits: Getty: Hill Street Studios/DigitalVision p. 44 (bottom); Lucy Lambriex/ DigitalVision p. 44 (top); Michael Prince/The Forbes Collection/Contour by Getty Images p. 17; Robin Skjoldborg/Stone p. 44 (middle). **Courtesy of Eric Nuzum** p. 15. **Steve McFarland** p. 230. **Shutterstock:** Alexander Lysenko (background patterns); Olgastocker (background patterns); Sylverarts Vectors p. vi. **Photo by Stephen Stickler** p. 16.

Workman books are available at special discounts when purchased in bulk for premiums and sales promotions as well as for fund-raising or educational use. Special editions or book excerpts can also be created to specification. For details, contact the Special Sales Director at the address below or send an email to specialmarkets@workman.com.

Workman Publishing Co., Inc.
225 Varick Street
New York, NY 10014-4381
workman.com

WORKMAN is a registered trademark of Workman Publishing Co., Inc.

Printed in the United States of America
First printing December 2019

10 9 8 7 6 5 4 3 2 1

For Calvin

Q: What does your Daddy do?
Calvin: He tells stories.

CONTENTS

Welcome 1

1 Story. Character. Voice. 16

2 The Only Ten Words That Matter 31

3 Function and Form 50

4 Asking Questions 76

5 How to Tell a Story, aka Don't Be Boring 106

6 Audience Building 149

7   Leading Creative Teams 193

8   Time to Go Forward 226

Bonus Episode
Four Pivotal Moments in the History of Podcasting 232

Acknowledgments 250

Recommended Reading 252

Index 258

About the Author 264

WELCOME

Hi. I'm glad you are here.

I've been told to set my expectations low for this introduction, that "no one reads an introduction." Well, thank you for showing that assumptions are dangerous things and rarely work out the way people think. (That's a theme we'll touch on a lot in our time together.)

Let's start off with a truth: I've never heard a perfect podcast. Ever. I've also never heard a podcast that didn't have lots of room for improvement (including my own, by the way).

Even the best work I've ever done never felt fully finished to me. I felt there was always something I could do to make it better. That's one reason that I rarely go back and listen to things I've produced in the past—all I can hear are the things I should have caught, tweaked, improved, or fixed.

The French poet Paul Valéry once said, "A poem is never finished, it is only abandoned." The same can be said for a podcast episode.

A good audio creator balances confidence and humility. They have a clear and confident idea of what they want to create and how to create it, yet they also realize that the podcast will only be as good as they make it. The true limits of its potential are the limits of their own skill.

I've also heard it said that "overconfidence is the enemy of good thinking," and I think that applies to audio production as well. Overconfidence can prevent creators from seeing the opportunities in front of them to make their work stronger and resonate with more people.

That's why this book exists. To embrace that truth and the realities that come with it. As a creator, I believe in boundaries. Not as in narrow thinking, but that the best creativity comes from working around purposeful restrictions. Focus.

Whether you are new to podcasting or have lots of experience, finding a balance—between confidence and humility, between being clear and focused, while remaining open, and understanding that there is always an opportunity to improve—is the nucleus of this book.

I want to review three things before we get into Chapter 1 that I think will make your time with me more useful and productive: a bit about me, a bit about you, and a bit about the thing that connects us— an interest in podcasting.

A BIT ABOUT ME

There are three dates that are important to understanding what led me to write this book and, thus, you to be reading it.

The first: July 25, 2008. It was a day that changed my life, though I had no idea of that at the time. I stood in the control room at National Public Radio's New York bureau watching a group of colleagues through a large glass window; they had their arms around one another, some were crying. It was the last broadcast of a show that NPR had debuted just ten months earlier called *The Bryant Park Project*. Before the show had even hit its first birthday, it was being shut down, staff laid off, and all the money, time, and energy that went into creating it was written off as a huge and expensive mistake.

The idea for *The Bryant Park Project* had come almost two years earlier as part of NPR's agreement to provide two channels for satellite broadcaster Sirius (now known as SiriusXM Radio). Sirius wanted something new and original from NPR, so we dreamed up *Bryant Park*—an alternative morning news and chat program to NPR's flagship program *Morning Edition*, which would be offered exclusively on Sirius satellite radio.

By the time it launched on October 1, 2007, new ideas and initiatives were piled on top of the original concept: In addition to being a morning program, *The BPP* was also a podcast, and a blog, and a video series, and was also broadcast on a few terrestrial NPR stations, plus a few other things as well. That was the hidden lesson of *The Bryant Park Project*. It became so many things that it actually was nothing at all. The project had bloated to the point that no one, including those who initially created it, could really define it anymore.

After telling the staff and publicly throwing in the towel, we picked the date for the last show: July 25, 2008. On that day, I went up to the NPR New York bureau to be there for the last show. During the final segment, host Alison Stewart brought Senior Supervising Producer Matt Martinez and the entire staff into the studio. They all talked about favorite moments, acknowledged one another's talents and dedication to the project, then said goodbye to the audience they had spent the last ten months building. I watched all this pain and remember saying to myself, "I will never let this happen again."

Even then I knew I could not prevent failure. But there were so many red flags on this journey—so many signs that things weren't right. There were so many questions that could have been asked and answered earlier. If that work had been done, it wouldn't have guaranteed a different outcome, but it certainly could have provided a stronger chance for survival. Having a clear definition of what the show was (and what it wasn't) wouldn't have prevented a once-in-a-generation economic event, but it certainly could have prevented a dozen talented young people in tears wondering why they had poured themselves into a project for a year, yet were told they had failed, though no one could clearly express how or why. You couldn't even have a real conversation about whether *The Bryant Park Project* was "good" or not, because no one could really agree what it was.

There has to be a better way to do this, I remember thinking. There has to be a way to mitigate a lot of this lack of clarity and these abundant unknowns. *I will never let this happen again.*

The second important date happened six and a half years later: January 10, 2015. On that day I was riding the Metro through downtown Washington, DC. The train was pretty busy for a Saturday, but it was still quiet enough that I could hear a conversation across from me. One couple was telling another couple about a story they had just heard on a new podcast, called *Invisibilia.* It was the story of Martin Pistorius, a man who had been trapped inside his paralyzed body for twelve years, unable to communicate. It was the lead story in the first episode, which had only debuted the day before.

Right then I knew that my work, as well as podcasting in general, had really taken a new and uncharted turn. And an exciting one, too. I was the executive producer for *Invisibilia*'s first season. It was a show I had just spent the better part of a year working on, and I was experiencing a holy grail/white whale/unicorn moment: hearing random people in public professing their love for something I helped make happen. The moment went by so quickly. I immediately texted my wife and told her about it.

"You sure?" she texted back. "Perhaps they were just talking about something that sounded similar. Trains are noisy, you could have gotten confused."

I didn't blame her for being skeptical; it was a really weird thing to have happened. The show was less than two days old. So, I reluctantly agreed with her. It couldn't have been, I thought.

Then, the very next day, my wife and I were out to lunch and, mid-meal, I realized that the woman at the very next table was sharing something familiar with her four lunch mates.

"I heard the most amazing story," she said. "On this new podcast . . . I think it's called *Invisibilia* or something like that." She told the exact same story about Martin and his paralysis.

I looked at my wife. She'd heard it too. Neither of us could believe it. Once, maybe, but twice? Within twenty-four hours?

A lot of people loved *Invisibilia*. That first season was downloaded tens of millions times in the weeks following those two encounters. And the reason this all made me so happy was because *Invisibilia*'s success wasn't really an accident.

My role in *Invisibilia* came about when one of its cofounders, Alix Spiegel, shared an early version of one of the episodes with me and asked if I could help her and her cohost, Lulu Miller, make this into a show. At the time, I loved the stories they were working on, and was really honored that they trusted me enough to help make their passion a reality. But a lot of the lessons of the past were very fresh in my mind.

The decisions we put into birthing *Invisibilia* were a culmination of the better part of a decade I'd spent creating new radio shows and podcasts since the end of *The Bryant Park Project*. Testing. Learning. Deconstructing. Trying again. Never letting "that" happen again.

I'd spent a lot of time thinking about podcasts, why they work, why they didn't, and what their appeal is. I'd also spent a lot of time making podcasts. I tried to infuse all I'd learned into this new show I'd helped bring into the world. I've heard it said that luck is preparation meeting opportunity. That was certainly the case here.

Not everything can (or should) be an *Invisibilia*, but many podcasts, or ideas for potential podcasts, or really all forms of storytelling, could be much better than they are.

That's why I wrote this book. I wrote it to make your work better.

Before you praise me for my altruism, know that I wrote this because I love to listen. So by helping you, I'm making sure there are more good things for me to listen to. But the reason I spent two years of my life writing this book is that I believe that in serving you, you will learn to serve others: listeners.

That brings me to the third date that is important to under-standing this book and me, which happened years before either of the other two: June 1, 1998. It was the day I started work as the pro-gram director at WKSU, a small NPR station in Kent, Ohio. I was thirty-one years old and in charge of the entire on-air staff, program-ming, and sound of the station. The twist is that WKSU was the radio station where I got my first job in radio when I was nineteen. So not only was I now the boss, but everyone who worked for me was older than me (some twice my age), far more experienced than me, and a significant number of them had known me since I was a teenager. This was all far from ideal for a new boss.

How was I going to be the leader of a group that had taught me a sizeable amount of what I knew? How could I be the authority in a room of authorities? In a momentary instance of smart thinking, I decided that the only way I could lead this station was by devoting myself to serving its staff. Together we would design an ambitious vision of what was possible and I would help them attain it. I would lead by serving. Their success was my success. It got us away from bosses and reporting lines and generational differences, and helped us all unify around clear and shared ideas and goals. I made sure I was on the front line of our quests, and made sure that I was the one working as hard or harder than anyone else to reach them.

That's both a philosophy and a way of leading that I have honed since then and still follow to this day: lead by serving. In my mind, cre-ators serve audiences, and I serve creators. That is what I do. It's been the basis of my entire career. That perspective has led me to many new ways to think and create, which form the foundation of this book.

I don't have all the answers and I certainly can't make any-thing a hit. In fact, sometimes it feels like quite the opposite. In my career, I've had a hand in birthing more than 130 podcasts, radio pro-grams, streaming channels, and other audio projects. I've made every conceivable mistake along the way and been responsible for some colossal screwups. But over the years I've come up with a quiver full of exercises, questions, processes, and ways to approach problems that have helped me avoid the most common mistakes I see and hear in my work and the work of others. They have also led me to a string of successes as well. Given the explosion in both podcast creation and listening in the past few years, it seems like the perfect time to share all of them, as well as the principles and ideas behind them.

So, if you are a really impatient person, the rest of this book boils down to two things:

- Know what you're making.

- Stick to it.

And, as I'm sure you can guess, neither is as easy as it seems.

A BIT ABOUT YOU

Obviously, I don't know who you are or anything about you.

However, I have written this book assuming that you fall into one of three categories:

- A curious novice interested in starting a podcast.

- An experienced maker looking to improve your skill or push your work to the next level.

- Someone from a company or organization interested in using podcasting as a means to connect with audiences, customers, or like-minded people who share your interest in a subject, issue, hobby, lifestyle, or, basically, anything.

I'm sure there are a lot of variations even among those three categories. Perhaps you want to start a small podcast with and for your friends. Perhaps you are an expert in a field or niche and want to use a podcast to speak to others who share your passion around the world. Perhaps you want to make podcasting your vocation and reach a large audience.

I've written this book trying to speak to all the above. And surprisingly, I'm happy to say that, for the most part, it wasn't hard to do. This is a book about ideas and principles. It contains no product recommendations or ten-step walk-throughs of technical processes. I have focused on ideas and concepts that apply to everyone, regardless of the scale or scope of what you aim to make in audio.

That said, I want you to understand that, every once in a while, I will speak to someone who is approaching podcasting differently from you, is doing it for different reasons, or is at a different skill level than you. When that happens, bear with me. First, it wouldn't hurt for you to understand some of those ideas, and second, we'll get back quickly to what interests you.

Regardless of who you are, when making audio, please be aware that what you are about to undertake is work. It is hard work. It is also incredibly fun work. It can be rewarding and exciting, and can always surprise you with the way it resonates in the world and in people's lives. But it is still work.

It's best to set that expectation up front. One of the compelling stats that led me to write this book for you is that more than 40 percent of podcasts are abandoned within a year. Sure, some of them were only meant to last for a handful of episodes or a short amount of time, but still, there are tens of thousands of podcasts every year whose makers have simply given up and walked away. To me, that means that the creators of these podcasts got into it for the wrong reasons, got frustrated with the results, didn't reach the audience they'd hoped for, or had trouble achieving their vision.

All those issues are fixable, and this book is designed to help you tackle them.

WHAT IS A PODCAST?

That is both a practical and an existential question, which we'll get to in a minute.

First, something you might not notice if I didn't point it out: The word "content" never appears in this book.[1] I hate that word. I hate it because it is a lazy, generic word that describes nothing. Podcasts are not content. Podcasts are podcasts.

---

[1] Okay, full disclosure. That isn't entirely true. The word "content" does appear in a few quotes from other people, but it is not a word I use myself, at all, in life or in this book.

Success in podcasting starts by embracing what a podcast is and what makes it different from other media, including other *audio* media.

While almost all the practices, ideas, and principles in this book can apply to almost any audio medium, this book is really focused on podcasts: specifically, how to take good ideas and make them into great podcasts.

So, returning to the question: What is a podcast?

From a rather concrete perspective, the easiest definition to use is: Are you using an RSS feed to distribute audio files?[2] Then yes, congratulations, you are a podcaster and the show you produce is a podcast. Period.

But even from its earliest days, the industry has struggled with a definition of podcasting. Many early podcasters were snobs about that definition. They were fairly elitist regarding who they felt could call themselves a "podcaster" and what could/should be identified as a "podcast." While I was at NPR, many of these precious podcasters would not refer to me as a "podcaster" nor the shows offered by NPR as "podcasts" because they were originally, or also offered, on other platforms, such as terrestrial radio. This even though the podcast charts were often packed with podcasts I created, developed, or distributed. To the podcast elite, we were interlopers from radio, not pure podcasters. They were similarly dismissive of others as well. To them, even the perennially popular *This American Life* couldn't call itself a podcast, because it had started (and, at the time, considered its primary audience) to be on the radio.

As new distribution technologies occur, the podcast definition gets even cloudier.

I often counsel radio broadcasters not to think of their product as a *technology* and instead see it as an experience. Stop thinking of yourself as a terrestrial FM broadcaster and start thinking of yourself

---

[2] "RSS" stands for "Really Simple Syndication," a data files format containing information and metadata. In the case of podcasts, RSS files contain episode and show information like titles, description, and the URLs where artwork and audio files are stored.

as someone who creates audio experiences that accompany listeners through their life, regardless of the platform it appears on. I find myself more and more saying this same thing to podcasters. As podcasts start to find audience through music services like Pandora and Spotify, as well as through new devices like smart speakers, it's easy to argue that the underlying RSS infrastructure of a podcast doesn't matter to listeners. To them, a podcast is a type of listening experience. To them, it is completely divorced from the delivery method.

I, myself, encountered some of this same thinking when I left NPR in 2015 to produce audio programs at Audible. Many questioned whether the multiple-episode short projects I was creating could or should be called a "podcast"—many including my colleagues within Audible, who thought we should abandon that term. In trying to avoid the word, the company came up with a number of alternatives, such as "short form audio," "audio shows," or simply "programs." But whenever we presented these shows/programs/projects to customers and asked what they thought of them, universally they'd respond, "Oh, this? These are podcasts."

I tend to be fairly liberal with the terminology, especially as the industry continues to expand. If you think you are a podcaster creating a podcast, great. You are a podcaster. All this said, I have to acknowledge that "podcast" is almost an impossibly broad and inclusive category.

For every mass appeal podcast like *Slow Burn* or *My Favorite Murder*, there are tens of thousands of other podcasts tailored to specific jobs and industries, like podcasts just for dentists or real estate agents. I've met creators of podcasts focused around very specific areas of interest, like those about chameleons and spiders.[3] There are podcasts about arboriculture (trees), crafting with plastic shopping bags, medical office design, and several about beekeeping. There are podcasts that go on for hours about every episode of every TV show you can imagine, including TV shows produced fifty years ago.

---

[3] That's two podcasts, fyi. One about chameleons and another about spiders. Though, I wouldn't be so quick to dismiss the idea that somewhere in the world someone probably does have a podcast about both.

You name something that someone is passionate about and I'll find you a show about that subject that also serves as the hub for a community. And all are "podcasts," too.

I want to return to an earlier thought, that podcasts are different from even other *audio* media. If you are willing to accept that podcasts are an experience rather than a technical platform or medium, what makes podcasting different? Lots of people have opinions on this and love to debate it passionately, but, to me, the key to podcasting's uniqueness focuses around *intimacy*.

Radio was always thought to be the ultimate intimate medium. The best radio broadcasters always made it sound like they had an audience of one—you. It's a one-to-many medium that sounds like one-to-one. But as we've come to understand podcast listeners, we've realized that the podcast medium fosters an even *more* intimate connection between creator and audience. I think there are two reasons for this.

First, and this may strike you as weird, but I really think a huge part of this is about earbuds and headphones. Almost all podcast listening is consumed through earbuds and headphones. It is a singular experience, physically intimate (you put earbuds *inside your ear*, for crying out loud), in addition to emotionally intimate. That changes the relationship to what you are offering the listener, which changes the show itself.

The second reason is that podcasting is active listening. Audio is often something you put on in the background while you do other things, a companion medium to make mundane activities like folding laundry or commuting to work feel less mundane. With radio, your attention can float in and out and you can listen for hours without you really paying close attention to what's going on. But podcasting is much more deliberate. Rather than tuning into a station, someone picks a podcast. Maybe they do it because of the mood they are in, or the type of day they've had, or some other itch they are looking to scratch, but it is purposeful and deliberate.

That conscious choice, not only to listen, but to listen to that specific thing, raises the bar on what you make. Listeners have different expectations for podcasts than they do for most radio content.

When someone tunes into a radio station, they are tuning in for an experience: I want to hear country music, or news headlines, or conversations about sports. As long as the programming that comes out of the speaker matches that expectation, the listener often is satisfied. When they want to hear something else, *they tune into another station*. Often when someone listens to the radio, they start on the station that was playing the last time they listened to the radio. They only tune away if they aren't in the mood for that experience. It is quite passive. That's the reason radio works so well in the car; it is simple and easy to navigate while driving. In the mood for classic rock? Press this button. Boom. Classic rock. In the mood for the weather and local news? Boom. One button press and it is easy. Podcasting is different.

Podcasting is more purposeful and granular. Not only are you interested in a specific experience, but you may want to hear only a specific episode from that show. The level of selection is much more intentional.

TWO FINAL THINGS

Here is an idea that permeates everything in this book. I believe that the key to success in podcasting and audio of all sorts is learning to create empathetically—to learn to think about creation in the same way a listener hears that creation. Listeners are why we do this work—to reach people with stories and ideas. They are the audience for our expression. To properly align your thoughts with a listener, all that's needed is to simply learn how to empathize with them. What do they want? What do they need? How do we put them first? There is a lot in here to help accomplish that too.

And no strategic objective, success measurement, innovative initiative, new feature, or idea is worth much of anything unless there is someone (or lots of someones) who listen to it, understand it, feel it, see themselves in it, and love it.

And finally, a note about the origins of this book's title.

In 2011, I created a trivia program for NPR called *Ask Me Another*, an hour of puzzles, word games, and trivia recorded live on stage at the Bell House in Brooklyn. The show isn't the largest success I ever worked on, but it is one that is closest to my heart for a number of reasons, mostly because the show spent the first several years of its life at death's door. It was created at a time where NPR still needed new programs that appealed to the next generation of NPR listeners, but we were just coming out of the other side of the Great Recession that killed *The Bryant Park Project*. Budgets were still extremely tight at NPR, and difficult decisions were still being made about what projects we could afford to do, and what we had to let go. Despite repeated queries about killing it, I managed to keep *Ask Me Another* alive.

One of my methods was to spend as little money as possible producing it. Pretty early into our pilot testing, we realized that we needed an Applause sign to cue the audience when we needed them to applaud. Simple enough, right? But a new Applause sign would cost SIX HUNDRED DOLLARS. For a show trying to produce on the cheap, we couldn't afford that. So I asked the NPR shop engineers if there was something lying around that we could rig into a workable proxy.

A few days later, an engineer came to my office with two white boxes with a few cords coming out of them.

"Maybe this?" he said, handing a box to me.

It was a square box with "Hey Tavis" in two rows across the front. They were cue lights for Tavis Smiley, to let him know that his mic was about to turn on during the production of *The Tavis Smiley Show* on NPR years before. Since the show ended, the Hey Tavis lights had been collecting dust in the shop. While we could scrape off the old letters, the biggest problem was that the light box was square. If we put "applause" across it, the lettering would have been so small no one would be able to read it.

"You need to think of something else for them to say," the engineer told me.

I thought for a moment.

"How about 'Make Noise'?" I said, off the cuff.

"'Make Noise'" it is," said the engineer, as he turned and started to walk away.

A few days later, I had two Make Noise signs for my *Ask Me Another* pilots.

During one of the recordings for the first season of *Ask Me Another*, I was sitting on the stage when it dawned on me that those signs were two-sided, one facing the audience and the other facing the show's staff and performers. While the original intention was for the side pointed toward the audience to indicate when they should make noise, I realized it was so prophetic that the other side also instructed those on stage to Make Noise too.

But they made noise for another reason. They were to Make Noise to be heard. They were to Make Noise to defy expectations. They were to Make Noise to rise above strategic shifts and churn. They were to Make Noise to show their critics were wrong. They were to Make Noise to be relentless, work harder, and make the best noise they could.

When I first started to circle in on *Make Noise* as the title for this book, my wife was not in favor of it.

"Your whole thing is about focus and definition," she said. "That isn't 'noisy.'"

But I told her the point was, in a crowded world, to make the biggest sound you could. Be loud. Refuse to be overlooked. You have something to say, and if you don't do everything you can to be as loud as you can, you will be lost. Don't be polite. Don't settle for what's handed to you. Make the loudest noise you can. Be impossible to ignore. Doing so is deliberate and purposeful and focused.

That is some beautiful noise.

Now, it's your turn.

It's time to make the best audio of your life.

Let's go make some noise.

Chapter 1

STORY. CHARACTER. VOICE.

L et me tell you a story about what propels me to come into work every day.

For almost twenty years, I've kept this poster of one of my heroes hanging above my desk in my workspace: punk icon Iggy Pop. This picture looks down on me as I work every day. I have it there because he is an inspiration to

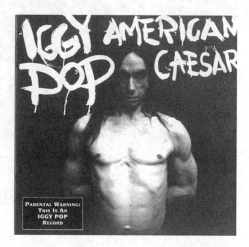

me. There are many things that I admire about Iggy, but there's one I want to share with you now: his hatred of broccoli.

Iggy Pop hates broccoli *so much* that he channels the thing he hates into inspiration to do his best. In the contract rider for his performances, he often stipulates that the promoter must place a bowl of broccoli florets in his dressing room, simply so Iggy can pick them up and heave them in the trash before going on stage. On days when Iggy feels he needs a jolt of motivation, he hangs a head of broccoli around his neck while performing (feel free to google "Iggy Pop broccoli" to see what I mean). That proximity to the thing he hates propels him to do great things and push the limits of his abilities.

I have my own version of Iggy's head of broccoli.

Richard Branson.

It isn't that I hate Richard Branson. I'm sure he is a very nice guy. But I keep this picture taped up next to my desk and, like my Iggy poster, I see it every day. Why?

Because, to me, Richard Branson is a symbol for what I despise and work every day to avoid: Richard is my avatar for "same-ness."

Over the past year, Richard Branson has been a guest on somebody's podcast no less than thirty times. More than thirty interviews on thirty different shows. To be honest, it is probably way more than that, I just got depressed while researching this and stopped counting at thirty. What does Richard possibly have to say that might inspire so much mic time? That's the thing—he doesn't.

Again, nothing wrong with Richard. My issue isn't really with him. It's with the lack of imagination his presence represents. To me, Richard the Podcast Guest embodies creative laziness. Richard gets booked for one of two reasons (neither of which have much to do with his thoughts on anything).

First, Richard is easy to book. Richard obviously *loves* talking on podcasts.

Second, Richard brings a celebrity halo to the podcasts he's on. Booking Richard brings cred. "Hey, look at me," a podcaster might mentally be saying with this booking. "I am such a *major podcasting celebrity* that I can book the well-known, charismatic, and mildly eccentric CEO of a major international conglomerate." Ergo the podcast (and its host) must be a big deal as well, right?

Let's keep in mind that while the podcast may be exploiting Richard's fame, *Richard is also exploiting the podcast.* One of the reasons that Richard loves podcasts is because it's an easy venue with generally soft questions and a host eager to bond and please.

Falling into this trap is so easy. Lots of podcasts do it. Whether it is literally Richard Branson, or Neil DeGrasse Tyson, stars on publicity tours, one of a hundred touring comedians, or other folks at different levels of celebrity. There are a lot of "echo" bookings and conversations in podcasts. "Echo" bookings are those guests podcasters book for no reason other than the fact that they are famous and available—and somehow it means something that celebrity X is willing to sit in a chair and pretend to be interested in you too (in addition to the twenty other interviews they are doing that day). You see this a lot when celebrities star in a new movie or have published a memoir. The celebrity shows up on tons of TV shows, radio programs, interviews in press, etc. They are everywhere. Why is it necessary to book them so many times? From a listener's perspective, the problem with "echo" bookings is that they produce almost indistinguishable conversations.

And, to me, "indistinguishable" is the enemy. As of this writing, there are more than 700,000 podcasts available today in 100 languages representing more than twenty million episodes. On one hand, there is a shocking amount of diversity: Almost every media outlet is experimenting or knee-deep in podcasting, and a wide variety of celebrities, companies, causes, enthusiasts, and interest groups have their own podcasts. It seems everyone from the President of the United States to the yoga instructor down the street has a podcast. On the other hand, there is a tremendous amount of sameness. The sameness is what I fight against in every project I do. That is why I keep Richard's picture at my desk. To remind me to never settle for sameness.

I hear this problem with sameness in narrative podcasts, too.

Podcast superfans can take a look at the top charts in Apple Podcasts, Spotify, Stitcher, or other aggregators, and pontificate for hours about the multitudes of differences between *Slow Burn,*

Radiolab, *Serial*, *Lore*, and *My Favorite Murder*. I've done research where we played excerpts of leading podcasts to people who aren't big podcast listeners. To them, it all sounds remarkably the same. There is nothing wrong with any of these shows, I (and millions of others) listen to them and love them. But how many Roman Mars or Sarah Koenig knock-offs do we need in this world? Judging by all the new podcasts, apparently a lot. At least according to those who create them. To those "eh" listeners in our research, they look at all these podcasts and see them as minor variations. To them, they all sound the same. To many potential listeners, these top podcasts have the same level of distinction as chocolate swirl has from chocolate chunk, and from chocolate chip, and from chocolate fudge, and from mocha chocolate, and so on.

Well, what if you don't like chocolate?

What if you are allergic to chocolate?

Many people ape the style and aesthetics of other podcasts because they think this is the pathway to success.

Newsflash: It isn't.

The pathway to success in such a crowded, fast-moving field lies in being uniquely different. Uniquely yourself. Uniquely precise, exact, and clear in your vision. Imitation may be the sincerest form of flattery, but it is really boring to listen to.

Why all this sameness? It happens because it's easy. It is so easy to do what everybody else does.

In this golden age of podcasting, there are so many new shows, inspiring ideas, and exciting voices. Yet, at the same time, way too many of them sound the same. Or, even worse, they sound unfocused, uncentered, and boring.

Doing something original? That shit's hard. But it doesn't need to be as hard as most people make it. That's why I'm writing this book and, I assume, why you are reading it.

The pathway to righteous originality, to creating something that expresses your vision and is unlike anything else in the world, all boils down to three words.

19

Story. Character. Voice. Stated more specifically:

- **Compelling stories and ideas.**
- **Engaging characters.**
- **A unique voice.**

Every successful podcast, ever, has delivered on each of these three tenets. Regardless of form, format, or style, I've spent years trying to find an exception to this, and never have. You should consider hitting these marks to be your gateway to success, too.

COMPELLING STORIES AND IDEAS

One evening, kinda out of the blue, my friend Heather and two of her friends decided to start a podcast (one of them wanted to learn to edit audio) and call it *Whiskey Cats*. The concept was magnificently clear and simple. They would plug a microphone into a computer and record. Then they would consume an entire bottle of whiskey and just talk. They'd comment on the whiskey while they were drinking it . . . while slowly getting tipsy. That's it.

In season 2 of *Whiskey Cats* (yes, there was a season 2), they even branched out to mix whiskey cocktails for their recording sessions.

Many of their listeners (yes, they did have listeners—not a lot, but more than you'd think) encouraged them to branch out and talk about other things, too. Why not? They were charming and fun to listen to. Listeners asked them to chat about movies or TV shows. Items in the news. Celebrities. How about expanding into trying out tequilas? Wine?

No. No. No. They really didn't have a passion for other subjects. They stuck to their vision: whiskey.

The lesson here: Everything needs to be about something. The best things are about something that is evocative and irresistible. Those best things articulate a vision that's compelling and clear. And the best of the best stick to that vision like it is dogmatic gospel.

Heather and her friends not only had a podcast, they had a podcast that was about something specific—and that's why it resonated enough that we are talking about it today.

Compelling stories and ideas can be about a lot of things. They can be about something that happens. They can be about a series of events. They can also be a question or suggestion. They can be about something that's at stake. Those stories and ideas can be expressed in narrative form or through conversation.

In Chapter 2, we'll spend time on a great exercise designed to help you come up with that vivid, unique, and high concept. And the higher the concept, the better.

People often confuse "high concept" and "highbrow." High concept is an immediately and strikingly clear idea. It's straight-ahead. Anyone who hears it will understand what it is. It's easy to communicate. High concept is unique—there can't be something else in the world like it. There is no vagueness in high-concept ideas.

Highbrow, on the other hand, means rarefied, intellectual, superior, and somewhat pretentious. Many high-concept projects are not highbrow. The movie *Snakes on a Plane* is about as high concept as you can get. *America's Funniest Home Videos* is a high-concept TV show. The novel *Alien Stripper Boned from Behind by the T-Rex* is equally high concept.[4] None of these would match most people's definition of highbrow.

However, for a story or idea to be compelling, it has to be about something specific, and the creator must give the listener a clear reason to care about the idea and be invested in it.

All listeners are narcissists about their listening. And why shouldn't they be? It's their time. They don't listen for any reason other than their own fulfillment and enjoyment. Period. They don't listen because knowing a story, character, or situation is good for them. They don't listen because they have nothing better to do. It has to pay off for them, every moment, every time. In a world of so much choice for entertaining things to listen to, it needs to be a pretty short walk to understanding what's in it for the listener and why it is relevant to them. The harder you make listeners work for that understanding, the fewer listeners you are going to have.

---

[4] And yes, there is such a novel (it's a novella, actually). It was nominated for a Hugo Award in 2017.

I regularly talk to creators who want to leave a little mystery to this. To give the listener a puzzle to unlock. That's a romantic idea, but it rarely works out that way. In fact, unless you have already built trust with an audience and have repeatedly delivered on the promise of your show, there is very little chance an audience will stick around long enough to rummage through an esoteric idea.

Think of a story[5] as a dark forest. A dark forest can be a scary and intimidating place. In a dark forest, filled with an almost unimaginable number of potential things going on, you have no idea what's there. Immediately your mind races through the worst possible options as if they were the most likely options. Ten feet in front of you could be an evil marauder, an angry bear, or a 400-foot cliff. You just don't know. Audio stories are the same, pockmarked with tons of rabbit holes filled with people, information, ideas, and possible next steps and outcomes.

Because of this, people step carefully, or not at all, and devote their mental energies to trying to spot and establish the importance of everything.

You, as an audio storyteller, are responsible for guiding listeners through that maze of horrible and distracting possibilities in the dark forest. You show up with your flashlight and illuminate a pathway. The presence of the bright light actually lowers the awareness and distraction of other possibilities, so listeners can step forward with confidence, paying attention to only the details you illuminate with your light.

A great audio storyteller will lead the audience 85 percent of the way to the destination, then let them finish the journey on their own. By this time they've gotten comfortable in the journey, have a better feel for what is going on, and taking those last few steps on their own creates a euphoric feeling of finding the destination without having it spoon-fed to them. But it is critical to note that the moment of discovery happens at the end of the journey, not the beginning.

---

[5] Be it a narrative story, an idea, or even a peek into someone's mind through a conversation or interview.

To understand why it is so important to start off with a clear and compelling direction, think of what your audience is doing while they listen. People are doing laundry and riding the subway to work. They are exercising, doing dishes, walking the dog. Podcasting is what's known as a "companion medium," meaning it is something you listen to while doing something else. It makes mundane activities less mundane.

Sure, there are listeners who will stop all other activities, sit in a chair, close their eyes, and listen to your show while doing nothing else whatsoever. In fact, there may be five or six people like that. It is far from normal behavior and you should treat it that way.

That means everything you do needs to be structured with the way 99.999 percent of your audience will hear it: passively. That doesn't mean it needs to be dumbed down—it just needs to give people a clear and well-articulated reason to listen.

If you have a compelling story or idea, and you tell it well, your listeners will want to hear what happens next. When they read an episode description, they'll be excited to hear your take on the subject.

This leads us to the primary vessel for your compelling ideas: your characters.

ENGAGING CHARACTERS

Michael Chabon's *The Amazing Adventures of Kavalier & Clay* happens to be one of my favorite novels. After first reading it, I was constantly trying to get my wife interested in it, too. Finally, probably more to get me to shut up than anything else, she started reading it on our vacation. It was a slow start for her, but eventually she became so immersed in it that our vacation was basically me watching her read. As she bolted to the end of the book, we had scheduled a rafting trip on the Colorado River. She brought the book *along on the rafting trip* and read the final pages as we headed down a deep gorge, everyone else on the trip admiring the beauty, with occasional glances over at this woman with her head in a 700-page book.

When she finished, she looked up at me with tears streaming down her face.

"What's wrong?" I asked.

"I just didn't want it to end," she replied.

When I asked about the tears, she said that she loved the main characters and finishing the book felt a little like a death to her. She was crying because she'd never get to spend time with them again. She spent the rest of the day in a low-grade funk. She was in mourning.

I mention that story because it set a standard with me for the importance of characters. In podcasting, a critical element of success is a deep connection to the individuals you hear in a show. It isn't that every character needs to be relatable and charm the listener, but there has to be some emotional anchor for the listener, someone they feel so interested in, connected to, and invested in. It is someone that they would (occasionally) sacrifice other activities for just to hear from them, understand them, relate to them, and learn from them.

While it's pretty obvious how this concept applies to narrative podcasts, engaging characters can be anyone in any type of show. The engaging character can be the host. Characters can be guests, subjects, profiles, and so on.

The essential elements of character in a podcast really aren't that different than in a novel, play, or movie, even when the project is a nonfiction podcast or a conversation/interview program. In a fictional story, characters are often more important than plot. In audio, the characters are avatars for the idea, theme, or premise you want to explore.

Just like in a book, play, or movie, characters are motivated and want something. And they want it badly enough to step outside their comfort zone and go on an adventure. They can be relentless in their pursuit. Perhaps, in the podcast, a character is on a narrative journey or guides the listener through a story. In narrative podcasts like *This American Life* or *Snap Judgment* we understand the world better by walking in someone else's shoes—seeing the world through their eyes.

In an interview or conversation, the adventure doesn't even require the host character to step away from a microphone set up in their garage. In these instances, the engaging character wants to understand an idea or another person or perhaps hear their story from their perspective. The host or interviewer has what I like to call "a hunger by proxy": they give voice to the curiosity of their audience and are insatiable, always pushing and exploring

Just like characters in books, plays, and movies, characters in audio can fail to connect with audiences, too.

A common weakness in a podcast's concept or idea is stories that focus on the weird. These podcasts fetishize quirky or enigmatic characters and fail to make them relatable and intriguing. In these stories or conversations, we end up with characters who are two-dimensional or flat. These characters never change, never reveal anything surprising or interesting.

Another common mistake happens when a podcast's host, their guest, and other characters focus too much on being likeable. A listener doesn't need to like the characters; he just needs to understand them. Ironically, trying too hard to be likable leads listeners in the opposite direction. The eagerness pushes the listeners away. It's a turnoff.

But above all else, the most prevalent way characters fail is that they don't feel authentic. They are two-dimensional, predictable, unrevealing, or clichéd. This is true for podcast hosts as characters. I've heard it said that you can hire for attitude and train for skill. I've found this to be especially true in radio and podcasting. You can teach someone how to read a script and speak into a microphone. You can train someone how to use ProTools or other editing software. However, you can't teach someone to be authentic. You can't train someone to have a great story. You can't fake your way through being interesting, intriguing, or charming.

This leads us to my third tenet: voice.

A UNIQUE VOICE

Often in life, just at those moments when you think you know it all, you are confronted by profound evidence that you, in fact, know nothing.

In 2013, I encountered one such moment that has affected my thinking about podcasting every day since—all thanks to Mike

25

Herrera, the singer for the punk band MxPx. It has nothing to do with his music, but with his podcast. At that time, I kept hearing people talk about it: "It's fantastic." "The conversations are so intense and intimate." "It defines authenticity." And on and on. So I looked up this podcast, which at the time was leading the "New and Noteworthy" section in iTunes, rising on the "top podcast" charts; it had high ratings and hundreds of fawning reviews.

I couldn't believe what I heard. And it wasn't like "I couldn't believe" in a good way. The show sounded so . . . un-showlike. It was loose, informal, almost rambling. It just started—and went—with no clear idea where it was headed or what was happening. Mike would simply introduce his guest and they would just . . . talk.

I couldn't stop thinking about this damn podcast. I was kinda obsessed with it. I kept asking: Why do so many people think this is "good"? What am I missing? Its production was so simple, so "amateurish." It was just two people jawing, for crying out loud. How can it be a viable competitor to *Fresh Air* or *Planet Money*?

That's when I realized that the problem wasn't with Mike's podcast. It was with my understanding of "good."

It's important to remember that podcasting is actually two very different audio experiences smashed into one platform, creating a bifurcated experience that isn't obvious at first. One experience is the professionalized and highly produced podcast. The second is podcasts like Mike's, niche podcasts.

The highly produced podcasts are things that most people rattle off quickly when discussing the medium: *99% Invisible, Radiolab, S-Town, TED Radio Hour*. These are the shows with big budgets and big staffs, who spend weeks paining over the editing and production detail for every minute they create. In the podcasting world, these are our Led Zeppelins, Beatles, and Beyoncés.

Then there are the small indies. While they may lack relatively huge audiences and download numbers, they have an incredible power that is really important to understand and respect.

Niche podcasters will often dismiss these highly produced

podcasts because they often are heard on other platforms, like FM radio. They argue that since these podcasts aren't native or exclusive to podcasting, they aren't "pure" podcasts. But the interesting thing is they aren't solely referring to distribution platform. To them, the purity of niche podcasts also refers to the communities these shows build around themselves.

I often refer to these niche podcasts as the "tribes." These are podcasts that are the literal voice of a community of interest. Podcasts tailored to niches, but often to microniches. Think of almost anything people are interested in—and there is probably a podcast to match. Think that's an exaggeration? Go search; you'll be surprised. There are even "tribe" podcasts focused on personalities. This is where Mike Herrera's podcast fits in. People, a fairly significant number of people, want to hear what he has to say, as well as conversations between Mike and others. The fact that it doesn't have a format, set structure, or other trappings of modern radio and audio doesn't matter to his audience because that isn't what they are there for. Consistency (something that all listeners secretly crave) comes in other ways. Mike's podcast is, in fact, just talking, and they are absolutely okay with that. That's because what attracts them is the show's unique perspective—its voice.

Voice means having something unique and authentic to say that sounds organic and genuine in the podcasting space. The concept of "voice" applies to both kinds of podcasts but in different ways. Professionalized programs, like *Snap Judgment* or *On Being*, which are heard on other platforms (primarily, radio), still need to feel like they fit well in the podcast space. Host tone, the way they speak to a listener, the way stories are framed—they all need to feel like podcasts, even if that wasn't their original purpose. Too many radio companies see the success of many of public radio's podcast offerings and (wrongly) assume that any radio program would do well as a podcast. They then post shows where hosts yell into the microphone, remark on things that happened before or after the podcast episode, allude to insider references, and other things that come off as exclusionary. These sound like a recorded radio show, not podcasts. The difference is the presence of that distinct voice.

The voice of a podcast is like a promise made to its audience: this is what we are going to do, and how it will be authentic and fit into the podcasting space. Sticking to that voice like it is sacrosanct is keeping that promise and demonstrating the creator's respect for the audience.

Here is a story about understanding a podcast's voice and what happens when you violate the audience's unspoken understanding about that voice.

In 2010, a few of my friends at NPR started up a podcast called *Pop Culture Happy Hour*, a weekly panel discussion of happenings in the world of pop culture featuring a recurring group of cohosts. One of the hosts, Linda Holmes, loves to say that *PCHH* was the one NPR project that was created with no meetings or any executive oversight. That's good, because if they had, no one in charge would have ever said yes. None of the four hosts had much experience being behind a microphone, let alone hosting a show. The conversation was loose, sometimes meandering. They sounded uncomfortable and unsure of themselves and what they were all doing (all true). But over time, a strange thing happened: They found a voice. With the first few years of weekly episodes, the four hosts learned how to talk to one another and to the audience. They developed individual roles and characters for the show. They'd have fun pursuing a segment idea, then do it again, and then again, until the segments grew into regular features. They established a crew of recurring contributors who eventually became substitute panelists. Linda emerged as the "host"—the leader among equals. Things really started to click into place. And with this evolution came something else: an audience.

I hadn't listened to *Pop Culture Happy Hour* for a while when I noticed that the show's monthly downloads kept growing, and at a time (before the second wave of podcast growth in the fall of 2014) when most other podcasts were largely flat month to month. I started listening again and was blown away by how good the show had become. The hosts had gone from being a bit awkward behind a mic to being natural and comfortable.

I suggested we start to work together. Perhaps we could find a way to put them on the radio more regularly. Perhaps we could put more into the show and see where it could go.

To make a long story interesting, I spent the next few months sitting in on their recordings, listening to the shows, making notes, hiring a producer for them, and working to give them a higher profile in the podcast ecosystem and within NPR. In short order, things really exploded. We could have made a million changes and directional focuses to "professionalize" their scrappy podcast, but instead we were militant in defining the core values of the podcast and sticking to what worked. We weren't trying to change *PCHH*; we were trying to amplify it.

About a year before we began working together, the *Pop Culture Happy Hour* crew had experimented with a live recording. They held it in an unused bank on the first floor of NPR's old building on Massachusetts Avenue in Washington, DC. Their only marketing was mentions in the podcast itself. At show time, with four mics set up on a folding table with nowhere for the attendees to even sit, the bank was packed with more than a hundred people.

We decided we'd try again, creating a more robust effort in NPR's black box theater in its new headquarters (this time with chairs for the audience). We sold out all 250 tickets in just a few minutes. So we tried a venue with 800 tickets, and sold them out in under a minute. On and on. Today the show has grown so much it does a national tour, selling more than 1,000 tickets an evening. All to watch the taping of a podcast.

This isn't all that unusual. Now, it is fairly routine for podcasts to host live tapings and events. It's an important part of their revenue stream and, even more important, a way to build that sense of community and connection with and among the audience.

Here is the really interesting part of the *PCHH* story.

We'd gone from an intimate panel discussion taped in a studio with four friends, and then occasionally we'd drop in these massive live shows taped in front of hundreds of people.[6] We wondered, What does the audience think of all these live shows in the podcast feed?

So, why wonder when you can know?

We did a survey. We learned pretty quickly that the podcast audience hated listening to the live shows.

Now, the audience in attendance loved these shows. As I said, tickets would disappear instantly and there would be long lines afterward for fans to meet and greet the four hosts. But as a listening experience afterward, it didn't work as well as we hoped.

In the survey, we learned that listeners felt the live shows violated the show's voice. To them, *Pop Culture Happy Hour* was an intimate experience, like sitting at a table in a bar with four incredibly smart, well-informed, and charming friends. It felt personal and "just for them."

The live shows were anything but "just for them." They felt big, impersonal, and the cheering, laughter, and applause from these increasingly large audiences violated the feeling of intimacy and, I dare to say, their ownership of the show.

So, at the time, we almost completely pulled back from including the live recordings in the show feed. The podcast was the intimate, personal, four-on-one experience for the hundreds of thousands of listeners. The live shows? They were great for the audience in attendance at that moment, but we decided it was best to mostly keep them that way. Almost any media executive would think this was dumb (well, except me) and a missed opportunity for efficiency and synergy. Except it would have ruined the show—completely and totally.

So having a voice is important, probably equally important as having a good story or idea and engaging characters. But it's hard to stick to your unique vision if you've never articulated that unique vision.

So, next, let's do that: Define your idea in a way that makes it distinct from any other in the world.

---

[6] This is an important footnote, folks. This is the first instance in this book where I have referred to a recording as "tape." You'll see a lot of similar references throughout this book. This is a holdover from when recordings were actually done on analog tape—usually ½-inch magnetic tape (similar to the smaller version you may have seen inside a cassette). Even though we long ago transitioned to recording digitally as .wav or .MP3 files, almost everyone in the audio industry still refers to it as tape. You "tape" an interview. You may ask another creator if they got "good tape" in a recording. When producers offer to give feedback, they often "share the tape." I'm not going to explain this every time I say it, but when you encounter it, you will now know what I mean.

Chapter 2

THE ONLY TEN WORDS THAT MATTER

Focus is a powerful thing.

A few years ago, the CEO of New Hampshire Public Radio asked me to come visit her radio station. A group of station employees had been working to develop a new podcast for ten months and felt kinda stuck. They'd piloted a number of segments and pieces, but nothing really seemed to click. They weren't getting anywhere. Instead, they spent a lot of time getting hung up on details. Details about the segments for the show; about its editorial voice. They would go back and forth as to whether "this" is a story for their podcast as compared to "that" story.

The morning I arrived, I asked them all to take out a piece of paper and describe the show they were working on . . . in ten words or less. And I wanted them to describe it in a way that captured their show and nothing else in the world. That exercise is a lot harder than you might think. It takes only three seconds to read ten words, but writing them takes a bit longer—or it should take a lot longer.

The group was done with their first drafts in about five minutes. They read them out loud and it was instantly revealed why they had so much trouble working on their new project: Their ten-word statements were all completely different. They had different visions and ideas of what the show was. In essence, they were four people producing four different podcasts.

The podcast, eventually called *Outside/In*, was about a lot of things, according to the group. It was about the environment. It was about outdoor recreation. It was newsy (though another staffer said it was definitely *not* newsy). It was about animals, plants, and insects. There were a lot of references to water: what people do in water, what people do with water, and what people do to water. It was about policy. It was about the impact of climate change. It was about people. And on and on. You get the point.

So we put aside everyone's statements and together tried to write a ten-word description that described their show and nothing else in the world. This time it took almost two hours. So why does this matter? The power of creative focus.

In his fantastic and inspirational book *Essentialism*, Scott McKeown includes this illustration to demonstrate the importance of focus.

In each circle, the same amount of energy is expended. On the left, it goes off in numerous directions. On the right, all the energy is harnessed in one direction and, as you can see, goes so much farther. Vision works the same way.

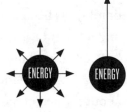

Take all the expectations and ideas expressed by the staff of this podcast in their various ten-word statements. Now imagine what they could accomplish with one shared statement.

In a moment, I'm going to ask you to write your own Ten-Word Description: Describe your idea in no more than ten words, and do so in a way that describes nothing else in the world. Whether you have an established podcast or just an idea for one, you, like many, many others, will find this more difficult than you think.

It's worth noting that, depending on who you are and your experience as an audio creator, you may find the order of this chapter and the following chapter—figuring out what form your podcast should take—to be perfectly clear. Or maybe it strikes you as kind of backward. It is one of the few times in this book that different people, coming to podcasting at different levels, need information in a different order. If this all makes sense to you, great. If not, it is probably best to take in the next two chapters, think about them, then adapt the ideas in a way that makes the most sense for you and your project.

I've been developing radio shows and podcasts for a long time. When I give workshops, I regularly speak with people who haven't been *alive* as long as I've been in audio. The reason I bring this up is that over the years I've seen a lot of people (including myself, I might add) invest a lot of time, money, and energy into ideas that never had a chance of succeeding. The primary reason they were destined to fail, almost to the exclusion of other reasons, is that they didn't have a clear idea what they were doing. Ten-Word Descriptions are a great first step toward building that clarity.

Let's look at a few examples for shows I've worked on in the past.

Ask Me Another: An hour of puzzles, word games, and trivia.

West Cork: An unsolved murder exposes the underbelly of a rural Irish town.

Invisibilia: A narrative journey through the invisible forces affecting human behavior.

Sincerely, X: Anonymous TED talks.

TED Radio Hour: Fascinating ideas, astonishing inventions, fresh approaches to old problems, and new ways to think and create.[7]

Radio shows and podcasts aren't the only media that have used this kind of focusing. Earlier I'd mentioned *Snakes on a Plane* as an

---

[7] Okay, I know this is more than ten words—when we wrote this one, the goal was something you could read in ten seconds. We've tightened the exercise up since then.

example of high concept. Its Description is embedded in its title. That's it. Four words. Only one breath required to utter what the whole thing is about. Everything you need to know. Everything that happens in that film is focused in that simple statement.

Even better? *Sharknado*. All you need to know about a movie, in just one word. It was so convincing that the movie's tagline was "Enough Said!"

And our friends at Outside/In? It was really tough for them. They wanted to avoid using the word "environmental," because it's a politically loaded word. They tried sandwiching "outdoors" into a few versions, but it felt too removed, like the show happened somewhere else rather than everywhere. They kept wanting to include the word "storytelling," but that word felt very convenient and unspecific.

After a long morning arguing about what words could work, they landed on this: *Outside/In*: A show about the natural world and how we use it.

To them, that statement captured what they wanted to do (and sufficiently safeguarded them from what they didn't want to do). A lot of people could see themselves in a show with that description, from environmentalists to sports enthusiasts to duck hunters. It was inclusive without compromising specificity. It worked.

So, now that you have some examples, I'd like for you to try to create a Ten-Word Description of your own. But before you do, there's one more catch. Following is a list of words, none of which can appear in your description. I call it Eric's Forbidden Word List.

Amazing	Curious	Incredible	Spectacular
Astounding	Diverse	In-Depth	Stunning
Awesome	Extraordinary	Lovely	Superior
Beautiful	Fabulous	Outstanding	Thoughtful
Best	Fantastic	Quality	Tremendous
Brilliant	Fascinating	Remarkable	Unbelievable
Classic	Fresh	Riveting	Unique
Compelling	Great	Sensational	World Class

I originally started this list in 2003, after reading Toby Young's memoir *How to Lose Friends and Alienate People*. In it, he shares that Graydon Carter had a list of 147 words that were not allowed to appear in *Vanity Fair* because they were "empty modifiers"—words so overused that they become devoid of actual specific meaning. One day, while listening to the radio after reading that book, I heard an announcer describe a Brahms concerto, the Goodyear blimp, the feeling you get when helping others, and the weather all using the same modifier: "beautiful"—and all within a few minutes. I thought to myself, "What do those things have in common?"

Nothing. They have nothing in common, outside of that dumb, easy word. I started my own word list based on Carter's idea, with the first entry being "beautiful." [8]

If you find yourself wanting to use one of these words, I have an easy anecdote. Simply answer why. Why is it beautiful? Why is it fascinating? Why is it spectacular? The answer to your "why" question is your distinct descriptor. Use it instead. (And I apologize in advance, as a "why" answer will invariably take up more words than your empty modifier.)

Now it's your turn. Write a Ten-Word Description of your show or your concept in a way that distinguishes it from everything else in the world.

_____ _____ _____ _____ _____

_____ _____ _____ _____ _____

Of course, I have no idea what you just wrote on the page. It would be weird if I did. Nonetheless, I can still tell you something about what you wrote: You weren't specific enough.

In years of doing this exercise with creators, I've never seen anyone who didn't try to describe their idea with the broadest possible

---

[8] If you are exceptionally clever and observant, you may have figured out that a few of the examples I've shared *themselves* contain some of these forbidden words (such as the use of "fascinating" in the *TED Radio Hour* description). This has been a living document over the years, with new words added on occasion. In fact, during the editing of this book, I added the word "fresh" following a conversation with my editor. So some of the Ten-Word Descriptions offered as examples were created before the offending words were added to the list.

language that they could fit into ten words. That's not surprising. Being specific is hard. Defining things in language so simple and clear that a stranger would understand, that's even harder.

Another common problem with first drafts of Ten-Word Descriptions is using jargon. I was once speaking to a group of journalism graduate students who were taking a podcasting course. I asked them to write Ten-Word Descriptions about their project ideas. When it came time to share, one young woman described her show idea as "issues involving intersectional feminism." While I praised her for only using four words, I asked her who she felt the audience was for this podcast.

Her response: "Pretty much everybody."

I asked her if everybody knew what "intersectional feminism" meant.

Her reply, "Probably . . . yeah, I think so."

I asked the class to raise their hands if they knew what "intersectional feminism" was. About a third of them did, and none of the men.

I confessed that, at the time, I, too, had no idea what it meant. I asked one of the women who had raised her hand what it meant to her.

"It means feminism for women who aren't privileged white girls."

I asked the woman who suggested the project if that matched her definition.

"Pretty much, but . . . not entirely," the first woman answered.

As feedback, I suggested that she would have an easier time with her project if she picked a lane: either use wording that everyone would understand or change her definition of her audience. After giving it some thought, she decided she wanted to change the audience. She and her cohosts would only be interested in listeners who already knew what intersectional feminism was, and she felt that was an important entry point for her audience. She could have just as easily gone in the opposite direction, but that would have been a very different podcast. In hers, she can assume a level of understanding, knowledge, empathy, perspective, and interest from her audience that a general audience program wouldn't possess.

I also pointed out that the other half of her statement, "issues about . . .," was kind of meaningless. What issues? What are you doing with the issues? Who is talking about the issues? How are they talking about these issues? Is this an interview program? A conversation among colleagues? Friends? Enemies? Is this newsy? Is it analysis? Is it things meant to surprise? Is it entertaining? Does everyone agree? Is there conflict? Does the cast of characters change episode to episode? It may seem strange, but almost all of these questions can be answered in the eight remaining words beyond "intersectional feminism."

Often, when you identify a soft spot and define it, that is where you find your truly distinct description.

Here are a few other real-world examples from previous workshops I've run:

A woman once offered this as a description of her show: "Raw Data. A show about how Silicon Valley is changing relationships between people and society."

I asked her, "How are they changing?"

This led to a conversation about how most people don't realize the amount of very personal information that can be learned from their digital history. Even though the subject has been covered a ton in other media, that felt more interesting (and much more specific) to me and to the other workshop participants.

After some more thought, she revised her idea to "Raw Data: A show about how our digital histories reveal who we really are." While I still didn't feel it was a particularly compelling idea, at least it was specific enough to work out the bugs in how to make it interesting.

Another student offered to share her Ten-Word Description. Her idea was for "White Rabbit Story Hour: Stories told by strangers I met by traveling." When I asked for more detail, the producer shared that she would meet strangers and ask them to tell a story about a piece of music, with a prompt question like "Tell me about the first record you ever bought." She had already recorded a few and was happy that many people's responses demonstrated how a shared story about a piece of music ends up unveiling a lot about a person's life and history.

Now, *that* was starting to sound more interesting to me. I suggested she change her Ten-Word Description to "Using a musical memory to unlock a person."

I remember that after I shared that suggestion, she took a deep breath and pulled her shoulders back, smiling. That was it. It made more sense, even to her.

She recognized that she needed to give it deeper thought.

And so do you.

I'm going to have you try again, and try to be exact, specific, and avoid generalizations.

_____ _____ _____ _____ _____

_____ _____ _____ _____ _____

Just as certain as I was about the first statement being too vague, I am equally certain that this one is better. Congratulations. It may not be final, but it's closer. I'd suggest you noodle on it a bit over the coming few hours and see if you can sharpen it even further.

After doing this, you may be wondering, why is the description so important? Because once you've finished it, that Ten-Word Description will be your North Star. For example, let's say that you are working on an idea for a podcast featuring kids talking about their favorite books. The only voices heard are those of kids. So let's then say that someone suggests that we could have R. L. Stine as a guest to be interviewed on the program. Is that "kids talking about books"? No. And that should be your answer to the booking suggestion as well.

Let's say that your podcast is telling the story of a championship sports team from the 1990s and what happened to them after their victorious season. Should you include a scene in an episode on the history of the stadium where they played? If it has at least a metaphorical relationship with the teams' post-championship lives, then sure! If not, skip it, even if it is a great story.

Most of your favorite podcasts and radio programs have not done this exercise, but that doesn't mean they don't have that sense of purpose. Ira Glass never set out to create a short description of *This*

American Life, but he states it at the beginning of every single one of his more than 600 episodes: "Each week our show has a theme, then we present several stories on that theme. Act 1 . . ." Joe Rogan doesn't have a Ten-Word Description, but there is a clear sense of purpose, perspective, and editorial vision of what his show is, what types of things he talks about, and what type of guests he has on his show.

Ira and Joe spent years coming up with their clear editorial vision. That's one way to do it, but most people, probably including you, don't have the time or resources to figure it out as you go, especially in a hypercompetitive world of 700,000 other podcasts. Your favorite shows probably got theirs through a lot of trial and error. So why not skip all the trial and error and start with a clear idea? Writing a Ten-Word Description isn't a guarantee that you'll have a successful podcast, but it will certainly increase your chances and can highlight some of the roadblocks that could trip you up along the way.

Your Ten-Word Description captures your vision, a clear distillation of your creative values. It should be treated almost like a piece of scripture. It's your purpose. It is a filter that everything has to pass through. It's what you stand for. Ten-Word Descriptions are exact and precise; they find a specific nerve and then pinch it.

And remember the old phrase: "If you don't stand for something, you stand for nothing."

Once you have your description finished, you should print it out in big letters and hang it on a wall. You should look at it every day. But most important, every time you make an editorial decision, you should ask yourself if you are keeping true to your vision. If you are considering booking a guest, and the conversation won't match what you've written in your description, don't book that person. If you are creating a multi-episode narrative and are unsure whether to include a scene or profile a character, think of your statement, and ask if what you're considering serves or forwards that idea.

This exercise forces you to do something we discussed in the first chapter: thinking high concept. When someone hears your Ten-Word Description, they can see it/hear it/understand it.

"Interview with celebrity" isn't high concept. When a celebrity is on a publicity tour, he will do dozens, if not hundreds, of interviews (think of my little Richard Branson picture hanging by my desk). What makes one different than the hundreds of others? Probably nothing of consequence. But let's say the interview is with a celebrity talking about early rejection stories—or first loves. Now that, even with an interviewee who is overexposed, would be interesting to listen to.

You basically want to avoid one thing when it comes to your potential audience: the So-What Factor. The So-What Factor is when a listener encounters your show, or a description of your show, takes it in, and consciously or subconsciously says to themselves, "So what?" If you describe your show as "Conversations with people fifty-plus about aging gracefully" and a potential listener says to themselves, "So what?" in an instant they are gone. Are the conversations meant for others over fifty to help them live better lives? Are they for younger people who want to understand what their parents and grandparents are living through? Are they for younger people as a window to understanding how the decisions they make today will affect their lives later on? Any of those ideas may be true—and they are all very different shows.

There are times when the So-What Factor is okay. If you are making a podcast for Hummel Figurine collectors (and, yes, there is one, I checked) and someone happens across the podcast who isn't a Hummel fan, the So-What Factor is a fine reaction. But if someone is a huge Hummel fan and doesn't care about your work, that is a shame.

FIND YOUR LISTENER

While we are thinking about listeners, why they listen, and who they are (and aren't), let me share something that may seem like a stupid little exercise, but those who've done it, especially creatives, find it incredibly helpful and illuminating.

Nothing will make a creative person's head explode like charts, graphs, and numbers. Put an Excel spreadsheet in front of a creative, or any layperson for that matter, and watch them glaze over. However, it is critically important to know who you are talking to in your show. You can either talk demographics and psychographics (spreadsheets and numbers) or you can just go find a picture.

In this exercise you are going to go to an image search engine (images.google.com is a great place to start), enter some terms that you think describe your target audience, and find that perfect picture of your listener—the *one* person who is your avatar. One picture. A photograph of the one person who represents your audience.

"That isn't possible," I hear you say. "My audience cannot be boiled down to a single photograph of a single person."

In doing this exercise with hundreds of creative producers and program hosts, I've never met one who failed at this exercise. Sure, it is hard at first, but you will find him or her. While you start to think about this exercise, let me share a story about how it works.

During the end of my time working at NPR, I was asked to spend some time thinking about the future of public radio and make a presentation to a combined meeting of the NPR Board of Directors and the NPR Foundation Board of Trustees. When my turn came to present in the meeting, I had one slide: a picture of a young woman who was staring directly into the camera.

It was a Creative Commons photo I'd found online. I had no idea who she was or what her life was like. I named her Lara. She was twenty-nine years old, had a master's degree, lived in Chicago, worked for a PR agency, and had never listened to public radio. I put the picture up on the screen and introduced Lara to the two boards.

All I said was that, to me, Lara was the future of public radio, in a photograph.

People like Lara should be easy pickings for public radio. In previous generations, people like Lara tended to discover public radio between the ages of thirty and thirty-five. They may have discovered public radio because they became more interested in news and world events, then sought out sources of information. Or they discovered public radio through "side channels"—programs like *Wait Wait . . . Don't Tell Me!* or *Radiolab*, then eventually looked for more programming from public radio, including its news offerings. However, Lara's relationship with radio and media was markedly different. The way she consumes media is different. If public radio didn't adjust itself to be ready to receive Lara, and others like her, in the next few years, then she would probably be lost forever. And if we lost Lara, there would be no next generation of public radio listeners, or at least a significantly smaller one.

Lara—her background story, and what she meant for the dilemma faced by public radio—was the avatar for years of audience data and listener research. No one wants to hear all that data and research, and they likely would not understand it, especially in a quick meeting presentation. But people understand people. And a photo of a person can personify a group or situation more clearly than any chart or graph. And even if they could grasp all the data, what is the point? By selecting an avatar, we could take that mental energy and apply it to generating the ideas that will serve them rather than trying to understand data.

You may have the same concern as many at that meeting initially had and as I've heard from those new to finding listener avatars: How can one person represent an entire diverse audience? An audience can cover an age range that spans decades, socioeconomic backgrounds, walks of life, races, ethnicities, and parts of the country. How can you expect to capture all this in one photo? To answer this, think of the avatar as a destination. If you get it right for Lara, the decisions, behaviors, and choices you've made along the way have made your project (or multiplatform network) accessible and enjoyable for many others along the way who will connect with Lara. In other words, what is good for Lara will be good for many others, perhaps even millions of others.

One of the best examples of this came when I was doing a workshop in Australia. A producer was workshopping an idea for a podcast featuring the voices and stories of incarcerated aboriginal women, recorded inside prison. Now, even from that one sentence, you can assume there is going to be a niche of people interested in this, but how do you broaden the appeal? The producer went in search of her listener avatar and came back with a picture of a happy, fashionable young woman she named Zoe. The producer said that Zoe was on her way to brunch to meet her equally fabulous friends Chloe and Josie. Why was this such a powerful choice? Because the producer said, "If I can produce this so Zoe and her friends care about the lives of these women in prison . . . if I can move them and have them understand and feel empathy for the prisoners, I've done my job." Indeed. And the real power of this vision lies in the journey. The decisions the producer will undertake to successfully reach Zoe (as well as Chloe and Josie) will draw in many, many others along the way.

Now you should go give it a swing. Go to a search engine and just start putting in words, then look at the people in the pictures that come up. If you don't like what you see, adjust the words. Keep adjusting the words until you come up with one image you feel represents the target audience for your project.

I was inspired to create this exercise by an activity I was asked to do several times when working in broadcast radio. At that time (it was a few years ago), we were all given a stack of newspapers and magazines, and told to comb through the photos and advertisements to find our audience. This wasn't a short-term relationship. We were then told to tape up our pictures at our desk. Then, whenever we had to write copy or figure if/how to describe something for our audience's benefit, we were instructed to look at the picture before writing, and ask, "What does this listener need to know about this story or conversation?" Or, "How do I describe this story or event in a way that *that* person will understand?"

Once you've located the photo that represents your listener avatar, sit for a moment and think about who they are and what their life is like. As I did for Lara, write a faux bio for them. Give them a name, occupation, and place where they live. Dream up more details of their life. How do they spend their time away from work? What occupies their thoughts? What things (besides your podcast) are they enthusiastic about? And how did they discover you?

Then, take it a step further. Once you have a fully realized avatar bio, take another look at the picture. Ask, why are they listening to my project? What role does it play in their life? If listeners are indeed narcissistic in their listening, what is this person getting out of listening to my show?

While it may come off as a hokey exercise, the kind that bosses love to make employees do at retreats or off-site meetings, it is a powerful tool to get you out of your own head and perspective and into the head of your audience. One I still use regularly today.

When I started writing this book, I did this exercise myself. I googled "bright enthusiastic podcast creator," found stock photos of these people among the results, and wrote a brief bit about each (that I totally made up).

This is Scott, a sports podcaster from Philadelphia who has been working on his fantasy sports podcast for three years and is thinking about starting his own podcast company.

And this is Anabel, who curates museum exhibits and is hoping to create a podcast about women's fashion from the 1950s to the 1970s. She is very comfortable in her creativity but has never produced audio before.

And finally, Aaron, who has a master's degree in journalism and wants to start his own storytelling podcast, so he can someday get a job at *This American Life*.

As I've been writing this book, I often look at my pictures of Scott, Anabel, and Aaron, and ask myself whether they will understand a particular issue I'm discussing, or whether it will be helpful to them. Do they need more explanation? Are they bored? What questions might they have?

They are my proxies for you. They are *your* avatar.

Whenever I do this exercise in groups, I ask the participants to share the keywords that got them to their final image (such as the "bright enthusiastic podcast creator" example I used for the images on the previous page). One of the things this helps safeguard against is a common mistake in this exercise: The podcast creator ends up googling an image with keywords that could be used to describe themselves. That is always a red flag to me.

This isn't to say that you can't create a podcast for people like you or who share your passion for a subject, but proceed with great caution. It is dangerous to assume that your audience is just like you. Let's say you are the podcast host for a show about collecting vintage baseball cards. It might seem reasonable to think the audience is just like you—you all love vintage baseball cards, am I right? You must keep in mind that you know more about the subject than your audience. Even if you have just learned something you are about to share with them, *your reasons for producing* the show about vintage baseball cards are different from *their reasons for listening*.

This idea applies universally to the difference between creators and listeners. You have information; they want information. You are living a certain kind of life; they want to vicariously live a certain kind of life. You have a worldview; they want to hear that worldview. You have a story to tell; they want to hear a compelling story. That is not only a big difference in perspective, but it is a big difference in the types of people who hold that perspective.

Here is another example: comedy podcasts. I wish I had a dollar for every comedian or comedy podcast producer who, when asked about the audience for their podcast, answered with something like. "You know, the people who come to shows and go to the comedy clubs." Here is some news: That isn't who listens to comedy podcasts. Well, let me be clear: I'm sure the people you see in the comedy clubs listen to some comedy podcasts, perhaps even yours. But they are such a minority of your listeners that they don't really matter.

So, if that is the case, who does listen to comedy podcasts? Nielsen recently released a consumer insight study that looks at the various types of products purchased by podcast listeners. Do you know the product category where comedy podcast fans are superconsumers?

Baby food. Yup, baby food. Fans of comedy podcasts buy 14 percent more baby food than the average US household: $727 million worth. The second highest category? Tea. Those comedy podcast lovers buy a lot of tea, more than a billion dollars' worth annually (which is 12 percent more than the average US household). And third? Pet care.

So, the fans of your comedy podcast: Are they the people you see in clubs? No. They are the people who don't have time to go to clubs. They buy a lot of baby food, tea, and pet care items because they are busy people with homes, raising the next generation of comedy nerds. They listen to the podcast because they want to experience comedy without having to go to a club. That is a completely different kind of person, and knowing and appreciating that difference can make the difference between creating a genuine connection with your podcast listeners and missing the mark entirely—making your podcast listeners feel like you are talking to someone else.

There is another great example from that Nielsen consumer product study: Health and Living podcasts. Not surprisingly, the number one product category for listeners to Health and Living podcasts is vitamins (they buy $2.3 billion worth every year). But the second product category? Booze. Health and Living podcast listeners purchased more than a billion dollars' worth of liquor a year,[9] significantly higher than the average US household. Takeaway: Sure, there are some vitamin-loving listeners out there, but there also are people

---

[9] And, oddly, when I've shared this tidbit with others, everyone asks if that statistic includes all alcohol. No, it doesn't include wine or beer, which they also purchase more of than the average household.

who *aspire* to be healthier and take better care of themselves (and probably enjoy a mean cosmopolitan in the process). The majority of Health and Living listeners are wannabes. That is a very different listener from the acolytes who would rather knock back a kale smoothie after work. Understanding that insight is key to understanding where your listeners are in their lives, and how you fit into that.

So what is the point of these avatar-seeking picture quests? To help get you in the right mind-set to be an *empathetic creator*, to think of the listener when you make creative decisions. To understand them and what they are coming to you for. To learn to think like they listen.

You need the audience, much more than they need you. You want them to feel welcome. You want them to feel like you are speaking just to them. They want to hear a small part of themselves being nurtured or nourished by what you do. They want you to help move them along on a journey to be a better version of themselves. If you talk down to a listener, talk over their heads, or sound like you are speaking to someone else, that bond is almost impossible to build.

There is an old bromide in radio that tells announcers and disc jockeys to phrase everything like they are speaking to only one person. It builds connection, makes the listener feel like they are a part of things. It demonstrates empathy. I'd argue that podcasting's need for an intimate one-on-one connection is ten times as important.

Does my theory about empathy and intimacy have any basis in fact, or an element of a scientific nature to it? Of course not. If resources aren't an issue, any number of consumer research firms will be happy to take a big pile of your money and do all this for you—they may even be able to do it with a certain degree of rigor and certainty. While I am a huge advocate for qualitative and quantitative audience research and I use it regularly in my work, when you are formulating ideas, I don't think that a big pile of money really buys you very much that you can't come up with by simply employing some clear-eyed thinking in this exercise.

We've established that listeners are not like you, the creator. We've also established that listeners are often far more complex than the primary-color versions of them we tend to create in our minds on the rare occasion we do think about them.

Before you print out your avatar and hang their picture in your creative workspace (and, yes, I do think you should print out your avatar and hang their picture in your creative workspace), there is one more aspect of understanding them that I'd like you to take on.

How do you want your project to affect them? What do you want them to think about? How do you want to make them feel? What is your project's impact on its audience? Basically, what do you want to leave them with as a result of the time they spend with you and your show? (And we talk about this in the next chapter.)

It is an important element of a project's design to think about the end point—the outcome. Why are we all doing this, all this creation and storytelling? I emphasize this element of the exercise because I find it so hard to map out a journey unless I know where I'm going. To me, the end is the effect on the listener.

You don't need to tell listeners this, but for you as a creator, it really is the point, isn't it? I mean, you want people to listen—most of your success metrics will try to measure that. But that isn't an end of the journey for your listener. To them, the act of listening is the beginning! They want more than noise to fill their ears while they do something mundane; even something light and fun has purpose for them. And you, as a creator, need to plan accordingly.

Journalists I have worked with often freak out when I mention this. They suggest that their work is objective reporting and they aren't trying to influence anything. I think that's a ridiculous position to take. Of course you want your work to have impact. Part of the journalist's mantra to "comfort the afflicted and afflict the comfortable"[10] is to provide a catalyst for change. When you report on abuses of power, you want to inspire someone to try to get the abuses of power to stop. It's the same with reporting on mistreatment, corruption, and other limits in accountability. You tell human interest stories to

---

[10] Originally coined in 1902 by humorist and writer Finley Peter Dunne, btw.

deepen a listener's understanding of the people in their community. News organizations spend millions to cover elections with the hope of creating a better informed electorate. It is troubling for journalists to suggest or advocate specific actions, but their job is to shine a light on something to help initiate change or action.

Creators of podcasts for hobbyists may want to inspire listeners to start their next project. Comedy podcasts want to make people laugh. Followers of a podcast about medical conditions or social anxieties may want to help their listeners realize they aren't alone in their struggles. Creators of a storytelling project in the inner city may want to make other residents understand their neighbors better. One time when we were working on an early episode of the *TED Radio Hour*, host Guy Raz articulated this beautifully when the team was working on an episode about advances in astronomy and cosmology: "If we get this episode right," he said, "listeners will never be able to go outside at night and see the sky the same way."

Most podcast producers don't stop to think about these issues: writing descriptions, identifying listeners, or having a clear idea what effect they are trying to create with their work. Often, that is why so many of them fail.

Let's go back to where we started in this chapter: the power and importance of focus. I place so much emphasis on this focus-based process because it addresses the most common error that new creators make. They spend so much time thinking about the mechanics of the "what" they want to create that they seldom give it the level of granularity it needs, especially when working with a team. Further, they rarely give much thought to "who" the idea is for or answer "why" someone would listen. The lack of thought on these points leads creators to waste a lot of time struggling to produce, overestimating the audience potential and growth trajectory for their projects, and making decisions that are completely ineffective and off the mark.

Going through these exercises won't prevent these things from going wrong, of course. But having a clear idea of what you are doing, *who* it is for, and why they will listen will undoubtedly reduce risk.

Chapter 3

FUNCTION AND FORM

FUNCTION

If you haven't guessed by now, I'm a big fan of using reverse engineering, especially when creating media. I believe that you start with your destination and work your way backward from there.

If we want to construct a compelling podcast, it is important to understand the roles of Story, Character, and Voice. An important key to unlocking those roles is a clear Ten-Word Description. So what informs the Ten-Word Description? A conversation (with yourself and/or your creative partners) about function and form. And for most people new to podcasting, understanding function and form requires answering some very basic questions. These conversations are also a great place to start for someone who is interested in podcasting but isn't quite sure where to start.

Take, for example, my yoga teacher, Joe. Joe is a terrific yoga teacher.[11] Joe has an uncanny ability to instruct a group of forty people yet still manage to offer one-on-one guidance to those who need it without interrupting the flow of the whole class. But Joe's style is

---

[11] Okay, I know everyone thinks their yoga instructor is awesome, but please bear with me.

what really sets him apart. Joe offers what I'd call narrative-based yoga instruction. He tells stories, often offering a short meditation at the beginning of class, sharing a reflection on a personal narrative from a student or himself, something he's read, or an idea he's been thinking about. The stories often function like a parable, allegory, or moral tale. Joe then structures the class so the poses and practice center around the core idea in his story. To be frank, not every theme resonates with me, but I really admire the way Joe's meditations and stories offer an understandable purpose and structure to yoga practice. So I always look forward to attending Joe's classes and I do it two or three times a week.

One morning before class, Joe stopped by my mat to ask if he could talk to me after class. My mind first went to what yoga faux pas I might have committed that now required a "talking to" from the instructor. After seventy-five minutes of mindful breathing and stretching, I completely forgot about Joe's request until I got home, then dropped him an email to ask what was up.

"I was wondering if you'd mind spending a few minutes talking to me about podcasting," he wrote back.

This may strike you as ironic, given that on many occasions, including in the opening of this book, I say ". . . today, even the yoga instructor at the studio down the street has a podcast . . ." as evidence for today's ubiquity of podcasting. Now, even my own yoga instructor was thinking about creating a podcast and was interested in my help.

Joe and I sat down about a week later. He told me that his students and acquaintances regularly tell him that he should have a podcast. They tell him that he has a lovely voice (he does), that he is a great storyteller, and that he has a lot to share—and that podcasting would be an ideal venue for him. Joe also shared with me that he was interested in expanding his brand. In addition to his yoga instruction, Joe is quite busy as a life coach. Between yoga and life coaching, he's become rather well known in our area. He shared that while he is very happy with his work and clients, he thought he has more to offer on a bigger stage and was wondering if podcasting might be one vehicle to get there. Yet Joe has little experience with creating any media, no production skills, no idea what specifically he wanted to do, nor any idea how a podcast was made or put out into the world.

On one hand, I was touched by the vulnerability Joe demonstrated in sharing his ambition. It took guts, and a fair amount of yet-to-be-earned trust in me, to raise this with me and ask my opinion, knowing that I could have simply told him how naïve he was and laughed him off. But on the other hand, I immediately saw that Joe had the only two elements necessary to create a fantastic podcast: He had something to say, and he was passionate about saying it.

If I had three hands, I'd say that on my third hand, I also slowly realized that almost every tool I'd created to define podcasts—Ten-Word Descriptions; googling listeners; being distinct; defining story, character, and voice—were all far too ahead of where Joe was. He couldn't define his unique Ten-Word Description because he didn't yet know what he wanted to make. He just wanted to make it.

Jumping in and creating a Ten-Word Description is great, but most people need to start earlier. They can't decide between different podcast formats, because they don't really understand the value and drawbacks of each, and how those formats map against who they are, their talents, and intended audience.

As I was sitting there talking with Joe, I realized that if I tried to get him to use some of my definitional exercises, I'd just end up confusing and frustrating him, probably making him feel stupid in the process, and he'd walk away without even trying to record anything. This, as you can probably imagine, is exactly the opposite reaction I'd want to evoke in a potential creator. It would be similar to advocating running a 10K as a curious runner's first jogging experience.

That's when I came up with the Four-Pointed Circle. While it was originally envisioned to help novice creators, it is now a part of almost every podcast development conversation I have, even with established talent and media companies.

Joe and I got together for another conversation, and I tried to come up with a different framing just for him. I started out by drawing a triangle on a piece of paper. Each corner of the triangle represented the "what," "who," and "why" we discussed at the end of the previous chapter. Each corner was a question I needed him to answer, the answers locking together to form a foundation for a potential podcast idea. But as we talked, I realized there were actually four questions, so on the fly I started calling it a quadrangle.[12] But as we spoke, I started drawing curved lines between the quadrangle points and soon realized I was drawing a circle, a Four-Pointed Circle. Imagine a circle with four equidistant dots on it, with each question leading into the next answer.

As Joe and I spoke, and I started to sketch the circle, I wrote a word at each point to represent the questions I needed Joe to answer.

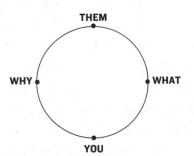

I explained what each point meant:

- **YOU**: Who are you?
- **THEM**: Who are you speaking to?
- **WHAT**: What do you have to say?
- **WHY**: What effect do you want to have on them?

And I expanded on each.

---

[12] I must admit that at the time I had no idea if there was such a thing as a "quadrangle" or if it was just a made-up thing, like a "gazillion." It is a real thing; any four-pointed geometric shape—like a square, diamond, rectangle, etc.—is actually a quadrangle.

WHO ARE YOU?

Not just who you are, but which version of you are you. I am a podcast producer. I am also a writer, an autograph collector, a father, an electric car enthusiast, and a number of other things. Which version of me do I want to host the podcast in question? Joe is a yoga instructor, a life coach, a husband, and other things, too. Which version of Joe is he going to feature in this podcast? He can combine things (and be a life coach who also teaches yoga, as opposed to a husband who also offers life coaching), but which version of the host will dominate? You have to pick a primary.

WHO ARE YOU SPEAKING TO?

Who is the audience? No cop-outs here either. A podcast about calligraphy can't answer "people who like pretty letters made with pen and ink." As I explained in Chapter 2, you need to get specific and envision a portrait of a person with a specific life and interests and needs.

For Joe, I wanted him to pick a target among his specific audiences. Was he making a podcast for his yoga students? Potential students? Life-coaching clients (current or potential)? Were they local? National? Global? Almost any answer here would lead you to producing a very different podcast. Pretty quickly, Joe focused on people who might be potential life-coaching clients. And he knew that he didn't want to limit himself to the local area. He wanted to reach people nationally. But even then, who? A podcast for those seeking life coaching can be very different if you are talking to someone who is seeking to rebalance their personal life as opposed to someone else who is interested in switching careers later in life.

WHAT DO YOU HAVE TO SAY?

Now that you know who you are and who you want to reach, what do you want to tell them? What is your message? What do you have to offer that's specific and of interest/use to them? You don't need to plot out the theme or message of every episode you'll ever produce, but what are the general ideas or themes you want to embody in *every* episode? For example, if you create a podcast with the framing of "Everything in life is amazing," that's a very different podcast from one produced under the idea that "Everything in life sucks." Determine and define your perspective.

WHAT EFFECT DO YOU WANT TO HAVE ON THEM?

After listeners hear your show or podcast, what do you want them to think? What do you want them to feel? A great podcast lingers and resonates far after you finish listening. Your mind returns to it repeatedly. You see, hear, and feel things differently after listening. It has altered you in some way. That is what you are shooting for as a creator. So what emotion do you want to invoke? Do you want them to laugh? Cry? Get angry?

What else might you want them to do? Take an action? Write a letter? Treat people differently? Vote? Adopt a puppy? Your aspiration should not be to keep them from getting bored while folding laundry or walking the dog. Get specific about what you want to have happen after the episode ends.

I put the four elements around the circle in a specific order for two reasons. First, I think having YOU on the bottom and THEM on the top is a symbolic hierarchy meant to reinforce that the listener always comes first and that you, as host, need to adopt a kind of humility to serve your audience. The listener is the beginning and end point. When you have questions, problems, or feel lost in the process of your work, always return to the listener.

Second, by starting with Them, then moving clockwise to What, You, and ending on Why, you establish the circular and cyclical movement through these questions, each informing the next. They are all interconnected.

Joe and I set a date a few weeks out to go through these in detail, as well as explore the "form" we wanted this to take, as outlined in the next section. We set aside a few hours and invited Joe's husband, Michael, and colleague Meg to join us. I often encourage creators to bring a friend to a brainstorming workshop. An extra person increases the energy and ideas. Plus, having someone else there who knows Joe's strengths, weaknesses, and abilities opens us up to having some clarity and ideas. I always counsel someone to bring a "truth speaker" in their lives to workshops—someone who knows you well, wants to help you, but isn't afraid to disagree and feels comfortable pushing back.

When I showed up Joe was already putting up printouts of his target listener. She was a stylish, somewhat feisty-looking young woman he named "Cate." Joe's faux bio for Cate was that she is thirty-three years old and lives in Chicago, working in public relations. She met her husband, Matt, in college and they were married two years ago. Cate and Matt love to travel, go to restaurants, and they have a gray French bulldog named Charlie. Cate has a strong sense of community, can be moody at times, and is outgoing.

When I looked this over, I told Joe and his cohorts that there was one thing that stuck out to me. I asked them to guess which attribute it was, and they couldn't.

"Being moody," I answered. "I wonder what causes that?"

I asked Joe to imagine what problems she has.

"She's insecure," he answered immediately. After some more thought, he added, "She's worried about how she communicates with her husband. There are some problems there she wants to address."

After more conversation, Joe added that Cate has these concerns about a lot of the relationships in her life. She believes she needs to communicate better to unlock the next levels in her career and personal relationships.

So before we even really started the rest of the exercise, Them was covered.

When we started talking about WHAT, Joe had a few answers he'd written down in advance, and they were all kind of generic and bland: "Getting people to think," "Teaching people how to live their best life," and "Taking people to the next level." While all worthy ideas, they were too broad. We needed something more specific. After some group conversation about how Joe interacts with people who meet him, we quickly circled in on Joe's core message to those he counsels as a life coach: Instead of battling with others in your life, there is a strategy to talking about feelings, ideas, and desires. Joe wanted to tell people how to be more present, be better listeners, and, thus, reframe their view to see situations differently. *That* is specific.

Joe had a list of You statements about all his various perspectives and roles in the world, including life coach, yoga and meditation teacher, husband, communication expert, world traveler, animal lover, avid learner, son, brother, friend, boss, employee, and lover of life. For the person he wanted to speak to and the things he wanted to say to them, it seemed like "life coach" was a given, but what other attribute of Joe should dominate? What should the listener identify and get to know first? The group had trouble deciding. Joe was all these things, and they were all important, they argued. I kept pushing them to get more specific, even within the descriptors Joe had written.

"One of Joe's many skills is he tells people the honest truth by asking questions," his husband, Michael, said. "He uses questions to help them gain perspective and connect to their feelings." That's better.

I asked what "communication expert" meant and pushed for more clarity. Joe said he was referring to his expertise in helping people communicate.

"You are a translator," I said. "You help translate the world to your clients and help them learn to translate their own feelings and ideas out into the world."

The group agreed: That was the Joe to host this podcast.

And finally, we got to the WHY. What was the point of this podcast for Joe?

During our conversation, I asked Joe what he might say to someone he was counseling. He offered several examples, and I asked if he would ever offer supporting reassurance.

"Would you ever touch someone on the shoulder and say, 'It's going to be okay'?" I asked.

"That really isn't my style," Joe said, after a short pause. "Because I don't know if it is going to be okay or not. I just want to help them reflect and see things more clearly."

As we talked about this, we swung back to our target listener, Cate. What would Cate want?

Cate is active and wants solutions. She isn't listening to be entertained. She wants to improve herself. Listening to Joe's podcast is a way to improve. She wants something prescriptive.

"She has her own toolbox," Joe said. "I'm just putting a new tool in it."

So we had Joe, the life coach and translator, who was going to help people like Cate, the thirty-three-year-old millennial professional from Chicago, by providing solutions for how she could avoid emotional battles by adopting new strategies for talking about feelings.

Four points on a circle.

That's a clear vision.

FORM

So now that we have all this figured out, what "form" should our idea take?

I find that most people are naïve about form—and really, why shouldn't they be? A podcast episode is roughly thirty minutes long, and they say, *How much time could it really take to make a thirty-minute podcast?*

That answer depends on the form you choose, but the answer is never "thirty minutes."

Before we dive deeper into form, I want to spend a moment more on this link between the form you choose and the time commitment required to produce that form well.

Half the meetings I have with experts in various fields, famous people, and other professionals who call up querying about podcasting begin with this misunderstanding about time. They love podcasting, or at least know that many millions of other people love podcasting, and they come to me to ask how to start their own.

A simple truth: It takes a lot longer than you think to create those thirty minutes. Even for podcasts with a simple setup, it can take many hours of time.

In one recent conversation I had with an Incredibly Well-Known Celebrity, she said that she was a fan of one of the podcasts I'd made. The core of those episodes was a thirty- to forty-minute interview.

"How long do those interviews take to record?" she asked.

The interview takes about ninety minutes to record and then we edit it, I told her.

Her face lit up. "That's terrific," she exclaimed. "I can fit that in every week."

Then I told her about the ten to fifteen hours of prep time the host of that podcast put into every interview, reading tons of books and material, working on the structure of the interview, and working with the staff to write and edit questions.

What most listeners and aspiring podcasters miss is that there is a big difference between being spontaneous and *sounding* spontaneous. There are often hours of prep work that go into a podcast episode, done by the host and/or producer before the microphones are turned on.

The Incredibly Well-Known Celebrity got a puzzled look on her face, as if she was about to ask, as many in her position do, if someone else doesn't do all that for the host.

No, I say. On that show, the host does the heavy lifting herself, which is one of the reasons the show is so good. And then there were the hours in postproduction to give feedback on the edits. And the marketing. It was a lot of work.

I asked Incredibly Well-Known Celebrity for some examples of podcasts that she loved, which she felt sounded spontaneous and recorded live. She mentioned *WTF* with Marc Maron and *Anna Faris Is Unqualified*. While episodes of *WTF* certainly are long (most clock in around two hours), the production team actually cuts out 20 to 25 percent of the episodes in postrecording editing. The producers of *Anna Faris Is Unqualified* often spend as much as twelve hours editing every episode to take out things they don't like, improve the pacing, and punch it up (make it funnier). Both these podcasts *sound* like they are loose, free-range productions without a lot of editing or behind-the-scenes work going into them. But they aren't. They are actually very sophisticated productions meant to create a vibe that sounds loose and free.

As you might imagine, I never had a second meeting with Incredibly Well-Known Celebrity.

Now, your mileage may vary. The examples she picked for her ideal podcast models were actually a heavy amount of work. Even in the few cases where a successful podcast is literally recorded direct to tape (meaning they don't edit afterward), a lot of thought goes into the preparations for the recording. Someone read/watched/listened to a guest's work. Someone thought through some questions. If not, then the host is often an expert in what they are discussing and brings years of learning and experience to that recording.

Most frustrating of all, there is no clear formula for time invested and how good your podcast can be, outside of acknowledging there is a correlation. No amount of time invested will save a crappy concept (but a lack of time investment can certainly kill a good idea)—and some talents just require less time than others to do a great job.

It's important to note that there are many thousands of podcasters who basically press "record," talk for however long, hit "stop," and then post the episode unaltered. However, almost all of those podcasts attract very small audiences. And you know what? That's completely fine. There is nothing wrong with creating a podcast and minimizing the amount of fuss involved. But set your expectations accordingly.

While we are on the subject of time, allow me a bit of an aside to discuss podcast length. The most common question I've heard over the past dozen-plus years from potential creators is "How long should my podcast episodes be?" I've been asked this question thousands of times.

If you have asked that question of a supposed podcast expert and they've given you an answer, never take any advice from that person again. They are an idiot. I'll give you the same answer I have given to everyone who has ever asked me that question: A podcast episode should be as long as it needs to be, but no longer. One of the many benefits of podcasting for creators is that you are no longer slave to a clock. Broadcasters live and die by the clock, but in the on-demand world, there are no such constraints. There literally are no rules, so don't make dumb ones for no reason. I've heard terrific podcast episodes that are three minutes long, and I've heard terrific podcast episodes that are—no lie—four and a half hours long. The episode should have pacing and rhythm and should convey a set of clear ideas, and that can take as long as it needs to, but not longer than it needs to.

And an important point about "as long as it needs to be, but no longer": Almost every podcast can be improved by editing to tighten and clarify what happens. It's worth the time it takes to pick up the pacing where it needs it, take out the dead weight, and get rid of what doesn't really work. It makes everything else that remains more vivid and resonant with the listener. If you do the editing well, no one will ever notice that you've done it; they will just think all your speakers, characters, hosts, and contributors are smart. A common refrain heard from a well-edited podcast is when listeners say, "Everything they say is interesting." You'll want to respond, "Yes, because I cut out all the boring parts!"

With that out of the way, let's talk about all the different varieties of form . . . both of them. The more than 700,000 podcasts available today fall into just two categories: *people chatting* and *people telling stories*. That's it. If I were being paid by the word, I'd wax on a bit more about that, but it really is that simple. Every podcast fits into one of those two categories.[13] Both categories have three subcategories:

PEOPLE CHATTING

- **RANT:** A rant is when a person shares an idea or opinion. That person is often a well-known thought leader, personality, leading voice in a field, or from a specific worldview, though sometimes it is just a regular person with something to get off their chest. Rants are one-way conversations from the podcast star to the audience.

---

[13] And I've even argued before that it's really just one category: people telling stories, as most times when people are chatting in podcasting, they are actually telling stories.

Sometimes there can be a foil present—a guest, cohost, or some other stimulus—but their presence is basically to give the star someone to talk at or to prompt them with questions. The term *rant* might seem a bit pejorative but it isn't. It is just meant to reinforce that this is a solo effort, not the work of an ensemble. (Examples of rants: *The Tony Robbins Podcast, Rise with Rachel Hollis, Dear Sugar, The Ben Shapiro Show,* and *TED Talks Daily.*)

- **QUESTIONS AND ANSWERS:** One person asks questions and another person answers them. While your mind might immediately go to interviews (which certainly are a big part of this category) there are a number of other types of podcasts that fall here, too, such as games and quiz shows. The difference between "questions and answers" and a "rant" is that questions and answers is a two-way exchange, a parry, while the rant is a peek into the worldview of one individual. In questions and answers the questioner can share ideas and perspectives as well, but the focus is on what the host and audience can gain from the answerer's offerings. The host or star of this type of podcast can be either the Q or the A—the one asking questions of others or the one answering the questions. (Examples: *The Tim Ferriss Show, Fresh Air,* and *WTF with Marc Maron.*)

- **CONVERSATION:** A conversation is two or more people talking to each other. While there may be a primary contributor (or hostlike figure), there is no other hierarchy. It isn't one interviewing others. No one person fully dominates. It is a discussion among equals where the conversation is generous, and everyone has something valuable to contribute. (Examples: *No Such Thing as a Fish, Culture Gabfest,* and *Pod Save America.*)

PEOPLE TELLING STORIES

- **SEASONAL NARRATIVE:** A story told over the course of multiple episodes, where its narrative arc emerges over the course of a season or a designated time period. You listen to each episode in sequence as the story progresses, and information given in one episode provides you with what you need to understand in the next episode. (Examples: *Serial, Slow Burn, Dr. Death,* and *In the Dark.*)

- **EPISODIC NARRATIVE:** Each episode of the show contains a single story that is told over the course of that one episode. Each episode follows a different story, often not connected to the stories featured in other episodes. (Examples: *99% Invisible, Embedded,* and *Revisionist History.*)

- **MULTIPLE NARRATIVES:** In this category, the shows have multiple episodes, each containing multiple narrative stories (sometimes wrapped together in a unifying theme). In other words, one episode could contain two, three, or more stories in that single episode. (Examples: *This American Life, Snap Judgment, The Moth,* and *Invisibilia.*)

Whenever I mention these categories to people, some argue with me. They try to point out examples of podcasts that don't fall into these categories. I have yet to find a podcast that doesn't.[14] Once you get past trying (in vain) to find exceptions, it is pretty easy to use these as a framing method.

When you think about the answers you've developed using the Four-Pointed Circle, which forms make sense? Given who you are as host, who your audience is, what you want to tell them, and the effect you want to have, does it make sense to tell a story or chat with someone? Is it a story that unfolds over multiple episodes, or do you have a number of stories to tell through the episodes? Are you asking questions? Perhaps you are *answering* questions. Is your idea better framed as a rant or do you think it's best to be part of a conversation?

There is no science here. You just go with what feels right. The great thing about audio projects is the production costs are fairly low, so there is little (besides time) that prevents you from experimenting

---

[14] Okay, there are some examples of things that don't fit, like instructional podcasts. I would argue that while they use podcasting as a means to distribute their material, they aren't really germane podcasts, but just audio products using podcasting's platform as a delivery method.

with different forms to see what feels right to you. Try a few versions and see which works best. As you grow more comfortable in your production prowess, you can start to work on some projects that combine different forms. For example, I was working on a podcast series with progressive Christian leader Nadia Bolz-Weber. The pilot presented a short narrative story, followed by a conversation, and closed with a short rant. Staying in one specific lane isn't essential to having clear focus. You can produce a show that follows one form, or you can mash them up—there is no right answer. It's important just to be cognizant and deliberate in your choices, and to realize that occasionally you may have to stop and question yourself and your initial assumptions to find what's right.

When my team and I were developing the podcast *Where Should We Begin?* with Esther Perel, we had difficulty deciding on form. If you are unfamiliar with Esther Perel, she is a leading relationship therapist who has given two stratospheric TED Talks, written bestsellers, and is considered one of the leading voices in her field. She has a reputation of being the relationship therapist of last resort; couples often go to Esther after trying (and failing) in other relationship counseling. Esther usually sees couples one time, in a massive three-hour session, and then sends them back to their other therapists. Though she would never say this about herself, if Esther can't help you, no one can help you. We knew Esther was a singular talent and that an audio project with her talking about relationships would be like nothing else produced.

When we first considered approaching Esther, we started rolling through a lot of fairly traditional choices for what form her podcast should take: For example, let's have Esther host conversations with other thinkers, let's have Esther answer listener call-in questions, let's have Esther be interviewed by a host facilitator, and so on. We considered every traditional template structure for a podcast showcasing an interesting mind. Nothing seemed to square very well. And even though Esther is a brilliant communicator who speaks nine languages, she isn't very good at reading written scripts. She comes off sounding somewhat uncomfortable and not the smooth, flowing, warm Esther you hear on tape. As a result, none of the basic forms felt right.

More out of frustration than anything else, Esther suggested we come and record a session with a couple. Esther has a massive waiting list to see her, and couples can "jump the queue" if they are willing to be anonymously included in Esther's research and writing projects. So we knew we could find a couple pretty easily. Esther suggested this so we could hear what she does with couples, in the hope that this would inspire us to think of the best form for her podcast.

So my staff mic'd up her office, Esther, and the couple (there were at least six mics in the room). We recorded with the couple and Esther in one room and the production crew in the next office.

While the show would eventually go on to record some pretty wild interactions between couples with significant fissures in their relationships, the first couple we recorded was fairly ordinary. They were young and Indian-American, struggling between traditional roles (with resulting expectations) and modern relationships. At first, we thought the recording was a bit of a dud, but then we noticed something. Listening to that recording carried with it a bit of a spooky contagion. Do you remember the movie *The Ring*, where every person who watched a video died shortly afterward? It was a bit like that, except no one died. Every single person who heard the recording with the couple and Esther, and I mean every single person, unprompted, did the exact same thing after listening. They had a conversation with their partner about what they heard, and it promoted a discussion about whether some of those behaviors and issues were present in their own relationship. Every. Single. Person.

Once we noticed it, we began to test this with a larger group of people. Everyone reported back that listening to that recording had prompted some level of conversation with their partners.

That was went it started to dawn on us.

Rather than simply serve as inspiration for form, to figure out what predefined box to put Esther into, or as a demonstration of Esther's skill, it became apparent that this was the show. While we had just recorded it to document what happened, we had stumbled on the conceit of the show itself. Esther. A couple. Alone in a room for three hours, later edited down and packaged.

While many called *Where Should We Begin?* an innovative approach, at its core it wasn't. It is simply people telling stories. The couple has their own versions of their stories, individually and together. Esther would try to help them reframe their stories and walk away with a different perspective. But at its core, they were just telling stories.

Again, there is no need to be binary. Someone who listens carefully to *Where Should We Begin?* would point out there are some elements of other forms in the episodes. Most episodes open with a short vignette to introduce the couple and familiarize the listener with the problem: a short narrative story. The edited recording of the sessions is often paused so that Esther, recorded afterward, can offer a small rant about what we are hearing and what it means, which is interlaced with the recording itself.

And even when you're innovating with form, you may not get it right on the first try. It might require tweaking.

Probably the largest project I've ever created (to date) has been *TED Radio Hour*. While it has been a massive success, its origins caused a lot of angst. TED had considered the idea of an audio program focused its iconic eighteen-minute TED talks[15] for years, but a lot of radio and early podcast makers had said it would be difficult, if not impossible, to create something that didn't feel derivative of the original talks, if not a far inferior experience to simply listening to the audio of a talk. So for years, that was what they did, just offer a podcast feed of TED talks that didn't rely too much on visuals to share their ideas.[16]

---

[15] So why are TED talks eighteen minutes long? Why that length? Very early on in my relationship with TED, I asked that question of TED curator Chris Anderson. He said that the number is completely arbitrary. He figured if they picked a number like fifteen or twenty minutes, the speakers would think that was a suggestion. But eighteen minutes feels deliberate—sending a message to speakers, "Oh, these people are serious." Thus, the speaker is more likely to make sure they hit their mark.

[16] Which, worth noting, was and still is an incredibly popular and beloved podcast.

At some point around 2011, TED reached out to NPR to make a broad inquiry about potential ways to collaborate. I was invited along to the meeting. I was told to come up with some ideas to share with TED, and I came up with exactly one. Once the meeting started, the conversation turned to possibilities, and I took my chance to lay it out.

"I think we should do a show together that can live on the radio and as a podcast and sound like it belongs in both places," I said. "We can use the TED talks as launching points for conversations about the ideas they contain. It could mix audio from the talks with new interviews and conversations we can record."

Looking back, it is shocking how closely that initial pitch mirrored the show we ended up producing. There were a few small details that never made it into the show. For example, I was just starting to develop my long-standing (and still in practice) dislike for recording in studios, instead preferring to record out in the world. So the original pitch was that if we were talking to a TED speaker about his talk on urban growth, we would record the conversation on a busy street. If we were launching from a TED talk about water reclamation, we'd record the conversation next to a stream or lake. My idea came from the sound of TED talks, which are incredibly clean sounding, but with enough ambience and reverberation to let you know it was recorded in a large live venue. But they all sounded, mostly, the same. Answer: Record out in the world where the sound palette would be so much more diverse. That idea became a logistical nightmare (as well as potentially expensive and difficult to edit), so we recorded most conversations in soundproof studios.

Once we'd settled on a form we liked, we produced the first series of ten episodes, and it was a hit from day one. Those first episodes were downloaded more than five million times in the first months (a massive accomplishment for a podcast in 2012) and aired weekly on more than 250 radio stations (a massive accomplishment at any time). It was lauded in the press, received amazing reviews, and was named the "Best New Podcast" of the year by Apple.

Then, much to everyone's surprise, we stopped. It was one of the largest, if not the largest, podcast debuts, ever, and we stopped it cold. For ten months.

Even though it had been almost universally praised, several of the people at TED, as well as myself, felt we had were being celebrated for getting a "B-." We could have, and should have, done better. Sure, it was fine, but as I have mentioned: I hate "fine." Fine just felt like a marker that it could have been better. Once we admitted to each other that we felt we hadn't achieved what was possible, we stepped back and dissected every element of the program. After some reflection, we realized we were pursuing the wrong form.

Those initial ten episodes of *TED Radio Hour* were built to be Questions and Answers. Our host would interview the speaker about their talk and expand the topic, but it would never stray very far from the ground covered in the original talk. They were just too focused on the original TED talk. They were always looking backward.

As we thought through it, we made one change in form: Let's abandon conversations and tell stories instead. Let's tell narrative stories about ideas, and use TED talks as the launching pad to go off in completely uncharted territory. Instead of asking and answering questions, we would tell stories and encourage those we spoke with to share stories, too. The stories would become the carriers of the ideas.

That one change in form led us to change almost everything about the show. Before, we used a staff split between New York (where TED is located) and Washington, DC (where NPR is located). With the change in form, we relocated the production entirely to DC. With that move, we had to hire a new host. We changed the flow and pacing of the show. We used much more music as a scoring element. On and on. Basically, when that was done, all we had kept was the name and two staff members. We changed everything else about the show. All originating from that one simple change in form.

The result was immediately apparent. Every success marker we had from the original series of ten episodes was blown out of the water. We had originally thought we'd created a massive hit, but the changes showed us that our first series had just started to tap the show's potential. We had thought that *TED Radio Hour* would be a concept with about three years of shelf life, now, more than seven years later, the show is still going strong, on more than 600 radio stations and downloaded hundreds of millions of times a year.

All from just a small perspective switch.

Going back to my discussion about my yoga instructor, Joe, we spent the second half of my workship with him focused on form.

We'd ended our Four-Pointed Circle exercise focused on Joe, the life coach and translator, who was going to help people like Cate, the thirty-three-year-old millennial professional from Chicago, by providing solutions for how to avoid emotional battles by adopting new strategies to talk about feelings.

But what form would that take?

I pulled out my clever "only two types of podcasts": *people chatting* and *people telling stories*. And I explained the three sub-categories for each (Rant, Questions and Answers, Conversation, Seasonal Narratives, Episodic Narratives, and Multiple Narratives). Afterward I asked if there were any that stuck out that the group felt Joe would be particularly good or not good at executing.

The group was not helpful, suggesting that Joe could excel at almost any of them. Even though I had just met Meg and Michael, I think they had already figured out that this thinking wouldn't fly with me. You can't do everything. Then Michael suggested that Joe could have a podcast that could, on occasion, dip into other areas. For example, he could create some kind of storytelling podcast, then have an occasional interview.

He could do that, I responded, but that would be unwise.

I said that, to me, it all goes back to the target listener and what their expectations are. Think of Cate and her search for self-improvement. Does an interview deliver that? Maybe. Don't decide to add something different because you can. Instead, add something new because it will delight your listener. It's all about them.

When pushed, they all suggested that one of Joe's key strengths was his use of narrative. It was how he facilitated reflection in his clients; it was what makes his yoga classes so special.

"Joe helps people navigate their own stories," Meg said.

"Yes," Michael interjected. "Joe outlines the experience, shares something he has learned on his own journey, articulates the challenges, offers suggestions on how to self-correct, and then offers a solution."

I pointed out to the group that what Michael laid out was almost identical to Joseph Campbell's monomyth, "the hero's journey," which serves as the backbone of almost all storytelling (something we'll get into more in Chapter 5).

So, we still didn't know the form, but we knew it had to use Joe's talents for storytelling.

After more discussion, we landed on a structure we liked.

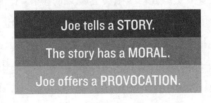

Joe tells a STORY.

The story has a MORAL.

Joe offers a PROVOCATION.

Story. Moral. Provocation.

It's a Rant but borrowing elements on an Episodic Narrative.

Joe shares a story. Something he has read. Something he has heard. Something he has thought. Something he has witnessed. Regardless of origin, that story has a moral to it, which Joe reflects on. The moral leads Joe to offer a provocation to the listener: It is meant to be homework for the listener. This structure is how Joe, the life coach and translator, is going to help people like Cate, the thirty-three-year-old millennial professional from Chicago, by providing solutions for how to avoid emotional battles by adopting new strategies to talk about feelings.

The provocation is key. The provocation is what makes it into an active experience that goes beyond the time spent listening. An example of this would be that after telling the story and considering that story's moral, Joe might ask the listener, "Today, make a list of three things that you've been unable to move forward with that you'd like to focus on this week." Or "Today, pay someone a compliment. Give it to someone who you normally wouldn't have said that to." Or "Who do you owe a phone call to? Make a promise to yourself to make that call before the weekend." Let's remember Cate. She wants something prescriptive and active from her listening. She wants to listen, learn, and know how to apply the lesson immediately. The provocation is aimed directly at her.

Further, since Cate is a busy person and doesn't want to (or have time to) indulge in long episodes, Joe's new podcast will shoot for a target length of seven minutes for its episodes. Joe plans to start his feed with four episodes and add a new one weekly. While adding even more is tempting and may make sense down the line as the show grows, Cate also won't have the time to listen daily.

As we wrapped up, Joe thanked me and said, "This is so clear. It makes sense and it makes sense for me to make it."

"That's the point, Joe," I said. "That's the point."

BONUS EPISODE: How Guy Raz Thinks about Form

When *The New York Times* ran a profile on Guy Raz, I jokingly sent him a text saying, "Guy, you are becoming the Steve Harvey of podcasting." Steve Harvey is a working comedian, hosts a daily radio show, and—at the time of this writing—also hosts six different TV shows. Steve Harvey is everywhere, and he is a busy fellow. So is Guy, the podcast host. Since he took over as host of *TED Radio Hour* when it became a weekly show in 2013, Guy has hosted no less than five podcasts.[17] He proudly holds the title of being the only podcast host to head three podcasts in the Apple Podcasts Top Ten chart at the same time. With all these podcasts, how does he decide what they should be? When he works on a new project with the kernel of

---

[17] Besides hosting *TED Radio Hour*, Guy fronts the entrepreneur interview program *How I Built This*, the kids' program *Wow in the World, The Rewind with Guy Raz,* and *Wisdom from the Top.*

an idea, how does he decide what form, or combination of forms, to utilize?

Guy is a veteran of working with me, as we spent several years working very closely to build *TED Radio Hour*. We both also did a considerable amount of teeth-cutting at NPR. All this is a way to say it shouldn't be a surprise that we have very similar perspectives, like the moment when I asked him what he thought was needed to make a great podcast, and he said, "Making a good podcast is about simplicity, and elegance, and a really clear idea." Amen.

"Making a podcast is not that hard. You can just get a microphone and start to record ideas into the computer," he continued. "But creating a podcast that sounds really easy is really hard to make."

Guy is a fan of beginning with the end in mind. He knows that his listeners are smart and, generally speaking, are engaged with news every day. But he is also (rightfully) aware that even the most hardcore news consumers need a break—they don't want to *just* listen to the news. But even while seeking out other types of listening experiences, they don't stop being smart.

There is a term that journalists and producers use to describe a certain type of production: a deep dive. A "deep dive" is a podcast story or episode (or long-form article, video, or other form of media) that explores a topic, happening, or event in great "depth": lots of context and detail, as well as getting into the "how" and "why" of a story. Guy likes to think of the role a deep dive plays in a listener's life by taking the term and using it metaphorically.

"If you are on a boat and it's very turbulent on the water, it's very choppy, right. It's very unpleasant," he says. It becomes a metaphorical reference to the turbulence and drama of daily news, which can often overwhelm people and cause them to want to get a breakaway.

"All you have to do is dive twenty meters beneath the surface of the ocean, and it doesn't matter if there's a hurricane, because it's always going to be calm. It doesn't matter," he says. "It's always calm twenty meters down. The motion of the waves twenty meters above doesn't affect what's going on deep down. It's calm. It's quiet.

And so that's sort of how I think about how we do our shows. I mean, obviously, we're affected by contemporary news issues, but we try not to let them distract us, because we want to take the long view on things.

"When approaching an episode of *TED Radio Hour* or *How I Built This*, we want to be in a place where our listeners can kind of go to step back, and to say, 'Okay, I'm getting some perspective here. This is actually more meaningful. This matters.'"

In other words, Guy sees his shows as the calm water underneath, the place where listeners can dive in to escape the turbulence.

That's actually a beautiful and thoughtful gift for his listeners. It's saying that you, the listener, come to this show to get away from the frantic news of the day. The show is not just an escape, but a provider of perspective. All the craziness of the day and the week—they are all just waves on the surface: distractions. They will pass. In the deeper, still waters, we will be safe until things are calm.

So, what does all this have to do with decisions about form?

As Guy and I spoke, I began to really appreciate the relationship he was highlighting between form and other factors.

"There's always a tension between resources and ambition," Guy says. "And we have always tried to push ambition really, really to the breaking point, with the understanding that, you know, there are limitations. Like, time is a limitation, right? The number of people is a limitation."

To be clear, a lot of people, especially in business, toss around the term "resources." And like a lot of things tossed around in business conversation, the term is really broad and can mean many things. "Resources" can mean money, cash you have available as a budget for a project or idea. "Resources" can also mean people, like paid employees available to work on a project. "Resources" can also mean physical assets, like a recording studio, theater, or small things like a computer, power drill, or chairs. Generally speaking, it is a term for things in the physical world that you can use to make something happen, assets outside of your mind, thoughts, and ideas.

As Guy was pointing out, when you are making decisions about what form a project should take, you need to factor in not only the limits of your imagination, but the limits of your resources, too. You must factor in constraints, and factoring in constraints to your ambition is one way of determining form.

As Guy and I were speaking, I started to doodle in my notebook. Whenever I'm dealing with things that relate to each other, I try to find a way to express that in a formula, like a math program.

I illustrated Guy's suggestion that form comes from ambition and resources like this:

Ambition + Resources = Form

It is worth noting that in my formula, if Resources were a number, it could be a negative number (a lack of resources), but occasionally it can be a positive number (we have more money, time, or assets than we thought).

As creatives, we always start with ambition. We imagine what we can create, and build the foundation of a vision in our minds, often largely divorced from the resources and constraints we have available. Then, reality sets in: We only have so much time, money, or assets to use to execute. But a smart maker doesn't let a lack of resources deter them; they apply their creativity to working around the resources, to make the most of what they have. Many in the podcasting ecosystem demonstrate this every day. Marc Maron doesn't own a fancy recording studio (at one time a requisite for production); he has a few microphones set up in his garage. The first episode of *Criminal* was recorded in the producer's closet (and who wants to count the thousands of other podcasters who recorded in closets, inside pillow forts, with towels draped over their heads, or just at a kitchen table?). A lack of resources doesn't stop you, but you have to factor that into your ambition in order to make decisions about which form you pursue.

But if that precious resource is time, it requires a different type of creative problem-solving. If your imagination and ambition yearn to create a beautiful, sound-rich narrative with a ton of location interviews, custom sound design, and an orchestral score, great. But if it is due in two days, that might be a tough prospect. So you learn to tailor your ambition by working with the resources at hand.

Guy learned this firsthand during his years as the host of *Weekend All Things Considered*. They strove to be entrepreneurial and enterprising in the way they would produce the show—to be very ambitious and present listeners with a deep dive on subjects meant to either end or begin their week (depending on your perspective on weekend). But they had two hours to fill, a small staff, and there was no way to extend a deadline. The show went live at 5 p.m. on Saturday and Sunday. So they applied their creativity not only to the editorial considerations of the show but to executing the best possible show, in the time they had, with the staff and resources in front of them.

"What I think we tried to do, and at times we were really successful in doing, was in sort of showing that even with a lot of limitations you can have big ambitions in producing content," Guy says.

As Guy transitioned into podcasting, he started to apply that same crafty thinking to how to produce new projects. When you have an idea, the decision to create a rich narrative experience, or a beautifully constructed interview, or a panel conversation, is not only dictated by your vision but has to account for the reality of what you have to execute it. But that doesn't need to be a restraint.

"In podcasting today, there are some very beautiful podcasts that are essentially produced in a black box. Many of them are one person in a black box of a computer," says Guy. "I think of *Song Exploder*. It's essentially one guy with a computer producing beautiful content. You know, huge shows like *Lore*; it's one guy recording himself and then producing it in a black box. The possibility to do ambitious things, even with limited resources, has been real and is even more real now because the barrier of entry is so much lower."

Chapter 4

ASKING QUESTIONS

n the summer of 1985, I managed to land an interview with one of my favorite bands at the time, the Violent Femmes. I was a DJ at our campus radio station and somehow convinced the record company PR person to schedule an interview, which, to me, was really a vehicle to get a backstage pass and a chance to meet the band. The show was at the Variety Theater in Cleveland, which had recently gained some notoriety as the venue where the English rock band Motörhead set a record for the loudest concert of all time. This wasn't an official record, since the *Guinness World Records* book had recently decided to stop "celebrating" this category for fear of promoting hearing loss. Thirty seconds of exposure to sound pressure rated at 110 decibels can induce permanent hearing damage, and the risk grows exponentially from there. The Motörhead show was measured at 130 decibels.[18] It was so loud that the plaster started to fall from the ceiling. But the plaster may have also been falling because the Variety Theater was a pit, a barely viable venue from a bygone era.

---

[18] Surprisingly, the record has been broken only a handful of times in the past thirty-plus years, with the current top honor going to a 2008 Manowar show in Bad Arolsen, Germany, measured at 139 decibels.

But on this evening, the mangy Variety Theater was transformed into a palace by my stellar interview with the Violent Femmes!

Okay, that actually isn't how I should characterize it.

After heading backstage at the appointed time, post soundcheck, I met the band, set up my recorder, brought out my cheat sheet of deep questions . . . and proceeded to do everything wrong.

Honestly, I've been staring at my computer screen for ten full minutes unable to even begin describing this travesty of journalism. It was horrible. After a few minutes, the drummer and bassist got bored and got up and left, so I sat with the band's singer and principal songwriter, Gordon Gano, for about forty-five minutes. I asked him a hot mess of dead-end questions, things he'd been asked probably hundreds of times before, coupled with some questions that looked good on paper but I had to try several times to explain out loud. I cracked jokes that no one laughed at (except me) in order to appear witty and quick. I walked in with no plan. I never asked follow-up questions or paid attention to what he was saying in response, just adding "Cool" whenever he finished speaking before raising my question list right in front of my face (and in a way that wouldn't reveal how badly my hand was shaking).

Worse yet, I was simultaneously trying to be cool around Gordon, yet also appear chummy and friendly to convey a false sense of familiarity with him. I wanted listeners to think Gordon and I were buddies—instant friends.

Even worse, I had brought along a girl I was trying to impress. So I was whiffing the interview, doing a cringe-inducingly bad job of establishing rapport with Gordon, getting crap tape, and God knows what the girl was thinking of all this.

And yet, of course, I aired the entire thing, uncut, on my radio show the following week.

The one saving grace of this is when I decided to share this story, I went searching through old tapes to find the recorded evidence of this debacle and thankfully, it seems to have been lost to the ages.

The only useful purpose this interview served was that periodically over the years I've thought back to that evening and pondered why it went so wrong.[19] The answer I've come up with brought me to an understanding of why most interviewers fail; and the fix for almost all bad interviews is extraordinarily simple. It isn't the questions. It isn't the lack of rapport.

I believe that the most common pitfall in interviews is the interviewer trying to play the role of "The Interviewer." The person conducting the interview walks in with a role in mind of how someone conducting an interview should act, and they, basically, act out that part. The Interviewer knows the subject so well they can recall even esoteric facts about minor things. The Interviewer asks deep questions. The Interviewer is buddies with the subject (or at least the subject likes The Interviewer). The Interviewer is clever and funny. The Interviewer is serious (except when The Interviewer is supposed to be charming). The Interviewer nods their head a lot and is deeply engaged. The interviewee being interviewed by The Interviewer often starts answers with "No one has ever asked me that before." At the end of the interview, the subject must thank The Interviewer for the best interview they've ever done.

I'm not saying that these are somehow wrong or shouldn't be a result of conducting a good interview, but being The Interviewer isn't the role you should play when conducting an interview. The role you should play . . . is you.

Here is another example. As I write this, I'm working on a pilot with a well-known author, which requires that she interview guest experts as part of each episode. When we got into the studio, she had a list of topics and questions, had read the subject's books, and did a fairly good job of mapping out the major chapters of the conversation.

Once we started recording, almost immediately things felt a bit weird. She was speaking in a noticeably higher voice than normal. She

---

[19] It's worth noting/admitting that it was many years before I admitted to myself how awful it was. I just thought the band wasn't into it, or had other things to do. Before I came to terms with it, it always brought about this weird, uncomfortable feeling, but I didn't understand why.

was stilted and stiff. Sometimes she would ramble on with the setup to a question. Other times, she'd reframe questions into a dead end, receiving only a one-word answer in response. It wasn't a total wreck by any measure, but it wasn't what we were hoping for or expecting.

Afterward, we had a debrief over lunch and I asked her what happened.

"It just didn't feel right," she said. "It just took me forever to get comfortable."

I asked what felt off about it.

"Well, I just kept thinking, 'What would Terry Gross do? What would Terry Gross do?'" she said. "And I just never felt like I got to the point of getting what Terry would get out of that interview."

I told her, "You know, I didn't want Terry Gross to conduct that interview, I wanted you to conduct that interview."

Maybe all interviewers aren't trying to be Terry Gross, but maybe they are trying to be Joe Rogan, Ellen, Trevor Noah, Ryan Seacrest, Oprah, Howard Stern—or anyone else they admire and think they should emulate. But too often, interviewers try to play a role rather than simply be themselves.

No amount of research or question-writing or prep will ever serve you better than just following your own instincts. You. Not The Interviewer. You already have everything you need to be a fantastic interviewer.

Well, you have everything you need, assuming you are a curious person. You can't fake curious. If you have to fake it, even a little bit, you should probably look at different forms for your projects.

Before I continue, another point of order here. I struggled a lot as to whether to put a chapter on interviewing before or after a chapter on storytelling. The two are so intertwined. You will never be able to tell a good story in audio unless you have strong skills as an interviewer—and you will never be a good interviewer unless you both understand the tenets of good storytelling and realize that interviews are, in essence, a means to tell stories. So my suggestion to you, as odd as it may seem, is to read this chapter, read the next chapter on storytelling, then circle back and read through this chapter again. You will probably get more out of it that way.

Moving on.

As a listener, I love interviews. I enjoy listening to them as a construct and form, and believe that some kinds of stories and ideas emerge better through an interview than through a traditional narrative. When it comes down to it, most times you hear someone talking in a narrative podcast (other than the host), that tape came from an interview. So, therefore, knowing what you are doing—and doing it well—will serve you regardless of the format of your project. Interviews are both formal and intimate; they are revealing and focused.

Interviews have given me, as a creator, an excuse to go places I couldn't otherwise go to and talk to people I otherwise couldn't speak to in order to ask questions that I have about them, their life, and their work. However, I've struggled with this a lot since that Violent Femmes interview,[20] so much so that many years ago I gave up on doing formal sit-down interviews, leaving it for others. I have the exact opposite feeling about doing "field" interviews, where I'm out in the real world interviewing people in their homes, at work, or in some normal environment. Perhaps because I'm using these field interviews to construct a story, I'm happier in my role and curiosity. But my thoughts on all this don't come from a place of expertise, but as someone who has spent a lot of time struggling and examining the work of others in order to learn. If anything, this chapter is a compilation of various things that feel true to me.

For the most part, I'm not going to offer you a list of questions to ask someone. There are plenty of books and websites specifically focused on interview techniques. Admittedly, 90 percent of them are probably garbage and you should just ignore them and follow your gut anyhow, but I'll leave that path of discovery for you to find on your

---

[20] Many reading this book may be surprised to learn that while I have built a lot of my reputation in audio, a sizeable portion of my creative output has been print (including this book, obviously), and a significant amount of that has been interviewing musicians about their work.

own. I'm not going to give you tips on how to get a subject to like you (outside of being courteous, friendly, and grateful). While this book is about teaching you to think like a listener, this chapter will also help you learn to think like an interviewer. Because what defines a good interviewer truly is someone who is comfortable using themselves as a proxy for the audience. Using your own natural curiosity as a proxy for theirs. Not to ask every question an audience of thousands might think to ask, but to ask questions that *you* want to know the answers to, and having the confidence that there are probably many others in your audience who want to know the same things.

SO I WAS WONDERING . . .

There's a common saying in courtroom proceedings that a lawyer should never ask a witness a question unless the lawyer already knows the answer. The lawyer should never leave the possibility for surprise, as there is always a chance that surprise may benefit their opponent instead. But as an interviewer, you should only ask questions that you don't know the answer to. *If you already know the answer, why are you asking the question?*

There are many tropes to interviews, mostly bad. But there is one trope that is worth emulating and almost guaranteed to elicit something interesting.

When someone starts a question with "So, I was wondering," the question is almost always going to get an answer worth hearing. The catch is that it has to be something you were genuinely wondering about.

Most interviewers think their job is to ask questions that evoke answers, which is slightly off. In truth, your job is to be curious. To be more specific, your job is to allow your natural curiosity to emerge in questions you choose to ask. Your job is to wonder.

The best way to utilize your curiosity is to simply ask what you want to know about a person, event, or idea. You've given a lot of thought to a person and what makes them and/or their work interesting, so after that, what do you want to know?

In 2001, following the publication of my first book, I was booked to be on the *Joey Reynolds Show*, a late-night talk show on WOR in New York City. I showed up and right before going into the studio the producer said to me, "Look, I need to let you know something before you go in there. Joey hasn't read your book. Joey doesn't even know the title of your book. Joey hasn't read anything about it. He hasn't even looked at the press release. In fact, Joey doesn't know anything about you."

"Okay . . . " I replied, somewhat hesitantly.

"And whatever you do," she continued, "when he starts talking to you, don't mention your book right away. He hates that. If you do it, he'll send you back out. Just follow his lead."

So, it's 11 p.m. I'm on a book tour and exhausted. I'm about to walk into the studio with a host who not only knows nothing about me or my book, but I have been told not to ever mention it.

"Sure," I said. "Let's do it."

I was supposed to be in the studio for twenty minutes. Joey started off talking about pastrami and various purveyors of pastrami. He asked me about my favorite pastrami sandwich in New York City and I told him that I didn't live in New York and had never eaten a pastrami sandwich. Then he somehow segued into talking about Britney Spears and Justin Timberlake, and then wondered what I thought about whether they were staying together. I said that I hadn't heard much from Britney lately, but I certainly hoped that things worked out for the best.[21] Joey thought this was funny and we continued in this mode: him just talking about things and somehow working in questions to me in the process. Joey kept me there for an hour and a half, just going back and forth. Without intending to and without any obvious transitions, we managed to talk about my book and many of the musicians mentioned in my book.

I walked in there expecting a shit show and didn't get it.

Why?

---

[21] Interesting aside: I, not surprisingly, don't know Britney and have never met her. Though several years later, and for no apparent reason, Britney started following me on Twitter, and she still does to this day.

Joey is just a curious guy and a generous talker. He has lots of questions and gives himself permission to wonder, out loud. Looking back, I remember him saying the phrase, "I wonder . . . " probably dozens of times. Joey's approach is a high-wire act, just allowing himself to fill several hours on the radio each night with no prep or advance work, not even knowing the guest's name. He also spent decades honing his craft and ability to do that. Admittedly, it's a rather extreme example, but it is dead simple. Joey isn't doing anything that someone else couldn't do. Everyone wonders. Joey just made a living learning how to do it out loud.

Now, the world already has one Joey Reynolds.[22] It doesn't need another. You don't need to try to do what Joey does and make him into your role model for The Interviewer. In fact, I really, really don't want you to try to be like Joey. Joey isn't especially a great interviewer either, to be honest, but he is a master of entertaining, off-the-cuff conversation. Joey is Joey, and you are you. But several hours a night, several nights a week, for decades, Joey's show is a great example of just how far you can go with a little bit of wonder.

SHUT UP

There is a phrase I've told my young son with enough frequency that he rolls his eyes when he hears it. While he is a bright kid who is comfortable talking with adults, he hasn't fully grasped that interrupting is a bad thing. When he does, I often say to him: "When you are talking, you aren't listening."

The same idea applies to interviews. While I stand by my assertion that the main requirement of an interviewer is to be curious, I'd say that a tight second place goes to listening. Great interviewing comes from great listening, listening by you. Your goal as an interviewer should be to do as little of the talking as possible. Just be quiet.

Unlike in a normal conversation, silence can be your friend in an interview setting. When someone is being interviewed, they, too, are playing a role, "The Interview Subject" (or perhaps "The

---

[22] As of this writing, in his fifth decade on the radio, Joey is still doing a weekly show on Sunday nights.

Interviewee"). However, in this case, having an assumed set of expectations isn't a bad thing, because the job description for The Interviewee is basically to talk. I find that whenever I interview someone, if I let some silence fall between their answer and my next question or statement, they realize they aren't fulfilling their end of the bargain and feel compelled to rush in and fill it by talking. *And often what they say to fill silence is the best part of their answer.* Beforehand, they told you the answer they had planned to give, but when there is silence, and they rush into that quiet to be The Interviewee, they say things that go beyond the early comfortable answer, offering something more, something deeper, something fresh that they haven't thought or said before. It's worth noting that you should save the silence for when you think it will reveal the most useful answer. If you allow silence between every answer and question, (a) your interviewee will probably catch on, and (b) it will create a lot of weird energy, pacing, and discomfort between you and the subject. Your goal is to keep them there, keep them engaged, and most important, keep them talking.

I've spoken with a few interviewers over the years who have all told me their goal in the interview is to talk as little as possible, just dropping in enough to get the interview subject talking again. By not dominating the conversation, not even taking up anywhere close to half the time in the conversation, you are forecasting to both the subject and the audience that the guest is the star of this interview. What they have to say is important, so I am just going to be present enough to keep the conversation going where I want it to go. Your quiet role is giving up the center stage to your guest, their story, and what they have to say.

Focusing on listening (and not talking) also will open you up to finding opportunities for follow-up questions. Often when you are asking questions in an interview, the initial question (and resulting answer) are not nearly as interesting as what a resulting follow-up question may evoke. Here's a great example: In a 1994 interview with actor Nathan Lane, *Fresh Air* host Terry Gross demonstrates a beautiful trick I've noticed in her interviews over the years. When guests on

Fresh Air make a statement, she simply interrupts with surgical precision to ask for an example:

> **NATHAN LANE:** *It was really my older brother Dan who got me interested in the theater. He's a teacher and he would take his classes over to plays in New York and he would take me with him and that's how I got interested in the theater. And so . . . yeah . . . eventually I moved to New York and became a struggling, starving actor and had all those strange jobs you have . . . you have to do.*
>
> **TERRY GROSS:** *Such as?*
>
> **NATHAN LANE:** *Well, I used to deliver singing telegrams . . . you know . . . ah . . .*
>
> **TERRY GROSS:** *Such as?*
>
> **NATHAN LANE:** *[starts singing] "Happy hysterectomy! Happy hysterectomy!" You know it was like ridiculous, and people hate when you deliver singing telegrams, and ah, I did this for a very long time. [Singing again.] "Congratulations, Shirley! Your stretch marks hardly show!" And it was terrible.*
>
> **TERRY GROSS:** *Who wrote the songs?*
>
> **NATHAN LANE:** *They did! They would tell whatever the occasion was and put it, set it to a popular tune, you know, one that you didn't have to pay any royalties on.*

Terry's contribution to that exchange is basically eight words—eight syllables—next-level Zen mastery that turned a toss-off (and almost cliché) anecdote about moving to New York into something unique, charming, original, and a revealing look into Nathan's creative mind. If Terry had just accepted the answer, or filled in space by talking, or simply moved on to her next question, that never would have happened.

I once heard that the function of asking follow-up questions is "turning the jewel," to show the various facets of the subject to the audience. While the initial presentation may be quite pleasing, turning the jewel lets light hit different parts, really demonstrating its quality and brilliance.

If you are worried about trying all this, you needn't be. There is nothing wrong with simply telling your subject about your objectives here. Before the conversation starts, as you and the subject are getting settled, it is very common to go over the ground rules for an interview: thanking them again for doing it, how to handle it if they need a break or want to do an answer over again, etc. During this exchange, simply add something like: "Look, I really want this interview to focus on you, so don't be surprised if I'm not saying much. I want to give you as much time to answer. So if I'm not stopping you or asking another question, please feel free to keep going!"

Remember that they know, sometimes quite explicitly, that their role as The Interviewee is to talk. That's what they signed on for, that is what they know they are supposed to do. So, if you say up front that they have the room and freedom to take as much time as they want answering, let them! You should be prepared to do a lot of editing on what they say, but what you will end up with will be more interesting, more revealing, and more fun to listen to than the short, pithy crap you may get with short answers.

Sometimes you will have an interview subject who doesn't want to be there, but most times, that isn't the case. People have an innate desire to be heard and understood. They want you (and your audience) to see it the way they see it (or at least the way they *want* you to see it). That is why they are disrupting their day to talk to you about something they know. They aren't going to learn anything from the interview. Most people often have other things that will be more personally beneficial to them than sitting for an interview. But they do it because they see the value in others seeing things the way they do. Understanding why they find it so interesting. Feeling the excitement they feel, or the enthusiasm, pain, or curiosity.

Since this is the case, why not help them achieve their goal by sharing what you want from them? This point applies far beyond simply explaining why you won't be talking a lot. By taking a few minutes before the interview starts to make sure you both share an understanding of the role of The Interviewee, you'll get better tape.

PREPARED VERSUS OVERPREPARED

It's always best to start with some research. Most novice interviewers approach this like they need to drink from a fire hose. They believe that to be well prepared, they have to ingest everything known on a subject or the entire body of someone's work. Read every book the subject wrote. Read every article written on a subject. Watch every film the subject wrote, directed, or starred in. Listen to every album or watch every episode. I'm not advocating for little or light research, but let's just say that becoming the leading expert on your subject is not a requirement for an interesting interview. You need to know what you are talking about and who you are talking to, but beyond that, there is a diminishing return.

If you are interviewing an author, read the book. Filmmaker? Watch the film.[23] You also need to dive into what others have written about them or what they have shared in another interview. And if you find yourself in the position that this isn't logistically possible, recruit someone else to do these things for you and have them help you prepare. Otherwise, frankly, there is no reason for you to be doing the interview.

It may prove useful to check in with your Ten-Word Description at this stage, too. You have a clear and concise focus for the project. So how will you apply it to this interview? More specifically, how will it inform the kind of preparation you do and the questions you will ask? That Ten-Word Description can save you time and help channel your energy.

---

[23] Surprisingly, it is really common for interviewers to not have seen the movie, listened to the album, or read the book. And the subject can tell this almost immediately in the interview.

If your interview is part of a larger narrative or story about some-thing that happened, then read and learn as much about the story as possible. You can't expect to find things to wonder about, holes in your understanding of the story, or fresh ideas to ask about if you don't know what you are talking about.

And here is a protip: An easy way to get fresh material is to walk your subject through some of the things you read, heard, and saw in the coverage of the story from others. At worst, you'll get back an answer like: "Yup, that's how it happened." But in my experience, more times than not, your interview subject will find the fresh angle on the story for you.

> **YOU:** *I read that you bought your first harmonica when you were in fifth grade and taught yourself to play over the follow-ing few years. Is that true?*
>
> **SUBJECT:** *No, that isn't entirely true. There was a harmonica teacher at the local music store. But he was a complete asshole. He'd smack me in the mouth every time I made a mistake. So I quit and taught myself to play. And every once in a while, I look back and think it was all because of that asshole harmonica teacher.*

Bingo. Something new and original—just because you gave them a chance.

All that said, it is really possible to be overprepared.

While it is good to know your way around a story or subject, you do not need to be a completist. Completists may still wonder, but they end up wondering about esoteric things that few other people would care to know.

> **YOU:** *I noticed that Paul Roman was your drummer for your first three albums, but then John Hammerstein played on your fourth, then Paul returned after that. Can you describe the differences in their drumming style?*

Who gives a shit? [24]

I could make a good justification for overpreparation by saying that the more you know, the less you have to wonder about, but in truth, overpreparation doesn't make for good storytelling.

The biggest resistance I hear from potential interviewers who deliberately leave a little white space in their understanding of a subject: What if I ask a question that they have answered before?

So what? It won't be the first time they've been asked a question multiple times. If you don't get something interesting or enlightening, or something that can move your story forward, you can edit it out later (more on the importance of editing, the interviewer's greatest gift, in a bit).

There is a difference between asking dumb questions . . . and asking dumb questions. Some questions are just straight up dumb: With a small amount of research, you could have avoided asking something you should have been able to figure out, has been discussed in other interviews with the subject, or has been written about and discussed ad nauseum by others. Then there is the good kind of dumb question: the expression of good old-fashioned curiosity about something that *should have* been understood before, but wasn't. The simple question about the thing that's glaring at you like a beacon. "I'm sorry if this is a dumb question, but I was wondering why . . . " If your natural curiosity, coupled with your preparation, leads you to wonder something, say it out loud. Don't worry about whether it is a dumb question or not. If you came to it after doing the right amount of prep, it probably isn't.

RAPPORT

Many new interviewers fret over the need to build rapport with their subjects/guests.

Don't.

I mean, don't be a thoughtless jerk. But don't worry about the need to get them to like you.

---

[24] Very few listeners, unless you are hosting a podcast about obscure session drummers from the 1980s.

As we've mentioned before, the subject doesn't have to do this. There are other things they can be doing. It is important to repeatedly remind yourself and everyone you work with that the guest is being generous with their time. Also, as we've discussed before, the best way to express your recognition is by being grateful, kind, and respectful. Grateful doesn't mean fawning or excessive thanks. Kindness and respect don't mean asking only easy questions or avoiding sensitive topics. It means be prompt, have your act together, and let them know you are taking their time seriously. It means telling them the ground rules of the interview, if and when they can stop to take a break or think over something they want to say, and so on.

Whenever I interview someone, I always say a variation on this before we start:

ME: *Okay, so a few things before we start. Do you see this thing I've placed in front of you? My microphone?*[25]

SUBJECT: *Yes.*

ME: *Okay. It is connected to this device over here, which is my recorder. This is all turned on, so everything we are saying is now being recorded.*

SUBJECT: *Okay.*

ME: *Now, some things you need to know. Everything you say is going to be recorded until I leave. Can you acknowledge into the microphone that you know you are being recorded and that I'm using this for my podcast?*

SUBJECT: *Yes, I am aware I'm being recorded for your podcast.*[26]

---

[25] For avoidance of doubt, I say this to make a joke. Of course they know what it is; I'm just trying to start things off in a light mood.

[26] Ninety-nine times out of one hundred, they respond as if this is a continuation of our joke. However, in fact, it is incredibly important to get this acknowledgment on tape. It provides you with some protection (and some states require two-party consent to record).

ME: *Great. Now, a few things you should know. If at any time you want to stop, start an answer over again, you need to take a break, or you want me to turn off the recorder, just say so— and I will.*

SUBJECT: *That's cool.*

ME: *The other side of that is that I am free to use anything that I record. There is no "off the record" while the recorder is on. But like I said, if you need to stop for any reason, just say so. I'm telling you all this so I can be completely clear with you—and I am grateful that you are doing this, so I want to be respectful of your wishes.*

Interviews are weird. It is important to embrace them for what they really are: They exist in wholly artificial environments and depend on wholly unnatural interactions with people who often don't have any business asking or answering these questions. It's weird for them and for you.

You don't need to be friends. It doesn't even matter if the interviewee likes you. Your objective should be to make them feel respected for the wisdom, expertise, and experience they are about to share with you. You should strive to make them feel comfortable doing so. But that doesn't mean you have to have a bond—even a fake bond—that has even a flicker of a chance of existing outside of the moment.

AN INTERVIEW IS A STORY

An interview isn't just questions and answers. It is an opportunity to learn—for both you and your listener. And like everything else in the world, learning is easier when it is in the frame of a story. That is why it is best to think of your interview as a narrative and structure it accordingly.

Whether you are filling in details of a story, or trying to tell a story with an interview, interviews are stories. Not only is this true, but it provides a lot of comfortable and productive ways to structure your interview.

When you think of the questions you want to ask and the story you want to tell in narrative order, it's easier to conduct the interview, as well as edit it afterward. When an interview isn't well structured, it requires you and the subject to go back and forth in time, or for you to ask about various pieces of information in a random way. Without that structure, the story you are telling won't build logically, and it will be confusing for you, the subject, and ultimately, for the listener. It helps the interviewee if you have a sense of direction and if the questions you're asking are building on the questions that you've already asked. That way you can just keep going deeper.

The best way to organize this is to think in chapters. For example, if you are interviewing a musician, you might have a chapter on their formative years when they were first starting to play. You could create another chapter on how they broke into music. Another chapter about what it's like to be on the road. Another chapter about how fame is both wonderful and damaging. Then you can take questions you already have and put them into each chapter, and fill in where you have gaps. When you are editing the interview, it makes it significantly easier, too. You don't have to move every question around. If a whole chapter kind of went nowhere, you can just easily lift that chapter out, as opposed to having to dissect it, question by question, from various parts of the interview. If you're building on questions that you've already asked, they become knitted together. And if they're not knitted together in a pattern, then it's hard to untangle them when you're editing.

And speaking of editing...

EDIT

Every once in a while, when I listen to a recorded interview, I hear an exchange where the interviewer remarks that the conversation will be distributed unedited. Either a mistake happens, a guest fumbles or reconsiders an answer, and then remarks, "Oh, I'm sure you'll edit this out." Then the interviewer announces that, no, they will not edit it out, because their podcast is *real* and *authentic* and doesn't need to be edited. I hear this on the radio (though it is often a function of the lack of time and/or resources to edit the interview), but it is really prevalent in podcasting. Some podcasters wear it like a badge of honor.

But this is like a chef considering it a badge of honor that their food is inedible, then justifying their "cred" by saying, "I don't use seasoning or do prep work before cooking. That isn't authentic."

Unless you are a live broadcaster who is offering an interview in the moment because of a sense of urgency and importance of the information being conveyed *right now*, there is almost no justification for airing unedited interviews. To be honest, it's actually rude to your audience and is almost certain to limit the appeal of your show to potential listeners. By saying this, I know I stand the risk of alienating the tens of thousands of podcasters who don't edit interviews. So be it. What you are doing is wrong.

And here is why it is so egregious: Ask yourself, "What is the goal of the interview?" Lean on your Ten-Word Description for help here too. Is it to offer listeners a look into the subject's life, way of thinking, or expertise? Then why aren't you cutting out all the junk that doesn't serve that, like questions that don't evoke great answers, the "umms" and "ahhs" that are often the vocal expression of a thinking brain, and the tangents that go on far too long and/or don't really amount to much? Is it to enrich or broaden the listener's worldview or understanding? Then why are you giving them something that contains irrelevant asides, conversational rabbit holes, and wastes everyone's time?

For a creative interviewer, editing is freedom. Have a slightly crazy follow-up that you want to ask on the fly? Go for it. You can always edit it out later if it doesn't land. That string of questions about their second book you've always wanted to ask, but the subject makes very clear they aren't interested in talking about today? Fine. Just take that section out. That time they remember something interesting to add on to a question they answered fifteen minutes ago? Cool. Go for it. You can move it adjacent to the rest of the answer later.

Editing things out. Rearranging the flow of the interview. Trimming answers to keep things moving. *That* is how you create an authentic *listening experience* for the audience. In all my writing, I tend to write a lot, often two or three times the amount I will ultimately keep. I do it to put everything in my head on the page, then I groom and trim it down to the most relevant parts, trying to offer just enough to translate these ideas to you. But, trust me, you don't want everything. Getting everything would actually make it less accessible and, ironically, *harder* for you to understand.

A filmmaker friend of mine recently told me that he had completed the first edit of his documentary film, and it was almost seven hours long. How was he going to spend the next four months of his production cycle? Editing it down to ninety minutes. When his audiences see it, no one is going to say, "Gee, I wish I could see the four-hundred-minute version of this story." My friend's job is to make sure the audience doesn't miss anything he is cutting out, and has a full, complete experience without all the details that, frankly, aren't worth it to most of his viewers.

Editing an audio interview is no different. A lack of editing also limits potential audience because the raw interview will only be of interest to some (usually hardcore) fans but it won't be for everyone.

To drive the culinary metaphors even deeper into the ground, raw interviews are a lot like the raw food movement. Some people do enjoy a raw diet more than cooked foods, but they are kind of extremists and their tastes don't represent those of even most health-conscious foodies, let alone the greater public. If a restaurant wants to cater only to raw food enthusiasts, that's cool. But be prepared for most diners to make other choices. That isn't to say your choice of offering raw food is bad. Just be prepared for the associated response.

Podcasters who offer only raw interviews can take heed of that same warning. There is an audience for that, but most listeners will make other choices because what you are offering isn't what they want. They want a curated experience—and that doesn't necessarily mean short. You can have a curated experience that's a ninety-minute interview, but that's because there are ninety minutes of good stuff and you got rid of the rest.

If you talk to a group of producers, they will all have their own variations and techniques on how to edit interviews, and will swear theirs is the best, smartest, and produces the best results. There really isn't a perfect method. What's best is however you were trained, whatever systems your colleagues use, methods employed by those you admire, or just whatever feels right to you.

Many of my former NPR colleagues have very specific ways of editing, which differ quite dramatically from my methods (which I'll share later in the chapter). NPR's methods of editing are built around speed, because often there are only a few hours, sometimes minutes, between the time an interview is recorded and when it airs. The producers and editors need to work fast.

Often the producer and editor will sit in on the recording, both taking copious notes. Then they will have a quick huddle after the recording to talk about how to cut it down, what points to highlight, which material to toss out, and a target length for the finished interview. Then the producer goes off and makes the cuts. Back in the analog tape days, a producer's tape machine, desk, chair, and sometimes even their body would be covered with streamers of magnetic tape, each a small segment of the interview, now cut up to be reassembled into its final form. After the producer would finish with the interview, an editor would listen through the interview, often at double speed (to save time), to make sure the edit came together as intended. Again, everything I've described could happen within less than an hour after the interview ended.

It's a high-wire act. Watching the process take place can make observers' heads spin, wondering how everyone can keep track of everything. But when you do this every day, and were trained on how to do it well, it is just a day at the office. Even on the occasions when NPR producers take days or weeks to put a piece together, they stick to a surprising amount of the process they use for their daily journalism.

Since most of the production I've done over the years has had a few days or weeks to come together, my methods are far less frantically paced and take advantage of the extra time to really understand the interview and its potential. That starts with re-examining its structure.

The interview structure you created as you were formulating your questions won't necessarily be the same structure you captured on tape. If your pre-interview prep was to create a narrative and structure for your *questions*, then post-interview editing is really about providing that same purpose, flow, and form to the *answers* you got to those questions. Simply put: Sometimes you don't get what you expected. Sometimes the answers were better or worse, and you may have skipped sections or asked questions on the fly.

The first thing to do when editing your interview is to really establish what you have. To do this, you should "log your tape" or create an outline (with time marks) for the interview you recorded. To some, logging is very close to transcribing (which I'll touch on shortly), but your first pass on logging is simply meant as a road map to help you get your hands (and head) around all the tape you've gathered (in some cases, many hours of it). If you are conducting your own interview, logging can be done afterward. If you are a producer logging an interview conducted by someone else, you can do a lot of your logging during the recording itself (more on this in the next chapter).

A tape log can look something like this:

0:00: *Recording starts, small talk and chitchat.*

02:35: *Q: So, when did you first encounter a clown?*

02:50: *A: When I was nine my aunt took me to the circus . . . first time there . . . right at the beginning of the show, a clown car comes out . . . twelve clowns come out of the* *tiny car. I was mesmerized.*

3:15:   *Q: This picture over here on your shelf, is that from that day?*

3:20:   *A: Yes.... Surprised you noticed that.*

[Sound of subject getting up and walking to shelf, pulls down picture . . . we hear them blowing dust off the frame.]

3:35   *Yes, there he is . . . Tumbo the Clown . . . who knew where our friendship would take us.*

The function of tape logging is twofold. It gives you a chance to listen to what you recorded, which often will sound very different from how it sounded while the recording was happening. Some parts are more interesting than they were in the moment; other parts not so much. Whenever possible, I encourage you to let some time pass between the recording and when you go back and log the tape. The space gives you a chance to hear the tape with fresh ears. And when you give it the space, the tape you recorded will almost certainly sound different. The second function of tape logging is that it provides a map of your recording. Let's say you record two hours of interviews with someone over two days. You want to find that funny exchange where the interviewer asks the subject about their first time on stage and the subject shares a hilarious story about stage fright. Where is it? Hunt through two hours of recording? Nope. Just look it up in your tape log.

An unintended benefit of tape logging is that it really helps you get familiar with your recording by forcing you to listen carefully and take notes on what was said and what happened. When I'm editing, I really need to have the entire thing in my head; I want to be able to navigate every corner of what was recorded. That way, when I'm looking at a transcribed bit of tape later, I don't need to listen to the tape very much while I'm making choices about what to use and what to toss. The log and transcript are just there to allow me to hear it in my head.

There is another unintended benefit of tape logging that my company's cofounder, Jesse Baker, credits with having a lot of influence on her as a producer. When she first moved to New York City, she called up a few shows and asked if she could do some tape logging. Most producers would *gladly* outsource tape logging to an interested novice.[27] Some shows even pay people to log recording tape for them. Whether you are doing so for slightly-above minimum wage or as a volunteer, logging tape gives you a chance to listen, unfiltered, to how others work. How do they formulate questions? How do they build trust with the subject? What tricks do they use to get great tape? For many, this is a massive opportunity to "earn while you learn"—by hearing other hosts and producers work.

When time and resources allow, I also suggest getting tape transcribed. There are a number of services that use AI to transcribe tape in near real time, often at little or no cost. The results can be mixed, especially if the subjects have accents or there is a lot of noise, but it is often workable. There are also services that transcribe tape using human transcribers for a fee. This can get pretty expensive pretty quickly, so consider human transcription to be a luxury and employ it accordingly.

Once it is transcribed, I use the transcript as my main editing tool. I do what we call a "paper edit" before I try to digitally edit the interview. First, I listen again to the interview while reading along with the transcript, and I make a lot of notes in the margins about things that go beyond words: emotion, interesting moments of pause or reflection, interesting sounds (if you are interviewing them outdoors). I also strike through everything that I know I won't use. Then it is a process of winnowing down. Highlight and make note of passages that work best. Continue to strike out others. Make notes about how to rearrange segments that need it.

---

[27] While a necessary tool for editing, let's be honest; tape logging can be a bit boring at times.

Sometimes the notes I put in the transcript about structure are enough (sometimes I number segments or paragraphs, for example, so I know how to re-order them). When needed, I often will physically cut up the transcript into segments. Some strips of paper contain just a line or two, and some strips are almost a whole page. Then I lay all the strips of paper on a table or the floor and literally rearrange the pieces into the order I want for the section or entire interview.

Regardless of how you work, from a tape log, quick machine AI transcript, or a full-on transcript, the last step is always the same: Take all your notes, pages, and strips of paper and begin to digitally edit your interview, using your edited log and/or transcript as a guide. Then listen through what you've done, make notes on what still isn't working, and do it all again.[28] And often, you repeat this process several times to get it perfect.

While this post-interview editing takes a lot of time, it is worth it. What you end up with is the best rendering of what you captured.

While impactful and valuable, and despite the emphasis I've put here on the importance of editing, it is also important to note that it is very easy to *over*edit an interview. A well-edited interview shouldn't sound edited. It should sound "normal" and conducted between humans who speak like humans. Some eager producers are quick to go a bit overboard on edits, eliminating every pause, "um," long breath, and stumble. I don't do this. While I want interviews to move along well, I often leave in an occasional "um" or stumble, so the interview sounds completely natural and organic. Editing should never be obvious. Never.

THE FULL SCHWARTZ

I want to share one of the most odd and unusual, yet also surprisingly effective, interview tactics I've ever encountered. It's called the Schwartz Technique, aka "The Full Schwartz."

The Schwartz Technique is a method to get everyday people to give vivid and evocative details in recorded interviews. The Full

99

---

[28] Worth noting that I don't purchase a fresh transcript for further edits, even though I still edit on paper. I will either use a machine AI transcript or simply create a new transcript out of my old edited transcript file.

Schwartz involves turning a recording studio[29] into a meditative environment, relaxing the subject and using visualization to pull out details that they may otherwise ignore or talk past.

Its creator, Stephen Schwartz, was an American who worked for the Danish Broadcasting Corporation for more than thirty years and became a specialist in documentary features produced without outside narration.

Over the years, I have often heard international audio producers discuss two different forms of audio documentary and feature production: the "American" style of production and the "Danish" (or sometimes referred to as the "European") style of production. "American" style audio documentaries feature a host/producer/reporter narrating the action (think *This American Life*, *Radiolab*, or *99% Invisible*). The host/producer/reporter is an intricate part of the story and is in the foreground of the action. The "Danish" style of audio documentary favors "self-narrated" storytelling, where the people being documented are the only voices you hear. There is no narrator or host reading scripted copy, asking questions on tape, or making observations. If the subject didn't say it, it isn't included in the production. They are the only ties holding it all together. Honestly, I'm not sure how set in stone and common are the terms "Danish" and "American," but I've heard them repeatedly for years, so I assume the use of these terms goes further than just me and the people I talk to.

When Stephen Schwartz started working for what was then called Public Danish Radio, he worked with the "father" of the Danish style of production, Willy Reunert (who, interestingly, was also an immigrant). They wanted to create productions where the subjects could speak directly to the audience, which was a pretty radical concept at the time.

But they quickly learned that not all subjects are natural storytellers. So how do you get John Q. Public to tell you a rich, captivating version of their story? A simple way to infuse emotion and make a

---

[29] Though, honestly, you could do this in just about any location.

well-worn story told in an interview more vivid is to tap into the teller's memory of details they probably hadn't shared in earlier tellings.

When someone first shares a story—be it something that happened to them, that they witnessed, or that they are reporting on, they tend to offer a chronological factual recitation of basic facts: what happened, who it happened to, and how it ended. It's surprising how many stories go no further than this. But we experience the world with all our sense and emotions, which provides you, as an interviewer, an opportunity to evoke new descriptive elements of the story as told to you. That's where the Full Schwartz comes in.

It's worth pointing out that Stephen Schwartz did not refer to his method as The Full Schwartz. He referred to his method as "Capturing the Moment." The eponymous term was most likely added by admirers later.

The Full Schwartz is pretty easy to execute.

1. In a pre-interview or conversation before going into the studio, work with the subject to identify some key scenes in the story. Imagine the moment as if it were a photograph, and go over a lot of what was going on in that scene. While it is the subject's story, it is really up to you to flag the pivotal moments in the story.

2. Prepare the studio (or other quiet place) for the interview by lowering or turning off the lights, putting cushions on the floor, and lighting some candles.[30]

3. Get the subject comfortable lying on the ground, and have your subject close their eyes. Do a bit of deep breathing to really get them relaxed.

4. Place the mic (on a boom stand) very close to the subject's mouth and encourage them to speak in a calm, quiet voice.

5. Tell the subject that you want to revisit some of the scenes in their

---

[30] Every telling of the Full Schwartz technique I've heard mentions the candle. It is important to make it nice for the subject and set an intimate mood!

story. Select the pivotal moments and have the subject talk about them as if they were describing a photograph. The key is to get them to describe every detail. After they answer, repeatedly ask them for more detail and what happened next.

6. In addition to describing the scene like a photograph, get the subject to focus on other internal details: What were they feeling at that moment? What were they thinking? Were there smells, sounds, or other sensations that stuck out to them?

Two keys to making the Schwartz Technique work. First, be prepared to really make them go over and over the pivotal scenes. Ask for more detail, then ask for even more. Evoke their full range of senses and emotions at that moment. Ask if they remember feeling hot or cold. Are there any smells associated with the moment? Was it very bright or dark outside? Was there music playing that may have matched the moment? Ask them if they remember what they were feeling at that moment. Ask them if they thought anything to themselves at that moment.

For example, if they are describing a touchdown catch that ended the championship game, ask if the receiver was running or standing still when he caught the ball. Did he jump into the air to catch it or was he on the ground? Were any tufts of grass kicked up during the play? How many other players were gathered around? Of course someone won't remember every detail, but don't assume they haven't retained *any* details. They will surprise you with what they remember. Dig deep and keep asking them what they saw and what details they remember. And be prepared to go over the same scene many times.

Second, and most important, coach the subject to speak in an active voice and ask them to rephrase their recollections accordingly. Instead of saying "I remember that the coach threw down his clipboard and I think he screamed out in joy," ask them to say, "The coach threw down his clipboard and screamed out in joy."

There is also a variation on the Schwartz Technique known as The Half Schwartz. It is a lighter, slightly less odd version of The Full

Schwartz. When using The Half Schwartz, you don't ask the subject to lie on the ground in the dark. Instead, you dim the lights and ask them to sit in a chair. You still ask them to close their eyes and focus on the scenes you've identified, but without the extra ambient flair.

STARTER QUESTIONS

Over the years, I've collected a few questions I keep in my back pocket for interviews, to ask when I get hard up for interesting questions. Unfortunately, I can't attribute them well, though every one of these I picked up by listening to interviews conducted by others. So, to those who first taught them to me, my apologies and thank you:

- When someone describes an event or happening, ask them: "How was this different than you expected or imagined it would turn out?"

- When you are talking to someone who is accomplished in a certain field, ask them: "Why do people fail doing what you do?"

- When interviewing someone who has been repeatedly profiled in the past, I like to ask: "What do people often get wrong about you?" (Or "wrong about your work," "wrong about your books," "wrong about people like you," and so on.) Not only does it often open up an avenue for your interview, but it helps you avoid mistakes made by others.

BONUS EPISODE: Terry Gross Gives Advice to Novice Interviewers

Terry Gross started her career in 1973 as an interviewer hosting a radio show called *Woman Power* at WBFO in Buffalo, New York. The show focused on the happenings in the feminist community around Buffalo, including topical conversations, recent speeches, and events. Even though she had never hosted radio before (she had previously been a schoolteacher), she quickly moved up to cohosting *This Is Radio*, a three-hour-a-day, five-day-a-week show. That's a lot of time to fill.

On *This Is Radio*, the Terry Gross we know sounded a lot different. There are a few clips of those shows that survive (Terry often plays them when she gives lectures or talks). I was curious about what she hears when she listens to them.

"I hear an uncertain voice," she answered. "I hear somebody who's not all that comfortable yet speaking on the radio. Whose voice is a lot higher." Basically, Terry Gross herself hadn't figured out how to be Terry Gross yet.

"Back then, I worked mostly on my curiosity," she told me. "I'm made of curiosity, and back then, working to fill three hours every day, that's about all I had."

Today on *Fresh Air*, Terry, assisted by a staff of producers, spends hours preparing for each interview: reading a mass of material on each guest; spending time with their work; writing, editing, and rewriting questions then spending many more hours editing the interview. And for every author who appears on *Fresh Air*, Terry reads each book. All of them.

But cohosting fifteen hours a week back in her Buffalo days, with no support staff, didn't afford much time for prep.

"Part of what we would do is go through the *Village Voice* classified ads looking for jazz musicians who were trying to make extra money by giving lessons," she said. "And we'd call them up and ask to interview them. We would have a short talk and then play some music. It wasn't very intensive. It wasn't as in-depth. I don't think I was working as hard as I do now to get beneath the surface of things. We didn't have time for that. Some interviews I could read an article, but that's about it."

In place of research was innate curiosity. "I always try to clarify in my own mind why this person matters, and why it's worthy of our listeners' time," she said.

As you can imagine, Terry gets asked for advice a lot on how to do interviews. She says that good interview prep starts with answering a simple question: "What do you want from them that you can't get from somebody else?" Beyond that, she suggests ordering questions in a narrative structure and planning to edit extensively afterward. She often gives a few other pieces of advice:

- You should know as much as you can about a person and their work or their field of expertise in the amount of time that you have to prepare.

- You don't need to know everything, and you don't need to be able to write a dissertation on it yourself. You don't have to become the expert, but you have to know enough to know what makes this person special.

- Ask "What do you want from them?" That might be their personal story. It might be insights into their field. But you have to have a sense of "Why am I talking to this person?"

- Map out how you will illustrate what makes this person special. Remember that if you just sit down and ask generic questions, you might never get there. Unless you've done some research, you won't know what they said a hundred times before that you don't need them to say again to you.

So what does arguably one of the greatest interviewers in the world hear as a common mistake with interviewers? Being slavish to your list of questions: "I think a common mistake people make, especially when they're starting, is that they've written out their questions and they're gonna stick to them no matter what," she says. "And as much as I suggest having a narrative order for your questions, I don't think that you should feel wedded to them. You should feel free to listen and ask follow-up questions, and follow the interview where it leads you, knowing that you have the structure to come back to, if and when you need it. But writing questions doesn't absolve you from listening and responding."

Chapter 5

HOW TO TELL A STORY, AKA DON'T BE BORING

I n 2008, I had just published a nonfiction book about vampires in popular and contemporary culture called *The Dead Travel Fast*. I was deeply invested in my audio work at NPR, but I was starting to get the itch for a new writing project. I thought to myself that maybe it was time to write a novel.

I'd never written a novel, nor much short fiction to speak of, and was looking for something to help me organize my thoughts. For Christmas that year, my wife bought me an item I'd placed on my wish list, a novel-writing kit called *You Can Write a Novel*. It's a box filled with a 200-page instructional book for outlining your novel, and a number of paper pads, each containing checkboxes and prompts to fill in information about your novel's chapters, characters, scenes, and so on. The back of the box promised: "Eliminate the 'where to begin?' trepidation that can ruin the novel-writing process. The *You Can Write a Novel Kit* gives you all the tools you need to turn your idea into a salable novel."

Today, in 2019, that box sits on my bookshelf in almost mint condition. The only sign of its use is the decade-old NPR business card stuck between pages 32 and 33, which was as far as I got. The paper pads are completely untouched, though I did remove the plastic wrap so I could look through them. The Scene Development pages ask you to check off a Scene Purpose and offer the choices:

- Move the story line ahead.
- Introduce/develop characters.
- Introduce/worsen the problem.

- Solve a problem.
- Set up later scenes.
- Create atmosphere.

The other section boxes of the pad ask the would-be novelist to write out Conflict In Scene, Setting Description, and Characters in Scene, among other prompts. The other pads contained prompts for filling out information on other elements in the process.

So, despite having everything laid out in easy-to-follow guidelines, as well as sitting next to my desk for a decade, *You Can Write a Novel* never helped me write a novel.[31] However, what it did reinforce to me is that there are components to great narratives. There are rules to telling great stories that have applied to tales told from the origins of language to the ones we tell and share today. They especially apply to the world of podcasting and audiomaking, where the story's teller provides the words, sounds, and voices that are the catalyst for the imagery invoked in the listeners' minds.

The most important skill of all, in podcasting, audio—and hell, in life—is knowing how to tell a story.

People love stories. People teach using stories. People connect by telling stories. People sell using stories. Multiple studies have shown that a person is much more likely to retain information and learn concepts if the information is presented to them as part of a narrative story.

---

[31] It's worth noting that this is, in no way, to suggest that *You Can Write a Novel* is some kind of inferior product. The fault totally lies with the would-be novelist in question.

As my friend Al Letson says, "People are hardwired for story. It is in our DNA. We just can't stay away from them."

So, given how essential stories (and, thus, storytelling) are to us, you'd think that we would be naturally as good at telling stories as we are at listening to them. Unfortunately, that isn't the case.

Now, it would be easy to write an entire book on storytelling and the components of great stories, and offer lots of compelling advice on how to tell stories. I know this because I've read many of them. If you look at the "Recommended Reading" list at the back of this book, you'll see I've listed a bunch that I think are particularly instructive, inspiring, and useful to audio makers. In this chapter, I will neither attempt to give you, in a few pages, what those books offer over an entire book; nor will I attempt to summarize or distill what they offer. I'd suggest that after reading this chapter, if your appetite is whetted, go read them. They will teach you much more than I can here.

That said, as someone who has been telling stories on the radio almost since I started in radio in my teens, I have found there are some important truths that you need to pay attention to in order to tell evocative stories in audio form.

If you, like me, have even the tiniest antiestablishment tendencies, I can already see you bucking against the notion that narratives have rules. But these rules are time-tested, not as in tested over recent years or decades, but as in tested over 10,000 years of storytelling.

I'm often asked by podcasters how to make sure something is interesting. My reply is always the same:

- Know the rules of storytelling.
- Follow them as simply and clearly as possible.
- Don't be obvious about it.

The last line is important. While most initially think it means not to let listeners see the structure of a story (it does mean that), it has a larger context, too. If a story's structure is its skeleton, then the components of story are the flesh around those bones. When you look at a person, you don't see a skeleton, though it is there. The appearance of the person is deeply influenced by the bones underneath, but you really don't want to see bone. When discussing narrative and story structure, those I'm talking with often love to point out narratives that "violate" the rules of storytelling. In almost every instance, their examples don't violate the rules at all; they are just super disciplined and purposeful about how they don't make them obvious.

I was speaking to a group of aspiring podcast students and played a documentary by my friend and former colleague Hana Walker-Brown called *The Spirit of Hessle Road*. The piece is a thirty-minute documentary (created in the non-narrated "Danish" style mentioned earlier) focused on her hometown, Hull, a seaside fishing town on the east coast of England, which Hana produced for BBC Radio 4. I played the first half for the class, which contains a mixture of voices sharing stories of the history of Hull, singing folk songs, and telling their own stories about their lives in the town. Hull is a working-class town that has seen its share of hard times. The voices and sounds are so rich and clear. It's a beautiful piece of work, but most of the students didn't like it at all.

"I hear voices but I don't know who they are," said one.

"I don't get what the story is," said another.

So we spent some time deconstructing the piece. Were there voices that aren't identified? Some, but not all. But did that matter? Did the lack of people's names prevent us as listeners from understanding their lives, hopes, and struggles? Did the style prevent us from empathizing with what they were fighting for, individually and as a community? Not at all. I even pointed to the classic Cormac McCarthy novel *The Road*, where the entire novel goes by without either of the two protagonists being named.

Was there a story? We spent some time outlining what we'd heard and you could slowly see the looks of recognition on the students' faces as they realized there were actually a number of narratives in the piece but they just weren't spelled out or obvious. And like many narrative stories, *The Spirit of Hessle Road* contains multiple narrative storylines. A story can be part of a larger narrative or contain a number of multilayered or interconnected stories. Take, for example, the first *Star Wars* movie. It was a complete narrative, with a beginning, middle, and end. But it was also part of a larger narrative (all the movies of the saga) that are presented in almost a dozen different films.

Most of the students walked away with a completely different perspective on the piece, or at least respected its craft in a way they didn't initially recognize. Nothing in Hana's piece violated or ignored the rules of storytelling; she was just super subtle and crafty about how she used them to her advantage.

When I first started to practice meditation, a friend told me that one reason new practitioners should trust the benefits of meditation is that it has had more than 2,500 years of testing and validation. That makes a lot of sense; meditation is done the way it is for specific reasons that have centuries of consideration behind them. Apply the same thinking to the 10,000 years of storytelling. The rules are there because they work.

When people fret over how to keep their work from being boring, I often tell them that "boring" is simply a side effect of a poorly constructed story. How can you avoid being boring? Simply make sure the story works on a DNA level by finding the parts that stray from the narrative structure and adjusting them back into place, as well as putting in the parts listeners will need to make the story relevant to them. As some wise person once said, "There are no bad stories, only bad storytellers."

WHAT IS A STORY?

One afternoon in the fall of 1999, I was on a phone call, pitching Ira Glass and one of his producers on an idea I had for a piece for Ira's new show, *This American Life*, and I was about to absolutely bomb.

A few weeks earlier I had run into Ira at some event, and in the course of our conversation, I started to tell him about this trip I'd taken over the summer to a place called Exotic World. Its full name was The Exotic World Museum and Burlesque Hall of Fame, dedicated to the burlesque dancing popular from the 1920s through the 1960s. It was located on an abandoned farm in Helendale, California, smack in the middle of the Mojave Desert. It was a collection of burlesque memorabilia, costumes, signage, and artifacts curated and put together by a group of now-retired former dancers, headed by a woman named Dixie Evans, known during her career as "the Marilyn Monroe of Burlesque," then in her eighties. Describing Exotic World as a "homemade" museum would be kind. The museum itself was in an old goat barn. The roof leaked. All the signage was hand-drawn and constructed using questionable technique and skill. It was a ragtag, yet completely endearing, hot mess.

Each year, as a way to raise money and awareness for the museum, Dixie held a Miss Exotic World Pageant around the property's pool (which was half filled with grit). During the pageant, young burlesque revivalists would compete for the title of Miss Exotic World, but the big draw was the retired older dancers from burlesque's heyday, who would go up on stage and revive their old routines. These women, now in their seventies, eighties, and even nineties, would bump, shimmy, and striptease, all the way down to pasties and a G-string.

It all was incredible. And you'd think it would make a great story. Except that it really isn't a story.

After I got on the phone with Ira and his producer, and told them about Exotic World, there was a lot of laughter and "wow"s. Then one of them finally asked me, "So, what is the story?"

"What do you mean," I replied. "I just told you the story."

"It sounds amazing," they replied. "But what is the story? What happens? What is the narrative?"

I was completely at a loss for words. My previous work as a radio producer, reporter, and writer was largely based on reporting events. Events are happenings. They are noteworthy because they have implications to larger ideas, reveal (or address) problems, and sometimes even have characters that you get to know well enough to love or hate.

Most news reports, events, and happenings are snapshots. They are notable moments in time. For example, you read on a site or see on TV that there was a house fire in your town. The reporters immediately tell you what happened to the occupants of the house and how severe the damage was to the property. But rarely do you know why it happened. You don't know anything about the residents. Beyond that immediate moment, you don't understand the impact of the fire on those residents or how this might change the direction of something they are pursuing in their lives. At best, the news "story" is a vignette. But it isn't really anywhere close to a full story.

Narrative storytelling follows the basic tenets of journalism, answering "who," "what," "when," "why," "where," and "how" within the constructs of scene, character, and action. Stories have a clear beginning, middle, and end. There are characters in search of something and encountering obstacles. There are scenes. There are themes and meaning. There is a moral. There are surprises, twists, and unexpected turns of events.

My pitch about Exotic World had little of that.

I had some jaw-dropping "who," "what," "when," "why," "where," and "how" bits, but I didn't have a story. Most news reports, anecdotes, and things we read, view, and share often contain elements of narrative story structure, but not the whole package. They are interesting moments, informative and revealing, but when you think of it, you rarely see more than a small piece of a larger story.

The Miss Exotic World pageant I saw and pitched to Ira was crazy and odd and surprisingly emotional and inspiring, but it wasn't a story. I had a sense of place, but no clear idea of what was happening in that space besides the pageant. I had bucketsful of amazing characters, but they were two-dimensional.

Were there real stories at Exotic World? Yes, there were tons. The museum itself had stories. The museum's founders and the retired dancers all had stories. The new revival dancers had stories. Over the next few years, I'd return a number of times, and though I couldn't see it then, some pretty amazing narratives emerged from the dancers and this history of burlesque they celebrated and shared. These were all equally valid types of stories, but they weren't necessarily podcast stories.

The expression of "story" in podcasting is narrative storytelling: Tell me about a situation where there are characters in pursuit of something, who then encounter obstacles, and are changed by their endeavor. *That* is a story.

ELEMENTS OF STORY

Anyone who has ever listened to a six-year-old recall a dream they had the night before understands what it is like to be locked into a narrative that lacks critical components. Stories have common attributes. As a storyteller—and, frankly, if you are speaking out loud, like it or not, you are a storyteller—you will never reach your full potential unless you are aware of how these universals work. They are elastic; some stories have more or less of each, but for a story to be an engaging and satisfying experience for a listener, these components all need to be present. Their presence is flexible, but they are all present. When you start to explore a fully realized story, you will find these necessary elements:

> Great audio stories contain SCENES.
> Scenes contain CHARACTERS.
> Characters have MOTIVATIONS.
> Motivations lead them to ACTION.
> They encounter RESISTANCE.
> The story has RESOLUTION.
> Ultimately, the story has a LESSON.
> And the best stories offer TWISTS.

Scenes, characters, motivations, action, resistance, resolution, and lesson, all even better with a twist. Every story contains its own unique balance of all these elements, and each is somewhat different for radio and podcast stories than they would be for text, video, or other media.

GREAT AUDIO STORIES CONTAIN SCENES

The power and effect of scene are almost criminally overlooked by many novice audio storytellers. In all seriousness, if there is only one thing you take away from this chapter, please let it be the importance of scene.

Think of scene like you would the set of a theatrical play. It is the world in which the action takes place. A great set establishes the play's tone. A great set enhances the drama, action, and emotion of a play. A great set is almost a character in the play itself. Scenes in audio serve the exact same role. Scenes are the lifeblood of great audio storytelling and have been as long as people have been telling stories on the radio. The scene is the basic building block of audio. Take any great audio story you've heard, and I know you could map it out as a series of scenes.

Scenes consist of images, images that exist only in the listener's mind, yet evoke places (where things happen) and actions (what happens there).

Here is how newer audio producers screw this up: When you are creating an audio story about a bank robbery, it is easy to focus on the mechanics of the crime: how the thieves enter the building, how they approach the teller, what the tellers put into the bag, and the getaway. But what about the bank? Is it a soaring marble structure or a threadbare low-ceiling seventies-era structure with chipped laminate countertops? Is it busy and bustling, or is it sleepy with a single gray-haired lady behind one of the dusty teller windows? A listener could set a number of expectations and inferences based on the scene where the robbery takes place. Yet many new producers spend too much time focused on the mechanics of plot, ignoring the vivid, revealing, and telling detail surrounding the characters and action.

Scenes can be a vessel for metaphor, allegory, and literary motion. Everything counts: not just the scenery itself, but the sounds, smells, and energy of a place where the action takes place. Scene takes that action and transforms it from a black-and-white image into a colorful environment that creates a vivid image of what happened in the listener's mind.

When you focus on scene, it is an environment filled with thousands of data points: furniture, items hanging on the walls, people, sounds, and so on. So which should you focus on?

You've heard the phrase "Show, don't tell"? It means to show someone being angry (or play tape of them speaking angrily) rather than say, "He was angry." Scene can be a great tool to do this. It shows what features are most revealing about the situation, the characters, what is about to take place, and what the thematic elements of the story are.

If you are profiling someone and notice there are stacks of newspapers and magazines strewn everywhere, mention the piles rather than saying, "She is a pack rat." If you are working on a story about a white supremacist and you notice there are Lou Rawls and Ray Charles albums in his record collection, mentioning that helps to set up the theme that this person is more complex than they appear. Which goes to show how scene is a great way to point out inconsistencies or things that contradict each other. Scene can exhibit ways to avoid sameness and predictability.

Scene is so important to radio because it places the listener in the middle of the story and takes them from one point in the narrative arc to the next. You, as a radio storyteller, are providing the building blocks to immerse the listener in the middle of a place they can't see, except in their mind. And your job is to make that as vivid as possible.

SCENES CONTAIN CHARACTERS

Scene is the underappreciated element of story, but it's character that drives your narrative and often *is* the story itself.

Characters, especially good characters,[32] are complicated. But they don't need to present their complications right away. A good character unfolds like a Russian nesting doll, taking on additional form with each revelation. Unfortunately, that isn't what you get in a

---

[32] And for the sake of clarity, when I say "good," I mean that they are rich, compelling, and engaging characters.

lot of journalism and reportorial writing. Most such writing is filled with two-dimensional apparitions of characters: subtle outlines and shadows of human form, lacking depth and detail. We learn little or nothing about them in the story. We rarely see them change. The journalist or reporter just does a basic drive-by of the protagonist, without adding more character or detail.

In podcast storytelling, the need is different. Intimacy is the primary ingredient in podcast storytelling. Cardboardlike characters don't resonate. Characters need to be deep, vivid, rich, multidimensional, and in full color.

Characters, as we see them, become the sum of their values, beliefs, and actions. What makes them interesting isn't just their strengths, bravado, and uniqueness, but it is their weaknesses, contradictions, and inconsistencies as well. But characters aren't enough: They need to go on some kind of journey; they need to be in pursuit of something.

CHARACTERS HAVE MOTIVATIONS

Everybody wants something, right?

In a story, the character's motivation is the fuel for the engine. The protagonist is in a situation, assumingly unchanged, but they want something more. Or something else. Or something different. That desire compels them to do something different. To break from routine. To defy convention. To take a risk.

That's when things get exciting. That's when they become interesting. A character that is "what you see is what you get" and unchanged or unchallenged . . . is pretty boring. They are two-dimensional. They are a cliché. But a vivid character is one who is capable of change, or at least capable of *trying* to change.

And as storytellers, we have an obligation to illustrate that desire, to show motive. It isn't necessary to always be direct and concrete about motive. A good storyteller can suggest it, or hint at it, or point the listener in the right direction. A *great* story shows how motivations morph and change, or how one motivation may be masking another. Rarely in life do characters get an idea in their head, driven by desire, and unflinchingly pursue that reality by any means necessary. Reality is a bit more complicated than that, and your telling of the story should reflect that as well.

Questions can also be motivations. An unanswered question creates a motivation to find an answer. An unanswered question creates suspense. As a creator, you should learn to value the power of questions. Questions lead to puzzles, mystery, paradox, and the unknown. As someone who creates for the mind's eye, these are your best friends. Revealing hidden motivation is also a great way to build twists into the story.

MOTIVATIONS LEAD THEM TO ACTION

Wanting something isn't enough; you have to do something to get it. Action is where things get real. A character's actions are a bit different from the "plot" of the story, yet actions make up the bulk of the plot in a story.

The plot is a series of cause-and-effect actions that move the characters through the story. Plot is literally when a story tells you what is happening, then here's the next thing that happened, and then this happened next, and then this other thing happened. The plot points are arranged and shared by the storyteller in a way to reveal their thematic significance to the story.

Plot can also include happenings that are not directly related to the characters (a tornado developing is a plot point, but no characters have control over that). However, most plot points you include in a story are either caused by the characters, happen to the characters, or move the characters to more action (here comes a tornado; let's go hide in the basement).

Action is different. Action is the literal acts initiated by the characters in pursuit of something. So, for example, when the tornado comes, and the characters hide in the basement (plot points), the protagonist decides this is the perfect time to try to kiss the girl (action), who he loves but is scared to tell.

I'm often surprised when I meet audio storytellers who take a very passive attitude toward action and plot. They lay out the happenings in a story based on the tape they have or the facts of the story as they understand them. If you are just reciting facts on tape, then a machine could do that. Deciding what action and plot points to consider can and should be a more active process, with creators researching a story, establishing the plot points, and focusing on plot points that match their thematic approach.

Your Ten-Word Descriptions can be of use here. Remember the Ten-Word Description I offered for a series I worked on, *West Cork* ("An unsolved murder exposes the underbelly of a rural Irish town.")? During the production process, the two reporters/hosts interviewed more than eighty people, gathered hundreds of hours of tape, and amassed reams of information and data points on every element of the story. How did we start sorting through it all? Which actions were the most important? Use the Ten-Word Description. If an action contributed to the idea of how this crime exposed the underbelly of the town, it stayed. If the action didn't serve that idea, it was put aside.

CHARACTERS ENCOUNTER RESISTANCE

While it would be terrific if everyone got what they wanted all the time, that never happens. If it did happen, it wouldn't be very exciting to listen to. Your protagonist, like everyone else in the world, needs to encounter resistance in order for us listeners to be invested. Only trouble is interesting.

When one person wants something, that often involves someone or something else giving it up. If nothing else, a character's change requires change from others, too. And it has been said that only a baby welcomes a change.

Though the character may not agree, obstacles have their benefit. Resistance builds and forms character. Pressure and tension can create something new and often more valuable than the base ingredients. Think of the process that transforms worthless carbon into precious diamonds.

The resistance, obstacles, and tension that characters encounter not only make the story better, and better to listen to, but the pressure also causes the story, character, and scene to become much more complex (in a good way), to become deeper, and ultimately to reveal more.

THE STORY HAS RESOLUTION

Resolution is a really interesting element in storytelling, because a story can still work without one. But that lack of resolution only works if it is purposeful.

You resolve complications and resistance in one of two ways: changing the world or changing yourself.

Robert McKee, in his seminal book *Story*, talks at length about the "Hollywood ending." There are two varieties of the Hollywood ending. There is the "closed ending," meaning that everything is answered, resolved, and wrapped up in a nice and neat, satisfying package. In short: There is a clear resolution. By contrast, an "open ending" is one that leaves a few loose ends; it isn't neat and tidy. Some questions aren't answered, and some questions are not resolved.

I have a soft spot for open endings, mostly because real-life stories rarely have that completely clean, buttoned-up quality to them—there is always something that goes sideways or doesn't land in the perfect spot. Sometimes I don't trust a closed ending, thinking that the producer just didn't dig deep enough to find the loose threads.

THE STORY HAS A LESSON

Every story has a moral. Every story has a lesson. Otherwise, what's the point?

Even capital-J Journalism, created by folks who generally avoid anything prescriptive whatsoever, often has a moral, even if that moral is simply "actions have consequences."

You will find storytellers who love to debate moral lessons: Should the moral be explicit, or implied, or left completely for the listener to discover on their own?

As I've stated earlier in the book, I believe in taking a listener 85 percent of the way toward an answer to a large theme or puzzle, but I don't want to spoon-feed it all to them. There is no joy in that. No sense of discovery. No self-revelation that lets the listener enjoy the beauty of figuring out the moral of the story on their own.

I've often told radio and podcast makers, if they can tell your story in a sentence, that is as long as it should be.

AND THE BEST STORIES OFFER TWISTS

When a creator is pitching me a story, or just telling me informally what they are working on, as I listen, I try to write the story in my head. Let's say a creator is working on a profile of a clockmaker who specializes in wooden clocks. I immediately guess (to myself) that the piece will include the story of how hard it is to practice a dated craft in the modern world, feature a symphony of ticking clock sounds, and include some exposition on the meaning of time.

Why do I do this? Because my hope is that the creator will put something into the conversation that I couldn't expect or see coming: a twist. Twists and pivots are the core of delight and surprise in stories. And every good story contains a number of unexpected twists, pivots, new dimensions, contexts, or complications that you couldn't see coming.

A good twist reveals what a story is *really* about. Sure, you may have been initially attracted to the story because it is a true crime tale about an unsolved murder. But once in it, you discover it's really about racism and cultural tensions. Sure, you may have initially been attracted to this story because it is about a crazy conspiracy theorist. But once in it, the story twists to reveal that the wacko conspiracy guy was actually right all along and the story becomes about how we treat outsiders and those who buck against cultural norms. Sure, you may have initially been attracted to this story about how an innocent man was shot by police in his home. But once in it, you realize it is actually an exposition on mental illness and how we expect law enforcement to deal with it.

A story with a twist that is predictable can be dull and two-dimensional. A story with unpredictable turns becomes delightful, surprising, instructive, and challenging.

One of my favorite recent examples of the power of a twist is in a story from a *This American Life* episode called "The Magic Show."[33] The story features Teller, of the magic duo Penn and Teller, explaining the invention of a magic trick called "The Floating Ball Routine."

The story is presented as an explainer on how the magic trick was invented, an act, many magicians will tell you, that can take years to perfect.

Teller shares that his inspiration for the floating ball routine came from a turn-of-the-twentieth-century magician named David P. Abbott. Abbott believed the best place for magic was in the parlor, so he exclusively performed in the living room of his home in Omaha, Nebraska. Magicians from around the world, including Harry Houdini, would travel to Nebraska to watch Abbott perform. Abbott was in the midst of writing an extended book detailing all the magic tricks he had invented when he died in 1934. His widow planned to publish the book, but died herself two years later. The book disappeared and became the subject of mysterious wonder. Many people searched for the book, but found little more than a few pages at a time until the rest of the manuscript was discovered in the 1970s. One of the tricks it contained was the floating ball routine.

Teller took the trick and spent almost a year perfecting it. He became kind of obsessed with it. Teller even took the ball on vacation with him to practice. Eventually, he staged the trick for his creative partner, Penn Jillette. Penn watched the trick from the back of the theater and when it was over, Penn walked out without saying a word. He hated it.

Penn felt it was "way too Cirque du Soleil" for Penn and Teller's act. He felt it was too arty and lacked an idea. There was no story to it.

---

[33] It's the *This American Life* episode #619, originally aired on June 30, 2017.

That is where the *This American Life* story twists. Instead of being about creating a magic trick, the story twists, to reveal that it was really about Penn and Teller's relationship as collaborators—about their dynamic. How they set standards for their act. How they communicate, and how they handle conflict. It gives you a peek into how they've managed to stay collaborators for more than forty years. Their personal dynamic takes over the story.

We witness that Penn and Teller are honest men and deeply committed to keeping the bar on their show extremely high. Penn hated the trick because he thought that while it was a great trick, it wasn't at the level of a Penn and Teller trick. And as was the agreement between them, nothing went into the show unless they both agreed.

What started off as an interesting premise about the anatomy of a magic trick became a model version of how to work with another person. In the end, despite feeling completely differently about the trick, they ended up working together to find a solution to raise the trick up to the level they needed. It was actually kind of sweet.

There is a line embedded in the story that Ira says in reference to the amount of work it takes to make a great magic trick: "Making anything good takes time." The same can be said about great audio stories.

STORY STRUCTURE

So now that you understand the elements and building blocks of story, how do you put it all together?

French filmmaker Jean-Luc Godard once said, "A story should have a beginning, middle, and end, but not necessarily in that order." He was right.

When looking at classic story structure, it is tempting to just start at the beginning and follow through sequentially to the end. Nothing is more stunningly boilerplate than a biography that starts at birth and ends at death. There are other ways. But before we talk about those other ways, let's look at some of the classic forms for storytelling, generally.

The Big Daddy of story structure was Joseph Campbell, a professor of comparative mythology and religion at Sarah Lawrence College, who rose to prominence following the publication of his seminal work in 1949, *The Hero with a Thousand Faces* (if you haven't read it, do so, it is worth it). Campbell theorized that all great narratives are variations of a single great story (aka the "monomyth"), which we repeatedly employ, even today. Basically, he argued that epic narrative stories all follow the same formula. Campbell forwarded the idea that the template "hero's journey" was the story of someone who prevailed through great suffering to return with newfound wisdom, experience, or some "thing" that would improve humankind. That's why this base structure has such endurance and appeal.

Campbell's vision of the monomyth template had seventeen stages across three acts:

ACT 1: "Departure," which includes the stages:

- The call to adventure.
- Refusal of the call.
- Supernatural aid.
- Crossing the threshold.
- Belly of the whale.

ACT 2: "Initiation," which includes the stages:

- The road of trials.
- The meeting with the goddess.
- Woman as temptress.
- Atonement with the father.
- Apotheosis.
- The ultimate boon.

ACT 3: "Return," which includes the stages:

- Refusal of the return.
- The magic flight.
- Rescue from without.
- The crossing of the return threshold.
- Master of two worlds.
- Freedom to live.

Some of the above stages may not make any sense without further explanation (and some are entirely misogynistic by today's standards). If it helps, there are many well-known stories that are considered to have the classic Campbell monomyth structure, such as *Star Wars, Moby-Dick, Jane Eyre, Lord of the Rings*, and Stephen King's *The Dark Tower*. If all this is a bit overwhelming, perhaps you can find understanding in a phrase Campbell himself used to boil all this down: "Follow your bliss."

The monomyth structure has been explored by a number of literary experts and writers since Campbell first published it in the late 1940s. One of the more recent and popular versions was offered by the creator and primary writer of the TV shows *Community* and *Rick and Morty* (as well as noted podcaster), Dan Harmon. Dan distilled the classic hero structure into a simpler, eight-step circular process, calling it his "Story Circle" technique.

The eight stages are:

1. A character is in a zone of comfort or familiarity.
2. They desire something.
3. They enter an unfamiliar situation.
4. They adapt to that situation.
5. They get that which they wanted.
6. They pay a heavy price for it.
7. They return to their familiar situation.
8. They have changed as a result of the journey.

He later distilled it down to just eight words: You, Need, Go, Search, Find, Take, Return, Change.

According to Harmon, the points should be arranged around a circle like the one on the right:

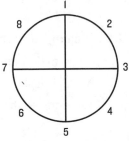

The two cross-section lines divide the story up into sections. The areas above the centerline and below the centerline (the centerline being known as the "Threshold of Adventure") represent the yin and yang opposites in life: order/chaos, conscious/unconscious, and life/death. The left and right sides represent the descent and ascent in the first and second half of the story.

If this all makes your head spin (it did mine, for a long time), there's an even simpler way to approach all this, a scheme for understanding story that requires only three words:

> There is a **PROTAGONIST** who encounters a **COMPLICATION**, then finds **RESOLUTION**.
>
> Protagonist. Complication. Resolution.

And make sure you throw in a few twists along the way for good measure.

But where do you start?

Anyone who has taken a literature course has probably studied the prevalent structure of a narrative arc: exposition, rising action, crisis, climax, and falling action. But don't be afraid to start elsewhere. In fact, picking the place to start, and how to roll out the story, is one of the most bespoke parts of the storytelling process.

A popular style in short fiction is to start the story as close to the ending as possible, then backtrack and tell the reader how we got to that point. I've seen this device used a lot in film as well (*American Beauty* and *Trainspotting* are two examples that pop to mind). One of my favorite tricks in telling narrative stories is to identify the defining moment in the story—the moment where everything changed, or came into focus, or the point of no return. That moment when a switch was flipped and nothing could go back to being the same. This approach raises many questions for listeners, and you can then fill in the answers (or strive to fill them in).

A textbook example of this is the omni-popular podcast *Serial,* most widely known for its first season, which focused on the investigation of the 1999 murder of a young woman, Hae Min Lee, in Baltimore. In its first episode, Sarah Koenig says that the entire series, and how you will feel about Adnan Syed's guilt or innocence, hinges on seventeen minutes on the day Hae Min Lee died. What happened during that time answers every question a listener will have. Throughout the rest of the series, Sarah takes the story in many different directions, but always ends up looping back through that initial question of what happened during that brief period of time. She ventures forth and loops back, almost creating a pattern like a child's drawing of a daisy.

Another example of this technique is the series we did at Audible that I mentioned earlier, called *West Cork*. The series starts with the story of a man named Len, a former accountant in London during the 1970s, who quit his job, sold all his worldly possessions, moved to West Cork, bought a dilapidated shack, a donkey, and a cart, and then embarked on a new, idyllic hippie life in the country. Len wasn't involved in the crime being investigated. He barely knew the people who were. He has little particular insight on the crime. So, why start there?

Jumping back to our Ten-Word Description ("An unsolved murder exposes the underbelly of a rural Irish town"), one might ask, what is the underbelly? Well, there are lots of messed-up things in West Cork, but most lead to or from an underlying cultural tension in the community between the native-born population and the "blow-ins" as they are called, people who moved there from other, often metropolitan, places. Both groups dislike and distrust each other, yet they also have an amazing amount of envy toward the other, often finding themselves running headlong into the other in pursuit of what they desire. The murder of Sophie Tuscan du Plantier there in 1996, in many ways, resulted from that tension and divide, embodied that tension, and remains unsolved largely because of that tension. So we strongly felt that we needed to start the story where that tension started, with the people like Len, who came to West Cork in search of something, as did Sophie, as did the man many believe killed her.

But, as I've mentioned, where you choose to start a story really depends on the story, and you. I think the best place to start puzzling this out is by diagramming your story. You may be old enough to remember when students were required to learn to diagram sentences as part of grammar instruction (newsflash: They don't do that anymore). Well, if you have any clue what I'm talking about with diagramming sentences, then this concept is pretty similar.

When I first work on a narrative, I like to diagram it. It's similar to creating an outline. I advocate starting out just listing off all the scenes, characters, actions, plot points, and other bits that you need to include in your story. Then, especially if it is a complex project, I will print that list out (often several pages long). And I will start to cut up the pages, each strip containing a single line (similar to what I advised for interview editing in the previous chapter, except this version is a bit more detailed and complex, not solely focused on the text).

Then I start to lay it out. One of the most important things you can do specifically as an audio creator is to start your story with a juicy, irresistible piece of bait. This is a moment when it benefits you to keep in mind that listeners listen while they are doing other things: driving, making lunches, walking the dog, folding laundry, and so on. You help keep their mind busy and happy while the body is occupied with mundane tasks. The one downside of this is that if you don't totally engage a listener, their mind will wander. At that point, you might as well be speaking gibberish, since no one is registering what you are saying.

So one of the most critical tasks you have in the beginning of the story is to give someone a reason to stay mentally tuned-in, to pay attention. Different producers have different tactics for doing this, with most focusing on picking the "hottest tape" they have (aka the best moment in a recorded interview). Just make sure that you never take that attention for granted or assume you have the listeners' attention. Earn it, deserve it, in every scene, but *especially* in your opening minutes.

When I edit stories and episodes with creators, they often remark how much attention I pay to the first three minutes of a piece. I probably spend more mental energy on those first 180 seconds than I do on the rest of the episode combined. Why? Because that is when the listener is making the judgment about whether they care to spend possibly hours with you and your story.

Another variation on this practice is to use sticky notes, writing an individual scene, character, action, plot point, etc., on individual stickies, then laying them out. Regardless of method, the idea is to lay out the pieces in the order that feels right, then move them around, and move them around again. Consider the recordings you have of sound and interviews, consider the ideas you have and things you plan to say woven between your clips of tape, then arrange again.

There is little more to help you here besides trial and error. Use The Six-Lunch Test Drive (detailed later in this chapter), use feedback from friends, and trust your gut. You'll know it's right when you see it. But you can't see it until you lay it out and rearrange and rearrange.

USE CAUTION WITH "IMPORTANT" STORIES.

I have difficult conversations with a number of journalists and news producers who have spent their careers chasing news stories, but are now trying to explore podcasting. While a lot of great podcasting employs journalism ethics, best practices, and principles, not all journalism makes for good podcasting. There are a few reasons for this.

In journalism, there are two basic kinds of stories: stories that tell the news and stories that forward our understanding of events and the people involved in them. Those stories that "tell the news" are basically covering the "who, what, and when" of a newsworthy event. Those stories that "forward our understanding" take a very broad look at the "why and how" of an event.

Headline news is a ubiquitous commodity. When an aging celebrity keels over from a heart attack, there are literally hundreds of sources who tell you, often as breathlessly quickly as possible, that the death has occurred. That's why a lot of journalists strive to break new stories or new angles on stories, if for no other reason than to separate themselves from the pack.

Journalists love the "forward our understanding" stories for the same reason: The enterprising nature of this type of journalism allows the journalist (and the organization they create for) to distinguish themselves. This is all well and good, but I'd argue that a lot of what makes good journalism good tends to focus on the relevance and importance of a story, not its ability to command an audience.

Let me provide an example. Recently a friend of an acquaintance called me for advice on starting a podcast. When I asked what the podcast was about, she told me they had done some investigative work on a local doctor who had been accused of molesting young female patients—very young female patients.

"So tell me," I asked. "Why would someone want to listen to that?"

"Because it is an important story," was the reply. "And we really dive in deep on who this guy was and what makes him tick."

I said that I didn't doubt its importance and praised her for her journalism and efforts to approach a difficult and highly emotionally charged subject. But none of that was a reason to listen to the story. And it wasn't a good reason to look at podcasting as the right way to distribute it.

I told her that it would be hard to imagine someone seeking out a podcast that was basically a biography of a serial rapist. I wasn't suggesting that their portrait of this guy and his crimes wouldn't be sympathetic, but that is really rough material.

"But no one else has this," she protested. "We have interviews with a lot of his victims, those who knew him, and many others. We basically own this story."

I told her that those were good reasons to cover the news story as a news story in their news programs on other platforms. But to create a stand-alone podcast, they were shitty reasons.

She just couldn't understand why I would say this. The story was new material on a heavily reported story. It had been so widely covered before, that had to be a sign that people were interested in it.

I told her that in broadcasting, there are thousands of examples of news stories, big, important, relevant, news stories that were widely covered every day in the press—that had been found to drive listeners away in droves. Syrian refugees. The Bosnian war. Famine. Ebola. All incredibly important stories journalistically, but they drove many listeners away.

To put it simply, people couldn't bear to hear that much bad news. It was too much.

Now, please understand, I am, *in no way*, suggesting that journalists shouldn't report these stories. However, their reporting ends up in news programs that contain a balance of information and stories. So even if there is a bummer story about child refugees, there are other things that balance it out. Plus, many news reports are just a few minutes. For the sake of being an informed citizen, many people can deal with a few minutes of bad news.

But what about six solid hours about child refugees? Or sexual assault of young girls? How about eight hours or ten hours? That's a podcast length. It's just simply too much.

And another important point that most journalists fail to grasp: Podcasts are things people seek out. If someone tunes in to the six o'clock news, watches the *Today* show, or listens to *Morning Edition* on their way to work, they are tuning into an experience. *Morning Edition* or the local news are vessels that offer a consistent customer promise: We will tell you what happened today, good and bad. It will be a variety of types of stories on a variety of subjects. If something isn't as relevant or interesting (or, God forbid, just straight-up boring), that's fine—there is another story, on a different subject, in a few minutes. These programs are, by expectation and definition, a variety pack. That's what news consumers want and expect.

Podcasts are very different. Listeners seek out particular podcasts because they are interested in the story or conversation. Sometimes this is going down to the micro level, where some listeners seek out specific guests on individual episodes, not even really caring about listening to the show on a regular basis.

So just because a story is important, or even great journalism, isn't a reason for a listener to care or be interested in listening (unless you are trying to reach an audience of fellow journalists).

To matter to listeners, stories and conversations need to be engaging, sticky, and really interesting; to be filled with compelling characters and conflict. They need to feel relevant to the audience. Most listeners do not seek out podcasts because they are important or enterprising journalism; they listen to be entertained and to learn. So seek out ways to make your important journalism interesting to them, find ways to make it entertaining and engaging, and take an approach that dares them not to listen. If you're planning to serve broccoli and have people choose it over candy, you'd better figure out how to put some cheese sauce on your broccoli if you want people to seek it out.

Interview podcasts are no different. The world is stuffed full of podcast interviews with "important" people doing "important" work, and no one listens to them. No one listens because they are boring as shit. A good producer doesn't sit back and hope the story or guest's importance is magically conveyed; they structure their episode, story, or interview so that it is as deeply engaging as possible. As with so many things, the less work you ask of your listeners, the more of them you will engage and the more they will get out of it (love it).

If the point of your journalism is to inform and enlighten as many people as possible, focus on how to tell the story in a way that engages them first, *then* informs and enlightens them. No one ever listened to a podcast because they "should" listen to it. That's work. That's not entertainment.

IDEAS

Another element that should be interwoven in all audio stories: thoughts and reflections.

The narrative podcasts people admire most, like *This American Life, Radiolab, Snap Judgment*, and others, contain more than just a great story and compelling recordings; they line the story with expository ideas. This can happen in big and small ways. It can be an inner monologue from the main character, or from the host/reporter. It can explain context or express meaning. Exposition offers a chance to share the meaning of what just happened.

The audio creator has the ability to put listeners into the middle of a scene, as well as the ability to pause that scene, or take the listener back out for a moment, or take the listener up to a lofty height to take a broader look around. They can stop periodically for a brief thought or idea provoked by a scene. As I often tell student

131

podcasters, when telling a story, it's good to stop every once in a while, look around, and share what you are thinking.

I generally don't believe in rules of thumb, because I think they lead to baseless habit. But if I did believe in rules of thumb, I would say that you should stop the action in the story at least once a minute and offer some kind of idea, or observation on an idea.

Sometimes a story can start with an idea and then go to the plot. And sometimes you'll start with the plot and then get to the idea. Ideas also help define a story's theme and meaning, as well as provide mile markers on the way to its moral lesson.

WHY AUDIO?

So you've put in all this work and what you have is definitely a story, but why audio? Do you have a justification for why this story should be told as an audio story, rather than text, video, or other format?

The answer to this question is driven by the tape you have. Who you have access to and their ability to tell their stories with vivid detail and emotion, express their thoughts and ideas, and generally be compellingly listenable. Do you have archival tape, ambient tape, and other sound resources that steer toward audio as the proper venue?

In other cases, audio may be a preferred medium simply because visuals may be distracting or might lead the listener to make snap judgments or draw conclusions. Regardless, answering this question is an important milestone in establishing your approach to your story and its structure.

SOUND

If I anticipate any criticism of this book, I expect that some will fault me for not discussing the role of sound and music in production in greater detail. Except for these few paragraphs, I have excluded it on purpose, even though I probably spend many hours every week wrestling with the use of ambient environmental sound, music, mixing, and scoring (often today collectively referred to as "sound design"). There are two reasons for that: First, it, like storytelling, could take up an entire book, and it's almost impossible to give it a full treatment in limited space. Second, sound design is an advanced skill. Even though I began my radio career as a sound engineer and sound mixer, today I don't sound design or mix my own pieces. The work is so advanced now, I often leave it to others. This book focuses on broader topics.

That isn't to say there isn't a lot that every creator should think about regarding sound and music. Sound and music are very powerful tools. They both evoke things that are unsaid, point a listener's attention to an important moment, provide emotional cues for the listener regarding mood and feeling, and provide the aesthetic of your work. When a story moves through scenes, the sound and music should move as well, and reflect the different environment of the new scene. Sound and music can be a signpost that things are changing, or that things are important. (There is a bad side to this as well, which is why many journalists detest the use of music in a piece.)

There are lots of great audio and video tutorials and resources online that can broaden and hone your thinking on the use of scoring elements like natural sound, sound effects, location ambient sounds, and music. They are inspiring and I'd encourage you to dive in; they will excite you.

I mention sound here for two reasons. Often creators think about sound too early, and often creators think about sound too late. Too early is often a case of putting the cart in front of the horse. Many eager producers will want to put in sound design elements like scoring and music when they first start working on a piece, even though they haven't put in the time yet to really figure out the story as a whole. That's kind of backward to me, as the story will often dictate the music and scoring you'll need in a piece.

That seems like deciding on the color of the car you want before choosing the size, features, and price. Well, you could decide you wanted a specific color, but starting off with that doesn't speak to your self-awareness of your needs as a driver. Same with stories. That said, I often do use music as inspiration while editing, and frankly, I've never met another audio creator who does this. I will often listen to music, or place quiet music inside my editing session files, *while doing the editing*. Sure, it is hard to hear fine detail (and I turn the audio off for that work), but it is not unusual for me to put on instrumental music while I edit, to help me hear the piece differently.

Those who think about sound too late often miss opportunities out in the field recording interviews and gathering sound. In the age of digital recording and rechargeable batteries, I often counsel students to always be recording. When in doubt, leave the recorder going. You will probably end up with countless hours of the noises inside the car as you are driving, sounds of walking and other street noises, and plenty of air-handling sound from air conditioners and noisy heating units. But when something remarkable or unexpected happens, or even when inspiration strikes with a thought you want to capture on tape, the recorder will be on. Capturing the sounds of place: birds and splashing waves in a tiny coastal community; the sound of laughing children at a playground; the clanging, music, and laughter at an amusement park. You will regret it later if you forget to capture these in the moment. Keep the recorder going. Don't shut it off until you are far away from your scene.

THE SIX-LUNCH TEST DRIVE

I came up with the Six-Lunch Test Drive almost by accident. I would go on a reporting trip, learn a bunch, meet a lot of interesting people, and get a lot of great tape. Then, when I'd be back at work, I would go to lunch with someone and my lunch mate would inevitably ask, "What have you been working on lately?"

I'd respond by telling them about the story I was working on. I began to notice that over the next couple of days, as I retold the story to different lunch companions on different dates, I began to adjust the story each time in order to tell it better. Then a lightbulb went off. I was learning how to tell an improved version of the story every time I told it. As I did repeat tellings, the story got stronger. The interesting parts became more interesting. The funnier parts became funnier. The moments of tension grew sharper. Everything grew more vivid.

So I decided to embrace this process full on. Rather than wait for someone to ask me about my work, whenever I had a new story, I would schedule a bunch of lunches, sometimes even offering to pay. And in exchange they would listen to me tell them the story.

Now this is a routine part of my story-building process. I've honed it over the years and happily evangelize it to others, who practice it themselves and swear by it. Here is how it works.

First, spend some time learning the details, events, scenes, and characters of your story. If necessary, go on reporting trips, talk to people, record sound, and really do some work to figure out the story elements you have at your disposal, as well as make some initial decisions about structure and what's interesting.

Then reach out to six friends and invite them to lunch. Be up front by saying that while you are always happy to see them, there is a purpose to this get-together: They are to listen to you tell a story. And a word of advice: Invite a cross section of people. Schedule lunches with some people who love your work, but invite some people who are harder to sell, and make sure to include a few people you don't know well (look at it as a bonding experience with a new coworker or friend). Then, during lunch, take the story for a test drive. Start where it feels right and work your way through the story.

Telling the story really isn't the most important part of the lunch. The most important part is *watching the reactions of your friend.* When do they seem engaged? When do they laugh? When are they moved? Do they ask any questions? Do they look off or seem bored or uninterested? Are there parts they don't understand? It is a bit tricky, but your mind has to be in two places at once: telling the story to your friend and being a careful observer of their reactions.

After lunch, think back on their reactions. Ask yourself how you can improve the telling of the story. Figure out how to double-down on what worked. Make the funnier parts funnier, make the moving parts more moving, and so on.

Then you take your revised story to Lunch 2 and repeat. Tell the story. Watch the reaction. Note the opportunities. Tweak. And on to Lunch 3. After repeating this six times, you should have a pretty refined version of this story and know it pretty well. Then, after all six lunches and storytellings have been done, and you've done six revisions of the story, sit down at your computer and write the story, *exactly as you would have told it to a phantom seventh lunch mate.*

Then you'll have it, a finished first draft of a pretty good version of your story. It will have great pace and rhythm. It will be funny where it should be, sad or emotional where it should be. It will hit the right notes, put the characters in the right place at the right time, and so forth.

Admittedly, this tactic will only work when you have some time. Unless you eat more than one lunch per day, it will take a minimum of six days. Except when you are on deadline, needing a few days to do this exercise isn't a bad thing. One of the core tenets of this exercise is to spend some time letting the feedback you hear roam around in your brain for the rest of the day.

If you are pressed for time, there are ways to do the Six-Lunch Test Drive faster. If you are looking for a good buzz, perhaps do it as the Six-Coffee Test Drive. The Six-Beer Test Drive. Perhaps even the "Hey You, I Need to Tell Someone This Story, Let's Pop Into This Conference Room" Test Drive. Regardless, the key is in telling the story repeatedly and then adjusting the story for the next telling.

GIVING AND RECEIVING FEEDBACK

Since so much in this chapter, especially the Six-Lunch Test Drive, involves feedback, this is a good time to talk about how to give it and how to receive it. Part of embracing that your work is imperfect is acknowledging that it can often, if not always, benefit from the input of others, aka feedback.

So why care about being receptive to feedback? It will make your work better. It will make you better. And look for opportunities to provide feedback to others. As a creator, it is important to set up a culture that openly gives and receives feedback, even if you are a culture of one.

Whenever someone asks me for feedback on a project, the first thing I ask them is why.

Most people immediately respond with some variation on, "I'd like to know what you think of it."

That's flattering and very thoughtful, but I often push back a little on the answer, because most people who ask for feedback don't actually want critical feedback; they are looking for praise and reassurance. They have put a lot of themselves into what they are sharing and they really want you to like it as much as they do. Perhaps they have put so much time and effort into it, they worry they can't evaluate it clearly, and they are looking for someone to offer a pat on the back.

There is certainly nothing wrong with praise and reassurance. In fact, I always encourage creators to practice praising good work as often as possible. You should even praise imperfect work where you see talent growing, ideas blossoming, or other creators making ambitious choices.

For many years I have made a habit to praise. I try to send out praise to other creators at least twice a week. At times, I send a notecard to congratulate someone on work that impressed me. You'd be surprised how many people remember those notecards and mention them, even several years later. If you are willing to take the time to get out a notecard, write out your thoughts, put a stamp on it, and put it in the mail—in the digital age—that feels like a lot of effort. It feels special. And that effort means something. Alternatively, I do it publicly at times, with a tweet or post praising work that I hear and appreciate. When I give workshops or speeches, I try to openly praise the work of others and use them as examples (as opposed to just talking about my own stuff). Plus, what goes around comes around. There will be a time[34] when you need this, too. Those you have supported will likely return this gift.

But praise is different from feedback. Feedback is utilizing the skill and perspective of others to find the weak spots in your work. It's

---

[34] Note I didn't say *may be* a time.

akin to asking someone else, "If you were to do the next edit on this, what would you do? What would you focus on?" The point of soliciting feedback is not to hear how great a piece of work is, but rather to compile a fresh list of items that need attention, hopefully a list you couldn't have created on your own. Those who are stuck and need help often just say so up front. They know what they don't like about it and are asking for help in figuring out a problem. That's a real request for feedback.

Here is a tip on giving feedback—something that makes it easier for both you and the person who created the work. Regardless of intention, creators are often nervous to receive feedback, even when they really want to hear it. Even though they want to improve the work, they do care a lot about your opinion. You are someone they respect and admire—and they are about to do one of the most intimate acts in a professional setting: show you something they have created that isn't at its best yet.

To calm nerves a bit, I often raise a subject, then immediately ask them for their thoughts before offering my own. I often find if I start off by asking them to share their thoughts on what works and what doesn't, they will often touch on almost everything I was about to mention. Be it a bit of nerves, or a bit of sudden self-awareness at knowing someone is listening critically to their work, they are often grateful for an opportunity to point things out before you do, thus preventing you from having to bring it up.

As they mention items, you can agree with them and offer thoughts, or comment that you agree but see it from a slightly different angle, or even that you think they are being too harsh and the problem isn't as severe as they may suggest. The point is to make it more conversational.

Most people imagine critical feedback as you coming to them with a huge list of their sins, oversights, and shortcomings. They are prepared to get pounded and beaten down. People assume "critical feedback" means negative or judgmental feedback. To soften it, some refer to it as "constructive feedback"—supposedly to make it feel like it is positive, and can help make things better.[35] Getting them talking, and providing things for you to react to, feels far less confrontational. And if their guard isn't up from bracing for a tsunami of negativity, the more they actually hear from what you are saying.

You can also use this trick to talk about specific editorial or production choices about microelements of the work. For example, "Let's talk about the scene on the boat. You started off with an explanation of how Frank got his captain's license. Tell me about the choice to put that up front in that scene and how you think it works." Or "I noticed that whenever you bring up a new subject, Guest A always talks first. Can you tell me why and if that's a deliberate choice?"

And over the years, I've heard people use a variety of ratios when giving feedback, such as saying one positive thing for every two negative things. Or to construct a compliment sandwich: Start off saying something positive, then directly address the negative, and close with another complimentary item. I think a lot of this is hogwash, kind of like the rhetorical version of crushing up medicine and mixing it in with a spoonful of jelly. The kid can still taste the pill—and that's all they can really taste.

These tactics that force ratios of positive and negative on the conversation are largely targeted toward dealing with the earlier group of people who are asking for feedback but actually just want praise and reassurance. Plus, I think it creates a false dichotomy. Good feedback isn't negative or positive. It is about the things that stick out to you as you are evaluating the work. They are opportunities to make the work stronger; therefore it is pretty silly to force them into being "positive" or "negative." If you speak plainly, don't tiptoe around the creator's feelings (again, if they are asking for feedback for the right reasons, there won't be any potentially hurt feelings to avoid), and if you keep the conversation focused on how to make the ideas clearer, the emotion more vivid, and the listener more invested,

---

[35] If you look it up, you'll see that "critical" has two definitions, with the more appropriate one meaning "thoughtful" or "analytical." Critical feedback simply means to take some time to give insights that are given time and consideration. "Constructive feedback" just feels like a silly redundancy to me.

the entire conversation should have a very supportive, nurturing feeling to it that doesn't need to be forced.

Often when I start off a feedback session to review work, I open by saying, "If there is anything that I don't mention in our conversation today, assume I love it and don't want you to change anything about it."

BONUS EPISODE: Ira Glass's Trick to Quickly Structuring a Story

This is the opening to an episode of *This American Life*:

This is Ira's outline for the ten-minute prologue from the "How I Read It" episode, first broadcast on December 7, 2018.

The prologue is an interview with the creators of The InspiroBot. The InspiroBot is an Internet bot that generates random fake inspirational quotes on top of peaceful, contemplative images. Or at least it was supposed to.

When Ira started out, he thought the plot would be asking, How do you even make something like this?

"What's interesting about the InspiroBot is the guys who made it. At first they thought they were making a bot that would make actual inspiring messages," says Ira. "And then once they got going they realized, 'Oh, what it's doing is so much stranger and more interesting.' It was making these things which had like a weird sort of eerie human resonance." For example:

"Become a personification of your most horrible mistakes."

"Love is an animal eating your brain."

An image of a man under a starry night, with the quote, "Your time on Earth is random."

A woman holding a lit sparkler with the quote, "You are average."

"An education can be like an angry child."

"All you need in order to travel to Mars is a boy and a flag."

So Ira contacted the creators of the InspiroBot, who had never done an interview or spoken about the bot publicly but agreed to be interviewed. Beforehand, Ira sat down with his team and thought through the story and where they needed to go. This is a regular process for the *This American Life* team.

Ira believes strongly that every story is told through the tape you record in interviews and in the field. Tape is at the center of his storytelling. "You're always organizing around the tape, you're structuring around tape," Ira says. "I've structured around tape the same way since I was nineteen. So basically, you get your tape and then you figure out what are the best pieces of tape, and then have to organize it."

"It's really important to have a clear idea about a story's structure before you do the interview, or you're not gonna have the right tape," he adds.

I've heard Ira say this before, about thinking through story composition, scenes, and structure before you go out into the field. At its core, I agree with him, but when I hear him say this, I have some concerns.

"Don't you run the risk of kind of boxing the story in to a preconceived image?" I ask him. "That you might miss unexpected turns or perhaps the story isn't what you think it is?"

"Absolutely, you run that risk," Ira answers. "But the fact is that the outline you're going in with is just your starting place. Obviously, the thing that you want more than anything else is that you're going to be surprised, and it's something different and better than what you're imagining."

"So, if you walk in with an outline, how do you prevent yourself from having blinders on?"

"Well, I would say first of all, most stories are just not that fucking complicated," Ira replied. "You know what I mean? It's like yes, there's a chance that it's going to be very different than what you thought, but really the more likely thing is the person is just going to have a lot of feeling about some part of the story that you didn't anticipate, and then the thing that they have the most feeling about will be the thing that the whole interview will sort of tip toward."

For Ira, recording the tape comes fairly late in the process. Before that, Ira and his team spend many, many hours researching, on phone calls, fact-checking, discussing, plotting, and coming up with scenes for their outlines. This provides them with a clear plan for what they need to get in order for the story to work.

This structure is freedom. With a solid foundation, they can follow tangents, go down rabbit holes, or follow curiosities, knowing there is a plan to return to (a theme you are no doubt seeing come up again and again in this book).

So, back to the InspiroBot. The producers agreed that there were a few things they needed in order for the story to work. "I knew that the plot points that I'm going to get is the step-by-step, like, how did you make this software, what were the early mistakes, what was it doing at first," Ira says. "But the obvious turning point, which has to be in the story is: When did you realize that it wasn't doing the thing you wanted it to do, but instead was doing something way more interesting? Obviously, if they can't tell that part of the story, the story is dead." The other thing Ira needed was for the creators to answer if they found the bot to be occasionally profound in a way that surprised them. Without those two points, there was no story.

The interview, recorded on a Tuesday. The show would be broadcast that Friday. Not a lot of time to structure and write.

During the interview itself, Ira had a production assistant sit in and make a live tape log. Following is a page of the tape log from the interview. Ira's questions are in caps, with the responses paraphrased afterward.

HOWEVER WANNA BE IDENTIFIED - IF WANT TO COME OUT AS PPL YOU ARE LIKE TO IDENTIFY W FULL NAMES BUT KINDA THING WHERE IF YOU DON'T WANT TO -

always been element of mystique that we've est and never told anyone who we are ppl wondering asking but we've never blown our cover when you contacted us we said why not just blow cover it's not a big deal anyway

always enjoy secrecy

DO YOUR FRIENDS KNOW?

not sure whether we keep it

DON'T HAVE TO DECIDE THIS SECOND - NOT GOING TO BROADCAST FOR FEW DAYS. DO YOUR FRIENDS KNOW

some of them - some get very surprised. parents finding out thought it was pretty weird

FRIENDS SAW INSPIROBOT THEN U REVEALED TO THEM

don't remember - yes ppl who knew inspirobot already but found out later we were behind it

friends who shared images from inspirobot and had not idea that i was a part of it

THAT IS SO EXCITING - THAT'S LIKE GET TO REVEAL NO NO NO I AM SPIDERMAN

laffs yeah

AND THEN SHOULD SAY WHAT COUNTRY YOU'RE IN

yeah -oslo norway

AND ARE YOU BOTH PROGRAMMERS

i'm a programmer -

I'm a writer

SO JESPER YOU'RE PROGRAMMER

no peter is programmer and me jasper is the writer and we've sort of developed system together where peter is handling the technical difficulties and i'm trying to put together the syntax and spellings ok and everything vocab and everything

HONESTLY JUST WANNA HEAR STORY OF THIS - HOW MANY YEARS AGO START ON THIS EXPLAIN WHAT IDEA WAS WHAT WANTED BOT TO DO

started in 2015 in spring. bc we saw lots of ppl posting around then and still really posting lots of inspirational images words on fb twitter instagram looked like system behind whole thing. no idea where it came from but felt like machine should be able to do this as well. give so much of what it does you kind of have to give meaning to it yourself in a way. so started exploring how a machine by using modern machine learning techniques try to figure out make computer do same thing

143

You'll notice about two-thirds of the way down the page a circled B next to a bracket, then a circled C next to another bracket. Those are quotes from the interview that Ira thinks might work in the story. He reads and marks the log as he listens back to the interview. When he's run through the entire alphabet, he uses AA, BB, and so on.

"You'll see I'm marking out anything that could possibly be a piece of tape I would use," Ira offers. "And then just to keep track because all I'm going to be doing is making a list of all the possible pieces of tape."

Ira creates a new tape list in his notebook that looks like this:

Part of Ira's system is that as he is making this list, he will put double asterisks next to the quotes he is almost certain to use in the piece (note them next to C and D).

"This isn't written for anybody else to read; the handwriting is terrible. It's just like a series of phrases for me to use," he says.

Ira knew that he wanted to structure the interview fairly sequentially, meaning that he would introduce them, then tell the story of these two wanting to create a bot that would make actual inspirational messages, and why they wanted to do that. And then the next beat of the story is they look at the bot, and it doesn't do what they intended. It does something way more interesting, and then, at that point, you read people what the bot makes.

Ira also knew where he wanted to story to land.

"If you go up to CC, 'It's hard to believe that a person had no hand in this,' this is another one that I thought might be an idea that we would drive to," Ira said. "BB is another one that I thought was an idea for the ending, and that is like, seeing the bot do this, it makes humans seem pathetic."

Eventually, Ira starts to arrange and rearrange the pieces of tape he has, creating this:

"The reason why it's such a jumble of things is because I'm kind of thinking it through, okay, well obviously we're going to start with C: 'How did it start?'" Ira says. "Then we're going to D: 'What's the formula?' But, then, like, there's a bunch of choices that I have for the jumble of stuff that's underneath that: H, and T, and so on."

Then Ira writes in between his tape cuts, creating a script like this:

From WBEZ Chicago, it's This American Life.

> Jesper: You can call me Jesper.
> Ira: Jasper
> Jesper Jesper. With an E
> Ira: Jesper.
> Jesper: Yeah. And it's peder here
> Peder: Yeah. Hi Ira.
> Ira: Are those your actual names
> Jesper: Yaah! It's not a joke.

Peder Jørgensen & Jesper Sundnes ... this is the first time they've agreed to do an inteview about this thing they created ... or even idnetify themselves as the creators ... they say it all began ... back in 2015 they were killing time together... scrolling through facebook bored ...

The location?

> Jesper: At work. We were supposed to be working.
> Ira: Because you had a lot of free time?
> Peder: No!
> Jesper: Yes!
> Peder: We were probably on a lunch break. We were working very hard.
> Ira: I love that one of you said yes and one said no.
> (laugh)

They were working in radio ... they live in Oslo Norway.

Anyway, they noticed on their friends' facebook feeds ... very common ...

> people were posting lots of inspirational images with inspirational words. And Peder it kinda looked there was system behind the whole thing. Like it felt like a machine should be able to do this.
> Yeah. Like a robot would be able to do that.

Could make an inspirational quote.

After all they're so formulaic! ... every day might not be a good day but there is good in every day. -If you fell down yesterday, stand up today. the secret to getting ahead is getting started.

And so Jesper and Peder set about to program a computer to create these ... to generate inspirational sentences and paste them onto stock photos of beaches and starry nights and people staring into the distance. ~~Neither had worked as computer programmers, but Peder had taught himself to code ... years before ...~~

~~And using a grabbag of standard programming tools ... they set to work.~~

And what's interesting is just how quickly the program sort of took on a mind of its own...

at first ... the computer really did generate very typical inspirational quotes ...

but as they gave it a bigger vocabulary ... and taught it to string together a wider variety of sentences ... the kinds of sayings it started to crank out started to evolve ... as they got more random ... they got funnier ... and darker ... and – I don't wanna oversell this but it's true ... actually sometimes kind of profound ... the bot started to take on the personality that it has now ... ~~pretty quickly!~~

~~And when these kinds of quotes started to appear ... Jesper and Peder were like ... whoa ...~~

This system—logging tape, assigning letters to quotes, listing the quotes, arranging the quotes, and then writing—is the system Ira has used for pretty much every script he's written for almost thirty years.

"It's basically sitting there at my desk for an hour, basically going through and turning it into this thing. I move from having an hour and a half of tape to having like a real outline that I can then write from very, very quickly, as quickly as it can be," he says. "The other thing that going through the log and making the ABC list does is that it kind of puts the interview into the random access memory of your own brain. That is, it forces you to categorize: These are the good quotes, these are the bad quotes."

What Ira's method is doing is forcing the producer to work through hours of tape efficiently.

"The advantage of the steps is that it takes what is essentially a creative and editorial task, and it turns it into an entirely secretarial task; that is, it turns it into a task with no creativity," Ira says. "The reason why that's really helpful is because I, like most creative people, really fear the moment of jumping in and making a decision on my story. And so we'll procrastinate and put it off and do anything but actually make a decision about what's first, what's second, what's third, and actually sit down to write. I think a lot of people have a hard time sitting down to write; this is entirely designed to make it get you over the hump, by giving you a bunch of utterly secretarial tasks to do on your way to making your decisions. If you just immerse yourself in the thing, the path will become clear. I believe this is the absolute quickest way to do it."

Chapter 6

AUDIENCE BUILDING

was listening to a veteran radio producer talk about her first podcast, which she'd recently started to develop. We'd run into each
other at a podcasting conference that she was attending to find a
network for this new project.[36]

"Why are you looking for a network?" I asked.

"Hey, I just make the stuff," she said. "I need to find someone else
who will sell it and market it."

My reaction to her will also answer why there is a chapter on
marketing inside a book about creation. I said to her, "It isn't someone
else's job. It's your job."

Many creators seem to think there was a mythical time when a
creator would create, then turn over the "dirty," "lower" work of selling and marketing to others. That isn't true now, and it was never

---

[36] And a note on this in case someone is confused. There are a lot of different hands that can touch a podcast
between leaving the creator's computer and landing on a listener's phone (or whatever you, he, or she uses
to listen). Some examples include podcast listening apps, hosting services (that house and feed the podcast
whenever listeners request it), and networks. Networks are companies that help podcasters make revenue
and build audience at scale, meaning that by serving many podcasts, they reduce costs and increase the
effectiveness at a fraction of the effort, time, and resource of each podcast doing this work by itself.

true. If you think you experienced this in the past, it's most likely that no one was actually doing any meaningful marketing. You were just under the illusion that it was happening.

Even when making a gargantuan blockbuster movie with a marketing budget in the tens or hundreds of millions of dollars, the maker and stars are still required to get out there and hustle.

When it comes to marketing, a creator needs to embrace something between harsh skepticism and clear-eyed reality: No one is better suited to market your project than you.

No one is as passionate about it as you. No one understands it better than you. No one is better suited to understand the right places and methods to use to entice its future audience to seek it out and listen.

It isn't someone else's job. It's your job.

Now, that isn't to say that professional marketers are useless. Far from it. But you simply can't expect them to care the way you care, work as hard as you have worked, or take the small amount of time they have to devote to your project and waste it relearning everything you already know about the target audience and what makes your project awesome.

If you are lucky enough to work with a professional marketer, good for you. That is a rare privilege that most creators never get, or never get enough of. For the rest of this chapter, I'm going to assume you are on your own when it comes to building an audience, either because you actually will be, or you are planning on being the literal or figurative head of any marketing effort around your project, regardless of how it is distributed or who you have working for or with you.

When you're a creator, it's easy to under- and overestimate the importance of marketing.

This always surprises me when I see creators dismissing the importance of smart marketing, and, unfortunately, I see it a lot. A person or group puts time and effort into creating a podcast, yet puts no thought into how it will live in the world and eventually find an audience. They just assume that if they put a podcast out into the wild, it will somehow be discovered (again, in a sea of more than 700,000 others) and become successful.

They justify this by saying they are going to produce it and "just put it out there and see what happens." I can solve that mystery for you now. Likely nothing is going to happen.

Historically, many creatives have felt that participating in marketing would somehow dilute the integrity of their work. These folks believe that you can't be both a creator and an advocate for that creativity at the same time. That thinking is completely backward and wrong. The reality of all digital media today is that creators need to learn to think like marketers and marketers need to think like creators.

Creation and marketing are codependent (in a good way), and each should inform and influence the other. They follow the Principle of Yin and Yang: inseparable and contradictory opposites that require the presence of each other to function. Neither is superior to the other and each has, at its core, the presence of the other.

Some will argue that I'm wrong and that the creator should not think about marketability or the audience in their creative process. If that is the case, then what you are creating is art, not mass media. There is nothing wrong with that whatsoever, but you then need to set your expectations on reach and impact accordingly. That isn't to say that all art is not accessible to the masses, but it is a matter of intent. Who is this for? The creator or the audience? If the intent is your own self-expression, then it may or may not be of interest to others. If, on the other hand, your intention is to reach a mass of people (and you can define "mass" at any scale you wish), then you need to make choices based on the best ways to connect to its intended audience. And you need to make sure that the work is easy to find by the audience most likely to hear it and love it. Some find it more palatable to call this "audience building"—but it is really just plain old marketing.

While it's critical for creators and marketers to work together and influence each other, it's also important for each to recognize that they aren't an expert in the other field. I've been guilty of this myself,

151

I must admit. I've been involved in so many marketing campaigns for new work that I, at times, start to think I know as much as my marketing colleagues. I don't. And many of my colleagues have had to remind me of this. It isn't to say I don't have ideas, but they are tuned in on things, best practices, and ways to innovate that I simply don't connect with. Same goes for marketers. I've met many who think they should be the ones calling the editorial shots. While they deserve respect for their understanding of audience, it's important for everyone to understand the lane markers.

Considering creation without the pathways for discovery is only doing half the work. Those who claim they want to "put it out there" are just copping to doing only half the work, and can expect to see almost none of the potential return.

Creators can also *over*estimate the importance of marketing as well. Let me explain this by sharing a conversation I had shortly after I started consulting. The executive producer of podcasting at a startup media company called me up one day and asked if I'd be interested in consulting with them on how to grow their podcasts. They had put out a small handful of podcasts previously and were planning to start about a dozen new ones in the coming year. They wanted advice on how to increase the audience size for their current shows and set the new podcasts up to be stronger at launch.

In preparing for the call, I gave their current shows a listen and prepared some light notes to help me during the call. Once we started our conversation, I brought up the shows and asked, as I suggested above, what the producer thought were the strengths and opportunities he heard in the shows.

"Oh, we love them," he said, and nothing more.

Okay, I thought, starting to bring a few items I'd heard from my own listening into the conversation. In short, I said the episodes didn't really have a clear structure, allowing listeners to get lost and unsure of why they were hearing what they were hearing. Also, there were a lot of strange editing choices that made things confusing and hard to follow.

Before I got much further, he stopped me. He told me that he appreciated my comments, but they wanted to know how to grow audience, not how to make the shows better. I told him that those two goals weren't separable. Most times, the pathway to building an audience is to make the show a stronger, better version of itself. Only then do you focus on how to evangelize that show to its potential audience.

He wasn't having it.

I asked what shows he considered to be his contemporaries: those that had a similar sound and feel and covered similar topics or viewpoints. He mentioned a number of documentary shows, like *Slow Burn, This American Life*, and ESPN's *30 for 30*. It is routine for episodes of these shows to cost tens of thousands of dollars each and take months to create. He had allotted $3,000 per episode for his shows and felt that was plenty.

"I just want you to tell me how to spend my ad dollars," he replied.

I told him that I had never seen a single dollar spent on marketing a podcast that I felt paid off. I told him there are lots of smart ways to market programs, but if you want others to talk about your show, it requires that you make sure the show is worthy of being talked about.

He said that was all very interesting and he'd get back to me about hiring me.

I'm still waiting on that call.

I want to be perfectly clear here: Spending more money is not necessary to produce great content, nor does spending more money guarantee great work. That isn't the point of this anecdote, either. However, there is a definite correlation between input and output in podcasting. Investment and return are related. Investment can be money; however, it can also be measured in time and effort.

If *under*estimating the importance of marketing is the folly of having no marketing plan, *over*estimating focuses on the belief that marketing is the answer to everything—or too quickly blames marketing (or the lack of it): for all woes. These people think all that's needed is for someone to spend more on advertising (aka paid media) or get more press coverage (aka earned media).

There are ways to make marketing work to amplify your efforts; but as has been proven time and time again, the best way to achieve goals, to build an audience, and to earn the revenue to make it possible is to simply be relentless in making your work as incredible as possible. Most marketing work actually starts in the production process. Nothing beats great stories and conversations. No marketing plan, no network effect, no tricks or tips, is ever a better investment than simply trying a bit harder to be a bit better than your last episode.

So let me repeat myself: I have never seen a single dollar spent on marketing a podcast that I feel paid off. To be clear, I mean traditional marketing. I've seen creators, networks, and distributors run print ads, produce slick videos, put signs on buses, do billboard campaigns, pay for social media posts, take over transit stops, print brochures, and create giveaway tchotchkes like keychains, T-shirts, buttons, and stickers. Among all this, I've never been able to find a single instance where any of this activity generated any quantifiable and measurable increase in listening as a result.

But that doesn't mean it is impossible or a waste of time to market podcasts. Quite the opposite. In fact, good news: The effective and proven ways to market your show and build audience won't cost you a dime.

If you are familiar with "guerrilla marketing," a lot of what we'll cover in this chapter will feel very familiar. I am not necessarily a huge follower or evangelist for guerrilla marketing; generally, it's fine. But when it comes to audience-building for podcasts, if you look at the proven tactics that work, they tend to fall inside the guerrilla marketing framework.

Guerrilla marketing was first popularized in a book titled, no surprise, *Guerrilla Marketing* written by Jay Conrad Levinson in 1984 and has been updated several times since. The core of guerrilla marketing focuses on two tenets. First, that while traditional advertising may work well for large businesses, it is often financially ineffective or impractical for smaller, scrappier businesses (like podcasts). Guerrilla marketing is tailored to those businesses that have to find other methods to build, grow, and maintain their customer base. Instead of investing money, guerrilla marketing encourages you to instead invest time, energy, imagination, and information. Guerrilla marketing replaces expensive efforts with less-expensive high-engagement efforts. Second, and more important, Levinson explains that guerrilla marketing is also understanding that "marketing" includes every contact you have with the outside world. It means that marketing isn't an event, but an ongoing process of engaging with your audience and potential audience.

I'm not going to regurgitate the entire book to you,[37] but its applicability to what we do is clear: Marketing isn't something you do simply to get new "customers" (in our case, listeners); it is about building a two-way relationship with your audience that will create tight bonds with your current customers and excite new customers to join the fold. That communication just doesn't happen when a show launches; it is something that has to be built into your project's DNA, almost from conception. It counsels you to do things that get attention, get your audience involved with what you do, and communicate with them regularly, clearly, and responsively.

Even beyond Levinson's advice on how to conduct guerrilla marketing, most marketers agree that you need to do a fairly similar, small number of things to be successful at getting the word out:

- Start off with a wonderful idea (and if you've been following along with this book, let's go ahead and check that box).

- Know what makes your offering distinct. (Check.)

- Learn who your audience is. (Check.)

- Then, the most important part: Get out there and engage.

That last stage is often the most vexing for creators new to audience building. Old schoolers are more accustomed to creating audio, then lobbing it over a wall toward the audience (like my friend from the opening of the chapter). To them, it is a one-way relationship: I

---

[37] Go buy a copy. It is a quick, inspiring, and provocative read.

create, you listen. Most introverted creators[38] are intimidated by the extroverted notion of directly reaching out to people and groups they don't know, even to talk about something they know and care about deeply.

Intimacy and connection between makers and audiences is created by bringing down walls and offering transparency into you, your creative process, and all that goes into making the project that they listen to. It requires you to be vulnerable and, occasionally, less than perfect. I'm not going to lie: It takes some getting used to and isn't always easy. But it is effective, rewarding—it has the bonus of often making you feel really good about what you do—and most important, it works.

Before you worry about that, let's start by finding out who these future listeners are. First, think back to our target listener we googled and wrote faux bios for back in Chapter 2. Let's expand on them a bit and take that sentence or two of fake biography and flesh it out in a detailed portrait about their lifestyle, interests, and how they've come to care about the subject of your podcast. Ask yourself where your target listener and people like them are likely to congregate, in the real world and online.

Here's an example of what you should end up with.

Let's say you are starting a podcast about collecting Hummel figurines. Specifically, it is news, history, and conversation targeted at serious collectors. It isn't an introduction or "how to" for new collectors. This is for hardcore Hummel lovers. You have your target listener from our Chapter 2 exercise. Let's say her name is Clarice and she lives in suburban Pittsburgh. She is a semiretired librarian who is very comfortable with technology and loves to listen to audiobooks and some podcasts, especially about crafts (she and her husband, Tom, both love craft pursuits). She started collecting Hummel figurines when her grandmother passed away more than three decades ago, leaving her collection to Clarice. Since then, Clarice has become

---

[38] And a disproportionate number of audio creators are introverts.

very knowledgeable. She has expanded her collection, attended conventions and events, read magazines, and frequented online forums and user groups, as well as read a number of blogs devoted to figurines and collecting. She has dabbled in buying and selling figurines on eBay, but doesn't like it as much as in-person interactions, where she can get to know other collectors and dealers. She even led a local Hummel enthusiasts' group that met at the library once a month for several years. While she loves all Hummel types and eras, Clarice is especially interested in collecting figurines from the 1950s.

If you didn't come up with that level of detail in Chapter 2, then take a few minutes and flesh out your listener's story. You can construct similar faux bios for fans of your true crime podcast. Or your podcast idea about Tom Hanks movies. Or your listener for the herb gardening podcast you've dreamed of starting. Or your podcast sharing the stories of first-generation immigrants.

You may notice that in constructing faux listener Clarice, I made sure to include a couple things: where she goes for information and how she interacts with others.

If you were writing a guerrilla marketing plan for a podcast about Hummels targeted at listeners like Clarice, all the information you'd need is in that paragraph.

So once you have written your faux bio, start a list of places that groups of people like your target audience congregate, online and in real life: online forums, discussion groups, newsletters, conventions, groups at the library, Facebook groups, meetups, Twitter tags, etc. For Clarice, I'd start with what I wrote into the bio, but then would push myself to think of other examples, such as antiques, vintage, and collectible shops; flea markets; craft stores; and community centers. While all those examples can be local to Clarice's community, make sure to think big, focusing on real gathering points for people from all walks of life and locations. For example, if you are thinking about a target listener for a podcast about women's fashions from the 1950s, perhaps you might choose a famous vintage store in Chicago or New York City, rather than a local store. Or, if you want to start a podcast featuring live storytelling, all about adoption stories, you might think beyond the local Moth event recorded at a club downtown to regional or national storytelling events.

Once you have that list, spend some time thinking about how people interact at these places. Perhaps there are group interactions (a conference or meetup), online conversations, one-on-one interactions (mentoring events), or one-to-many (blogs, stores, or teaching events).

Then you need to do two things simultaneously. First, become an active member of at least some of those communities. Not a member promoting something, but a member who participates, interacts, and comments generally. You probably won't have time to engage in all the places where these people congregate, but find some entry points that feel like the right places to start, then plan to expand to others with time. Be present and engage as a member of that community. This is so important because when you do start to evangelize about your project, people will know you and be much more receptive to hearing about what you are working on (and support it by listening and helping to spread the word) if they know you, a bit about you, and you've taken opportunities to be interested in and engaged with them as well.

Second, you should start to work on making your Ten-Word Description and other descriptive material to form your pitch to potential listeners. There is a great exercise to help you develop a pitch at the end of this chapter, and the same pitch can be used for many different uses, including attracting new listeners.

Join online communities, but do your best to find ways to engage in the real world, too. For example, if you are working on a piece of scripted period audio drama and one of your target events is a book club that meets at the library, go. Try attending a convention or large book festival, as well. And so on.

Once you have become a member of the community, start to engage early in your project. Don't just wait until you have finished episodes and suddenly say out of nowhere, "Hey, strangers, I've got a podcast, it's available now, please listen to it!" Even when you are in the planning and production phase, engage your community. Ask them for advice. Let them help you make decisions. Give them an opportunity to provide input and feedback, which makes them even more invested in your show (and more likely to help). There is a section later in this chapter called "Opening the Kimono," which explores this concept in a bit more detail.

Every once in a while, I hear reservations from makers about this kind of openness and engagement, fearing that someone might steal their idea. I appreciate the confession of vulnerability, but to be honest, that's kind of nonsense. First, if someone else could hear your idea and then immediately duplicate it, the show concept either isn't very distinct, or perhaps you (and/or your talent) aren't the ones who should be doing it. Second, by the time you are building connections and relationships in communities, you are so far out of the gate that it probably isn't realistic to worry that someone else would be able to get it produced and out into the world before you.

159

And finally, while you are out building connections and relationships with potential listeners, you should also make a list of people whom you believe *influence* your target listener, like media, opinion leaders in your subject, perhaps even politicians and celebrities. For my fictional Hummel-loving Clarice, I'd reach out to the writers of the blogs, editors of the magazines, hosts of the conventions, and owners of the stores she frequents. When you reach out to these influencers, tell them about your project, your aspirations, and goals. Perhaps even solicit these influencers to be guests on an episode, if that makes sense. Regardless of how you utilize them, it will be some of the best investments of time you'll make. The influencers hold a lot of sway and impact in their niche. One post, tweet, display in their store, or guest slot at *their* event can translate into a huge bumper crop of new interest in your show.

So what I've just laid out over these past several pages sounds like a lot of work. That's because it is. Done right, there will be a feeling of a communal quality to your production. You are still very much in control of what happens, how you solicit engagement with the wider world, and how (or even if) you implement that feedback. I'm not advocating that you turn your editorial decision-making into complete democratic or anarchistic chaos, but I am saying that opening yourself up to audience interaction and input gets them invested in your project. They will listen, they will tell others about your work, they will defend you if necessary, and they will be your greatest supporters. And who knows, they may even have a good idea now and then.

Now you can probably see why my reaction to assigning marketing work to others isn't someone else's job, it is your job. That's because effective marketing and relationship building needs to come from the same source. You.

Since *making* your thing and *talking* about your thing are so interrelated, you might start to believe that marketing and creation are not two separate functions. As I've advocated to teams and other creators for years, marketing and creation are indeed two different components of the same action—like the yin and yang, two interrelated mutually dependent halves that fit together to make a whole. When I am pressed to point to why many of my projects have been successful, this is usually where I attribute a sizeable portion of that credit. I always say that in order to be successful, a maker has to be both Barnum *and* Bailey.[39]

Again, the main reason I so strongly advocate for this approach is because it works. And it just doesn't work occasionally or regularly; it works pretty much every time you give it a serious try. It isn't to suggest that every single tactic will net new listeners every time you do it, but if you put in the thought and effort to execute a smart campaign, you will find listeners.

The reason marketing feels hard is because it requires real commitment.

---

[39] Not to get too deep into something best left to a Web search, but P. T. Barnum was often seen as an innovator and showman. It's true that he was the showman (the marketer), but his partner, James Bailey, was the innovator (the maker) who invented the modern concept of the circus.

I want to share something that was introduced to me by Steve Pratt, one of many wise people at Pacific Content, a podcast and audio production company located in Vancouver and Toronto that specializes in creating podcasts for brands. Steve is a fun guy to be around, not only because he is so smart about audio, but because he is such an optimistic, positive person. I wouldn't be surprised if Steve has very few bad days in his life, if simply because he finds ways to turn things positive quickly. One great example of this is his use of "The Chart" to start projects off on a positive footing.

One morning over breakfast Steve shared with me a chart that his colleague Rob Leadley came up with to frame conversations with prospective clients. Steve and his colleagues called it the "Recipe for Podcast Success" chart. Though once they realized that name didn't roll off the tongue very well, they decided to refer to it simply as The Chart. They use it to align expectations with potential clients about what is possible and what it takes to make things work.

It's worth noting that this chart was developed for the specific type of podcasts that Pacific Content specializes in, known as "branded content" (meaning the type of podcasts paid for by brands to help promote them as well as the subjects and stories that they have in common with their customers—kinda like advertising, but without any direct message or call to action. It's confusing, I know. Even though it was created for companies and brands interested in making branded content, the ideas embedded in The Chart are really useful to almost anyone in any size project. It drives home the idea that there are no shortcuts. Every item of your marketing plan requires effort, and effort is synonymous with commitment.

When using The Chart with clients, he draws a chart with two axes: Creative Bravery and Commitment.

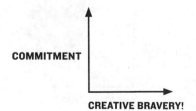

Creative Bravery is a pretty easy concept to get your head around. You mark on the axis how comfortable you are with creative risk-taking. Two people recording themselves in a twenty-minute conversation? That would go pretty low on the Creative Bravery axis. Want to push boundaries and create something challenging, bold, and new? You would go farther out on that same axis. The Pacific Content team did define a few other elements of Creative Bravery, such as going the extra mile to hire a phenomenal host for your show (as opposed to having a company employee do it), not putting deadlines and budgets ahead of quality, and asking if you would honestly listen to this show if you weren't part of the team making it.

It's important to note that there are no incorrect answers, just truthful ones. There is nothing wrong with picking any position on that Creative Bravery axis as long as everyone around the table agrees. To the Pacific Content team, Creative Bravery is making sure that your podcast is "a gift for your audience."

Then comes the more challenging idea: Commitment. For many potential clients of Pacific Content, they want to create a standout podcast that really extends their brand and reaches more people. They assume the commitment required of them is to write a check to fund the production, plus contribute some early editorial ideas and perhaps provide some feedback on the episodes. Most potential clients are surprised to see that Steve and his team would place that level of Commitment at about one-tenth of the way along that axis.

The underlying message: Having a brand and paying to create a podcast isn't going to get you where you need to go. As Steve says, "If Creative Bravery means making a great show, Commitment means making sure your desired audiences knows about it."

How do you move farther along the Commitment axis? For brands, it means making the podcast an institutional commitment, not just something you write a check for out of your marketing budget and you're done. Your organization should point every gun it has at the podcast. You can start with looking at every touch point you have with your potential audience: social media, online groups, websites, email newsletters, and events. If you are a company or organization with a physical location or store, how can you use that physical space to draw attention to your podcast? If you aren't working for a big organization, this thinking and approach can still apply to you. With every new enterprising way you use your network and "secret strengths," you get to move another notch up the Commitment axis.

The goal of The Chart, and the inspiration and action that result from using it, is to make sure, from the get-go, that your podcast project plots as far into the upper right corner as possible.

7 AUDIENCE-BUILDING TACTICS

Beyond the outreach we've been exploring, there are seven specific tactics that merit some attention. These are some of my favorite audience-building tricks that I've seen used to equal effect by big organizations and one-person independents. You are, of course, welcome to steal them all and implement them exactly as I and others have done in the past. Not everything will work for everyone, every time. Yet I hope they also spark your own imagination to try new approaches to reach your next batch of listeners.

TACTIC I: DIY NETWORKING As I've mentioned before, the most common question I get from new creators is, "How long should my episodes be?"

The second most common question I get is, "Should I join a network?" That's a really complicated question. For most podcasters, especially new podcasters, my answer is usually no. Joining an established podcast network makes sense only when your podcast has grown beyond what you can do for yourself. The notion that a network is going to spot raw talent and scoop it up, making you wealthy (or at least wealthy by podcast standards) and famous (or at least famous by podcast standards) is a myth. Networks gravitate to talent that shows the potential to be amplified. You have to create that initial spark and early success all on your own. Often, to capture a network's interest, you need to be making some money and doing fairly well audience-wise before they even want to talk. They don't make you money; they make you *more* money. They don't make you famous; they make you *more* famous. They are not star makers.

When I talk to creators about what they want from a network relationship, they often cite money, but more often cite an interest in building an audience.

Well, even though networks might not make sense to you, taking advantage of a network effect is relatively easy. I often counsel network-queriers to just start their own network, completely DIY.

Doing so is simple.

Gather a group of four or five other podcasters. You should pick others you believe might share an audience with your podcast. They can either produce a show that shares a lot in common with yours or that you believe would appeal to similar audiences.[40]

Finding them should be pretty easy. You can look for people at conferences and festivals (it seems like there is one every few weeks in cities around the country and world). There are podcaster meetups in many cities. You can find them via message boards, Reddit, social media groups, or newsletters (again, there are plenty of each). If nothing else, you can simply noodle around in podcast directories looking for like-minded folks and then reach out to them directly.

Then you make an arrangement to promote each other. You can create a thirty- or sixty-second promo to insert into an episode of their show or feed, provide the host with some copy describing your show, and let them figure out what to say to encourage their audience to check you out, and/or you can promote each other "off air" via

---

[40] Let's say you produce a podcast about beekeeping and they produce a podcast about building beehives. Or let's say you produce a live storytelling podcast and they produce a live improv comedy podcast. Or perhaps you both produce podcasts that focus on things happening in your hometown or area.

social media, websites, newsletters, and so on. Regardless of what you pick, agree on how often to do it.[41]

Another variation on this will be to do it "round robin." Pick your group of co-promoters; let's say there are four of you total. Each week, three of you promote the fourth program. The next week, you rotate. By taking turns, everyone gets promoted by the others once a month. Try it for a few months. This trick is simple, but it really does work.

TACTIC 2: ANSWER BACK Emily Post would be proud of this one, plus it is dead simple to understand and implement. Whenever someone emails, tweets, or mentions you or your show, respond. Every time.

I've written four books over the past two decades and have received many thousands of emails from readers. I have answered each and every one. I even openly post my email address and have always had a form on my website as an easy way to send messages. The volume is often light but regular. Around publication time, it can get pretty heavy as people discover and read the books in larger numbers. But I answer every one.

Conversely, I also respond on Twitter and via other channels. When I give talks and workshops (usually a dozen or so times a year), audience members live tweet it. Sometimes I just like a post, but often I'll retweet (as long as it isn't getting too redundant).

When you do respond, it's smart to ask them to write a review or post something to share their feelings about your show with others. Often they will be so impressed that you took the time to respond, they will do what you ask right away.

Nothing I've mentioned here is particularly time-consuming. It takes a few seconds to like or retweet something. It takes a minute to write a short reply thanking someone for writing. But it means a lot to them. While you might grimace at the notion of being considered a "celebrity," to your listeners, that's exactly what you are. And for you to like a post or tweet, for you to answer an email, or otherwise show

---

[41] A piece of advice: do it regularly and over a period of time, i.e., weekly for six weeks, at least!

them a bit of attention and appreciation, it is a big deal. It builds loyalty with your audience, and loyal listeners are regular listeners and those most likely to help spread the word.

A word of caution here—it is really easy to overuse and overliteralize this type of audience interaction. While engagement is important, it is more important to keep it in context: Those who respond are part of your audience, but they do not speak for the entirety of the audience.

Whether it's emails, tweets, phone calls, or comments made at public events and dinner parties, creators are constantly using these anecdotal chunks to justify doing or not doing something. This has been going on way before podcasting. In fact, I'm sure as long as there has been mass media, there have been creators confusing anecdotes with meaningful and actionable data. I imagine that when Early Man was creating cave paintings, I'm sure that someone showed up with a stone tablet left by a visitor asking them to paint more pictures of horses and the tablet-bearer announced that this was evidence that everyone wanted to see more paintings of horses.

When you question why a guest is used so regularly, one of the creators says, "Well, the audience loves her." What is that based on? Answer: tweets to the show. When you question a segment, or suggest a change in approach, or frequency of when something does or doesn't happen? The creators respond based on what they are hearing at events or reading in online comments, and so on, thus using it as an Infallible True North. The implication here is that the host or producer or other member of the creative staff has a magical, intimate relationship with their audience, and therefore understands them better than you.

On one hand, I applaud the intent. This whole book is focused on listening to the audience and adjusting your creative process to be responsive to them and their needs. That isn't what's happening when someone uses the inbox or mailbag as a justification for doing something based on the apparent will of the listenership. In fact, it is often dangerously off the mark.

Why would it ever be a bad idea to listen to feedback from the audience? Well, let's be clear; I'm not saying that. I think feedback from the audience is really important. When they talk back at you, regardless of form or format, you should treat it like it is, a brief one-to-one experience as part of your large one-to-many show or podcast.

I think these kinds of personal responses and touchpoints with your listeners are probably the most effective marketing tool you have at your disposal. The problem is when you take the feedback of *some* listeners and conflate it with the opinion of *all* listeners, or even a majority of listeners, or take it as really anything more than one person's thoughts and opinions. The reason it is a problem, is what you hear often represents nothing.

Even if you hear this feedback *all the time,* that still doesn't make it a valid proxy for the will of the audience. I often ask creators who claim to hear overwhelming responses from listeners how many responses they have actually heard. 100? 300? 1,000? Often the number is way on the lower side of that range, usually far less. Then I'll do some quick math to show that often the "overwhelming" feedback count represents a fraction of a single percentage of the whole audience. Even the most resistant talent has to admit that hearing from 100 people out of an audience of 100,000 (equal to one-tenth of 1 percent) is a really small slice. To be fair, what they're hearing *could be* a bigger truth, but using a bunch of anecdotal feedback is not the way to figure that out. There are a number of tools available today to create cheap or free online surveys for your audience.

Do something as simple as preparing a listener survey. It's simpler then you think. First, get an easy-to-remember custom URL to direct people to the survey and include a "callout" announcement during a few of your episodes to get people to take the survey. And here's a tip: Offer a prize drawing for those who respond, preferably something that they can't buy that's associated with your show—such as tickets to your next live event, a memento from a recent guest, or an autographed something. Stuff like that. That information that you can have more faith in. It won't be perfect, but it's real. But all the casual anecdotal material can lead you in the wrong directions.

If you are interested in digging in, there is a lot of academic research that looks at online comments and feedback, especially those found on retail and review sites, which clearly demonstrates that this type of feedback can't be used to represent the entire customer/listener experience. In feedback environments like comments, as well as tweets, email, and in-person comments, you hear from a subset of the audience, who often have strong sentiments and are most comfortable sharing them. That certainly isn't everyone.

When I created NPR's puzzle and trivia show *Ask Me Another*, I was really worried about the staff conflating the live audience at the recording with the larger listening audience out in the world. The show was recorded live in front of about 300 people at The Bell House in Brooklyn. Naturally, the guests and talent would often cater to the crowd in the room during the recording. I would always tell them that the people in the room weren't the real audience. The almost one million people who listened and downloaded the show every week—they were the real audience. I would tell the crew that for every person sitting in The Bell House, there were more than 3,000 people in the listening audience. Just because people laugh or react in the room doesn't mean it will be a home run for the whole listening audience. To drive this home, Jesse Baker, the show's producer (and my cofounder at Magnificent Noise) created an audience proxy, Rhonda Radio, which was a shelf-top FM radio with Mrs. Potato Head parts glued to it. Rhonda was placed on the front of the stage, largely out of the view of the live audience but easily seen by everyone on the stage. We put it there as a constant reminder that the live audience was actually a prop to provide laughter and energy to create something that the larger whole listening audience would enjoy.

But what I think is the most compelling reason not to overemphasize casual listener feedback (and this is where I often win back the reluctant anecdote-loving creators) is that by making decisions based on casual feedback, you are listening to your audience today, not your future audience.

Many creators are interested in expanding their listenership and growing the audience. One thing that creators must embrace is that their large future audience may be a bit different from their smaller current audience. Audiences are not monolithic. They may be different ages, have different interests, or come from different backgrounds and walks of life. The only thing they all truly have in common is *you*. With that in mind, you can safely assume that as you add additional audience members, that range of diversity will grow, too. Those new listeners will be different. First, they won't be as familiar with your show as established listeners. They won't listen as much or as frequently, at least at first. And, they will have different needs as listeners. And what works with your current audience may not work with or be as welcoming to them.

Therefore, when you make decisions based on what your loudest, most comfortable/confident listeners tell you, you are excluding the opinions of your next wave of listeners. Plus, listeners are incredibly resistant to change. They like you and your show the way they are. They want it their way. That is why whenever a podcast, or a website, or a store makes changes, at first all they hear is negativity and complaints.

So while it is good—smart, in fact—to have exchanges with and connections to your audience, do it for the sake of respecting your listeners and their relationship to your work. You need them to be successful and should be humbled by the fact that they listen and are often your best defenders and supporters. Just be careful not to take away too many assumptions based on what you hear, because it isn't what you think.

TACTIC 3: ASK THE AUDIENCE TO HELP I had a consulting client with a small podcast he wanted to grow into a bigger podcast. He was consistently garnering about 5,000 downloads an episode and was ready to grow. His goal was to be ten times larger. I thought that was a great goal, but we should take it in stages. So we spent our first conversation talking a lot about what his next 5,000 listeners were like, how they were the same or different from his current listeners, and what they'd need to fall in love with his show. He envisioned that his next 5,000 listeners weren't all that different from his current listeners. I told him that wouldn't be the case when he was planning for his 30,000th listener, but for now, it was a first step.

We agreed there were some structural things to change in the podcast, which contained a lot of insider information targeted at long-time listeners, and we made a list of changes to the first five minutes of the show to make it more inviting to new listeners.

Then came what he thought was a tough question: Where are you going to find those 5,000 listeners?

He looked at the ceiling, scrunched up his face (to indicate he was thinking), and grimaced, saying, "You know, I have no clue."

I asked him how he got his first 5,000 listeners.

Ceiling. Scrunch. Grimace.

"Again, I have no clue. Perhaps they just stumbled on it."

I told him that 5,000 people rarely just stumble on something, especially something in a directory with 700,000 other things.

I told him that many in his current audience found his show because someone told them about it: Someone shared a post, gave a review, or told others how much they enjoyed his show. So I told him he simply needed have the same thing happen again.

"How do I do that?" he asked.

"Just ask," I told him.

I suggested that for the next four weeks he should open the podcast with a simple request: If the audience enjoyed the show, tell someone. You can send a tweet, post something on a network or discussion forum, or just send an email or tell a friend over lunch. So he did.

A few weeks later I emailed him to ask what happened.

"My downloads are up thirty-five percent," he said. "It has to be a coincidence."

I knew it wasn't, but said we should try it again for a few more weeks. The 35 percent increase roughly held up over the next several weeks. He'd noticed a lot of people posting the episodes to social media, a really big increase over normal. While correlation doesn't prove causation, it was a pretty compelling case.

The lesson to take from this is: Often the best, most passionate marketers of your program will be its listeners. They love your show, and they'd love to help you out. All you need to do is ask. It costs nothing, and helps build that relationship with them. And as I mentioned earlier, when you see this activity on social media, make sure to "like" it. Listeners love that you "liked" their tweet or gave them a "thumbs-up" on Facebook.

TACTIC 4: OPENING THE KIMONO Social media has a way of making one-to-many communications feel much more intimate. Engaging the audience is an inexpensive and effective way to build audience and fervent supporters for your work. When you make it an organic part of your production process, it can create a powerful foundation for your program when it launches.

Many years ago I was involved in the creation of a 24/7 folk music streaming service called *Folk Alley*. We engaged brand and marketing consultant Ben McConnell (also the coauthor of the pioneering book *Creating Customer Evangelists*) to advise us on how to build an audience for the budding service.

Ben had a lot of advice for us, all with a familiar return: Ask the audience what they think and put as many decisions in their hands as possible. Ask them what features the service should have and how to make the service engaging, exciting, and fun. Have contests (with prizes) for those who suggest ideas that get implemented. Use fame economy[42] as a reward. Ask them to take surveys, look at prototype site pages, listen to demos of shows and hosts, and even nominate and vote on the service's name.[43] Expecting an artist to do an in-studio

---

[42] Fame economy is simply giving them credit publicly for their ideas and contributions. People will do a lot just for some loud and public praise.

[43] Yes, *Folk Alley* was a listener suggestion and was selected in a poll of folk music enthusiasts we engaged before launch.

performance? Ask the audience what songs they should play and what questions you should ask—even minutia like if, when, and how often to play holiday music during the month of December. Just ask them.

We went in search of folk music listeners and enthusiasts in online forums and started to recruit them to be our beta audience. This was around 2003 or 2004, many years before Twitter and social media made this kind of interaction much easier.

To say I was resistant to Ben's suggestions at the time was an understatement. *We* were the experts, I reasoned. If anyone should be deciding how to put together this service, it should be *us*. Ben was so patient with me, which I'm grateful for now, because once I let go of my hubris, I learned a ton that I still use to this day. If Ben's patient coaching didn't convince me, then the results certainly did. While the number of interactions with our beta audience were modest at first, every time we asked them something, the number of responses grew and grew. The beta audience really started to be deeply engaged and cared about how the service took form. At first it was hundreds of people, but quickly grew to thousands and then tens of thousands. By the time we were ready to launch, we had a *real* audience—on day one. And they were a real audience that knew the service, were excited to listen and tell their friends, and were willing to support it, even financially.

Today, you often hear this kind of audience engagement and involvement referred to as "opening the kimono," meaning that you let them see behind what the public is facing, behind the facade. By letting them see what's going on while your project is coming together, you invite them to get invested in you and your work. It will pay off repeatedly down the line.

Some might worry, "But aren't we spoiling everything by letting them know who we are interviewing or talking to, or what the subject of an upcoming episode will be?" I certainly hope not. Look: If you can tell someone in a tweet what an episode is about, and you don't deliver anything surprising, twisty, or unexpected, then your episode probably is destined to disappoint anyhow. You aren't thinking deeply enough about what you should cover in that episode. If you tweet out, "Next week we are talking about the Chinese economy" or "On our next episode we are going to talk about Quentin Tarantino movies"—and all you deliver is a two-dimensional recitation on the ups and downs of the yuan or *Reservoir Dogs*—then you have a problem.[44] Regardless, it's important to keep in mind that these fiercely loyal, deeply engaged listeners will always be a small minority of your audience. That's actually healthy.[45] So even if you are letting them see quite a bit of what's happening, that is their reward. Regardless, there will still be a large percentage of your audience that is surprised when the new episode shows up in their feed.

TACTIC 5: BE MY GUEST This idea works best for podcasts that feature people talking to each other, like panel discussions, chumcasts, roundtables, or chat shows. One of the tried and true ways of promoting a podcast, which goes back to the origins of podcasting itself, is if you want to promote yourself as a host, be a guest.

173

You have interesting things to say, subject matter expertise, and a unique spin on the world. Why not offer yourself as a potential guest on someone else's podcast? Chumcasts need chums to talk to, so why not you? You'll find that a surprising number of similar podcasts will be open to this. It often works best to arrange a "quid pro quo," where you can be guests on each other's podcasts over the course of a month or two, allowing you each to introduce your audience to the other.

TACTIC 6: LIVE EVENTS I was invited to go to Australia to speak at an annual audio creators conference called Audiocraft. It's a long trip to give a forty-five-minute talk, but traveling to another country to meet and speak with so many talented producers who are eager and excited

---

[44] Perhaps a better idea is an episode looking at what *Reservoir Dogs* can tell us about the yuan.

[45] As any radio programmer will tell you, it can actually be very *un*healthy to have too high a percentage of your audience as diehard loyalists. If you are growing and thriving, you should always be adding new listeners (who generally listen less and less often, but grow over time). If all you have are diehards, you are starting a process that ends in a death spiral. So while deep loyalists are important, don't listen to them *too* much.

to be part of the burgeoning audio industry in Australia turned out to be truly exciting.

One of the most intriguing parts of the trip was attending a live event for *The Allusionist*, a terrific podcast about words and language, hosted by Helen Zaltzman, that's part of the Radiotopia network. Helen, who was also speaking at the conference, decided to host a public live event while in Sydney and invited me to come.

I thought to myself, "How many people in Sydney, Australia, are willing to come out in a torrential rainstorm to see a live event for an American podcast hosted by a British woman about lexicography?" The answer to that is at least 200 Sydneysiders.[46] I say "at least" because the event sold out a few weeks in advance and I saw a significant number of additional people show up, in the pouring rain, to see if they could score a last-minute ticket.

The show itself was Helen performing some stories that had been featured in previous episodes (read: you could go and listen to them for free in the podcast feed) and then doing some Q and A with the audience. Those in attendance *loved* every single minute of it: They hung on every word, laughed at every joke, and would have stayed even longer if Helen had remained on the stage. It was charming and fun and so full of positive energy between Helen and the audience that I had a contact high for hours afterward.

I don't care how long I've been in podcasting; that still impresses me. For some reason that no one has been able to definitively explain to me (despite mountains of theories), podcast audiences are quick to jump at a chance to attend a live taping or live event tied to their favorite podcast. Now, I'm not advocating that you travel to a different hemisphere with a thirteen-hour time difference to host an event, but perhaps something with fewer associated frequent flier miles might make sense for you.

Even small podcasts can do surprisingly well with live events. One of my former producers, Eleanor Kagan, started a just-for-fun

---

[46] And yes, this is the term for people from Sydney, though some prefer "Harboursiders," which is even weirder, in my opinion.

podcast featuring discussions on feminist film that she and her friend recorded in her apartment. They had done only about two dozen episodes before booking an evening at The Bell House in Brooklyn, and they filled the house. I've heard many stories of large podcasters selling out major theaters for live events, and small indie podcasters host really fun nights in the back of a local bookstore.

If I had to guess, I'd point at two factors for the overperformance of podcasts as live events, one interesting and one boring. The boring one: Given that the average age of podcast listeners is still pretty young (late twenties to mid-thirties), these young folks are free to go out and enjoy a live event without worrying about obligations that might keep older listeners home, like kids, dogs, or other domestic responsibilities (including just being exhausted). The interesting factor: We've talked earlier about podcasts being the hub of a community comprised of those interested in a niche subject, talent, or worldview. The live event gives those people a chance to come out and be among their people—to see, experience, and be together with other members of the tribe.

There are three clear reasons for hosting a live event, even something as low scale as a meetup at a bar. First, it really helps build bonds with the audience. Strong bonds equal loyalty, and we've discussed many advantages of having a solid base of loyal fans for your show. The second reason is revenue. You won't retire off money from live-event ticket sales for your podcast, but it can be an important component of how you make a show financially viable. And third, the benefit of the event goes far beyond those who attend.

When I was promoting my first two books, it was still common for an author to pack a suitcase and hit the road for a book tour. At first, I hated them. I would arrive in a city and spend all day doing media, from the morning zoo show to the 6 p.m. news. Then I'd go to the bookstore for the event I'd been promoting for the past thirteen hours, and there would be a grand total of twenty people sitting in folding chairs. All that effort for twenty people felt like a waste to me. But my PR handler counseled me that all those media hits, all day long, had nothing to do with those people who attended. The book-store signing was an excuse to get media talking about me and my book. The real audience for those media hits wasn't potential attendees; it was potential buyers who would look it up, order it, or stop by stores to pick up a copy later on.

Events for podcasting can serve the same purpose. While a limited number of people will attend the event, many more people will hear about it through the event's promotion. Those who hear about it may not be able to attend, but they may check out your show to see what all the fuss is about.

TACTIC 7: TAKE IT TO THE LISTENER Instead of having your own event, why not go to someone else's? I don't mean to crash another podcaster's event (though actually, there is nothing wrong with doing that), but any event where your listeners may gather. This is an extension of the advice in the first half of this chapter, but with a more expansive view. Once you are up and running, seek out events that may attract people in your target audience.

But here is the key (as counterintuitive as it may seem): Don't promote yourself there. Don't hand out brochures, CDs, thumb drives with MP3 files, or pitch the people you meet to get them to listen. Instead, just talk to people and get to know them. If they ask what you do, tell them, but let them lead the discussion about how much you share or don't share. If they don't ask, you don't tell. You may be thinking this is the dumbest marketing tactic ever conceived. The key is to build relationships at the event, but do no "marketing."

Then, after the event, follow up. Get an email, phone number, or business card and tell them *afterward* about the podcast you do. This will take you from a *zero* percent chance of getting them to listen to at least *some* chance of getting them to listen.

I'll use myself as an example of this. Whenever I attend events, I usually encounter a lot of producers (sometimes dozens) who seek me out and try to hand me a CD, a thumb drive of MP3s, a brochure, or some other collateral about their project. As a matter of policy, I never accept them. This isn't about being conceited or inaccessible. I just don't have the time or ability to deal with it. This is the same reason I caution creators from placing CDs and thumb drives in conference, festival, or convention tote bags as giveaways: 98 percent of them never make it out of the attendees' hotel rooms, let alone get listened to.

Instead, whenever someone wants to give me something, I hand them my business card and invite them to follow up. I'll try to make time to listen, but send it to me once I'm at home, so I don't have to lug around a bunch of plastic stuff. Some producers will *still* try to hand me things—you know, just in case I'll have time. I won't. I don't accept them. Those who follow up with me often get way more of my time and attention than they do when they try to hand me things at gatherings. I'm giving an honest reaction, since most people will take the item with a smile, then chuck it the first chance they get.

Use the in-person opportunity to build a relationship, then follow up later. The result is a much better chance that you'll make a real connection.

HOW TO PITCH

I don't care who you are, if you are engaging in the making of creative work, you need to know how to pitch. To me, it is the most critically undertrained element of being a journalist, producer, or talent. We train these people for technical skill, editorial decision-making, journalism, on-air performance, and production technique, but we don't teach creatives how to sell their work. Just as with the other skills we *do* train for, it is equally essential to know how to engage and excite others about your work so they will support you and do things to help you and your work advance.

The classic role of pitching in the production process is a maker pitching to an editor, commissioner (a term applied to a network executive who approves or green-lights projects), development executive, or other gatekeeper: getting an audience with them, often just a few minutes, to convince them to get behind your project (which often translates into funding or resourcing your project). You share a quick (often just a few minutes, possibly less) pitch of your story, hopefully answer a few questions from an at least semi-interested gatekeeper, and then await your fate.

However, pitching skills are far more applicable than that. They can be used to seek a partnership or network relationship, sell advertising, and secure grant funding, as well as receive press coverage and marketing for your project. If you look at the creators who get grants, get picked up by a network, or have articles and posts written about their work, they aren't necessarily the best creators but they are the best at knowing how to sell their work.

I made sure this section appeared late in this book because so many of the exercises, frameworks, and principles you've learned throughout the preceding chapters will be helpful in building a great pitch for your project. You'll recognize a lot of it in the shorter versions of the pitch-creation recipe I'll share here.

Many years ago I was out to dinner with a friend, Ole, who told me that whenever he is trying to get a quick read on the quality of a restaurant, he asks to see the dessert menu. When I asked why he does this, he proclaimed: "It's possible for a restaurant to have good food and bad desserts, but you will never find a restaurant with great desserts and bad food."

In Ole's mind, the dessert menu is the ultimate barometer, better than service, better than reviews, better than ambience, and better than the interior design. If the dessert menu is good, eat there, because the rest of the food will be equally good or better.

Ole argued that the dessert menu reflected the chef's attention to detail *about food*. Were the desserts thoughtfully paired with each other and the menu? Were they handmade in the kitchen or generic food service items? Were they just a bunch of sweet things or were there delightful and surprising choices, flavors, textures, and combinations? Did the restaurant seem to delight in its dessert menu, crafting tempting and intriguing descriptions, or do they just offer "cheesecake" with canned strawberry glaze for an extra dollar? I've shared Ole's wisdom with many over the years. Many start off doubt-ful, but no one has been able to cleanly disprove his logic.

The same thinking applies to the relationship between pitches and the stories/series they describe. It is possible to have a great story and a lousy pitch, but it is rare to find a great pitch for a terrible story. I say this because the essence of a pitch is being able to *quickly* grab someone's attention with a refined synthesis about your story or idea and what makes it powerful. That requires a degree of thought and attention as to what makes the story good.

To be clear, there are lots of crappy stories that have some tit-illating anecdote about them that can catch attention. Let's say someone came up to you and said, "Did you hear the story about the guy who lives in a converted mausoleum?" That's a weird nugget. You may be drawn in and want to know more. After a few questions, you realize that the pitch is the extent of what's interesting about the story. The guy doesn't have a particularly interesting reason for living in a converted mausoleum. Nothing very remarkable has happened to him while he was living in a converted mausoleum. How he came to live there isn't a particularly interesting story. He is just a strange dude who lives in a converted mausoleum. That's it.

If all you have in a pitch is a sugar rush (to drive our dessert met-aphor even further into the ground), then you will most likely not get greenlit, supported, or approved by the person being pitched. And what do we call someone receiving a story pitch? A catcher? A pitchee? A pitch receiver (that sounds a little naughty for some reason)?

Regardless, to test my own preferences and biases about pitches, I turned to a number of other pitch catchers: friends and colleagues in the podcast and radio industries. I asked their thoughts on how to make a great pitch and where most pitches fail. I spoke with Chris Bannon of Stitcher, Andy Bowers from Panoply, N'Jeri Eaton of NPR, Nazanin Rafsanjani from Gimlet, and Mohit Bakaya from BBC Radio 4. Combined, they hear literally thousands of pitches for audio stories every year. Though we are all very different thinkers and create audio for different audiences and platforms, there was a surprising amount of consistency to what all these story pitch catchers had to say. Their advice basically boils down to four points:

- Know your story.
- Know your audience.
- Answer why *you* are telling this story.
- Land your ending.[47]

So for the rest of this section, I'm going to walk through each of these, and share a mini-variation on The Six-Lunch Test Drive that you can use to quickly get a pitch in order.

KNOW YOUR STORY

Most novice creators think that a pitch comes before the work. You find a story, pitch it, *then* you go out and do the work. It rarely works out that way, or well for the creator. Creating a pitch that will resonate requires that you do some of the work before you approach an editor or commissioner. That may seem unfair—that you have to invest your time and effort on spec, aka for free, just to be able to pitch something successfully. But life isn't always fair; get used to it.

To suss this out, I often ask people pitching me how they came to learn about the story. If the response is something like, "Oh, I read about it in one of the back sections of the *New York Times*," it's a pretty clear sign that the only work they've done on the story is reading a back section of the *New York Times*. On the other hand, if the reply is, "I read about this, then spent a few weeks digging into it and learned so many interesting things. Then I followed up with a phone call and learned even more," that pitch sounds enterprising and original, instantly elevating both the story and the pitcher in my mind.

My friend Mohit Bakaya, a commissioner at the BBC's domestic news and information service, Radio 4, put it well. He told me that a pitch is a story in itself. "Treat the pitch like you treat the story," he

---

[47] See what I mean about connecting to themes earlier in this book?

says. "You would never air a story without doing the work, so what does it say about you if you aren't willing to do at least some of that work for the pitch?" While knowing the ins and outs of a story is good, you also need to be prepared to define how to demonstrate that your take is unique.

"Be prepared to say, right at the top, 'This is *the* show that . . .'" Stitcher's Chris Bannon told me. "If you can't answer that, your pitch isn't ready."

Think back to our Ten-Word Descriptions. What Chris and other pitch receivers are asking for is very similar. What makes your project different? In a crowded field that may see a number of others attempting a similar story or idea, how are you distinct, and the one that listeners will gravitate toward over others? If you expect a network to be able to go out and sell you, or a PR person to generate interest in your show, you need to be able to answer this. You just can't expect a busy network exec or marketer to magically come up with it on their own.

Something that many creators don't realize is that before someone can sell or market your show, they have to be able to understand your show. As we've discussed throughout this chapter, that is your responsibility. The most successful creators have been able to share their vision and generate interest. That starts with you articulating why it matters, in a way that your sales and marketing partners can understand and repeat. You can't expect others to be able to tell that story unless you can.

KNOW YOUR AUDIENCE

"Who specifically is the audience for this podcast? I always ask this question," says Andy Bowers, Chief Innovation Officer at Megaphone. "Often the response is 'Well, everyone, really.' That is not a useful answer."

Since understanding your audience is a core tenet of this entire book, we don't need to spend much time on it here, except to note a few things. Many eager producers will want to ask an editor, commissioner, or executive to share their vision of who their organization wants to reach. I was guilty of this early in my career, too. I wanted to tailor my pitch to the audience that the radio show or magazine served. But there are problems with this approach. You are making the assumption that the audience they have today is the audience they want in the future. And it shows a lack of clear vision in the idea and story approach. If you know the story, you will know who it is for and who will enjoy listening to it.

Also worth noting that, just like when we googled our audience in Chapter 2, the target audience should be considered a destination and isn't to the exclusion of other potential listeners. The audience will contain a lot of people who don't resemble the target; those are the people you reach along the journey to your target listener. There are lots of people who will listen who fall outside your definition, and that's fine. But understanding that target, having a clear perspective on who they are and why they would listen, is critical to getting buy-in from a decision-maker.

Also, knowing and defining the audience is an important step to establishing your authenticity and credibility as a teller of this story.

ANSWER WHY YOU ARE TELLING THIS STORY

Of all the producers and reporters in the world, why should you be the one to tell this story? More often than you think, these commissioners and editors have been pitched stories with a lot of similarities in subject matter or approach. Why you over others?

Sometimes that answer isn't the sources you have, or the access you have, or the research you've done. Sometimes that answer is you, yourself. You are the defining asset.

I don't want to date myself, but I've been around long enough to watch a few trends come and go and then come back again. Denim jackets, aviator sunglasses, arpeggiated synthesizers in pop songs—I've seen these before. I've even seen these cyclical trends in the marbled principles of journalism.

At one time it was considered sacrosanct for a journalist

to remove themselves from a story, to free their work from their biases and opinions. That has changed, to a degree. Let's be honest: Objectivity, while once seen as a nirvana-like goal for attainment, is really a bit of a farce, and often unfair to your subjects and your audience. It is pretty much impossible to fully remove yourself from your work. Now, rather than scrub yourself, your perspective, and your experience from your reporting, it is considered more important for a journalist to be aware of where they sit in a story and be transparent about this with the audience. You will never be able to be "objective" enough to answer for every bias and shortcoming you will have in telling the stories of others. So rather than attempt the impossible, just be honest. In short: Name it and own it.

This healthy change in attitude about you and your reporting isn't just about controlling negative influences. Who you are, the experiences and worldview you possess, can be a potential positive as well when pitching work. The perspectives that journalism schools tried to beat out of students may be the reason why you should be the person telling the story.

According to my friend Mohit, "I much prefer it when someone says, 'The reason I'm pitching this is because this happened in my life and that's how I came across this.' Because almost always it's an interesting story."

This isn't just a matter of acknowledging perspective and worldview. Your connection to a story can also answer why you are the one to tell it, or the only one who can tell it. Mohit once told me about a pitch he received from a man who brought in an old bomber jacket to a pitch. During the pitch, the reporter said he wanted to do a biography of an old letter he found in the breast pocket of the vintage jacket shortly after he'd purchased it at a thrift store. The guy reaches into the pocket and pulls out the letter itself. The pitcher had already done some work to figure out where the letter came from and who sent and received it. Having the prop in the pitch meeting was a brilliant piece of showmanship, but it also helped sell the commission on why the reporter was the person to tell the story.

Destry Sibley, a producer at my company Magnificent Noise, once pitched a terrific series telling the stories of a group of Spanish children who were relocated to Mexico during the Spanish Civil War, and through a calamity of world circumstances, never returned home to their families and grew up as orphans in Mexico. During the pitch she revealed that the reason she wanted to share these stories was that her grandmother was one of these orphans. So by investigating and telling this story, she was understanding her own history. It was a fascinating twist that made the story come to life and established, super clearly, why she was the person to tell it.

Under the rules of old-school journalism, that personal connection would either have been buried (never mentioned) or would disqualify Destry from being the person to report and tell this story. Nonsense.

LAND YOUR ENDING

Gymnasts and figure skaters will tell you how critical it is to land your final move. If you screw it up, it will color the judges opinion of the entire routine. The same goes for a pitch.

As someone who has heard many hundreds of pitches, I'd say that for more than half of them, when I ask the producer how the story ends, or how they plan to end it, they haven't even thought about that enough to fake their way through an answer. They think the power of the story is interesting enough, so the resolution or ending will magically present itself.

It is a high-wire act to start producing and sharing a story without a clear idea of where it will end. Two well-known examples of this were the iconic first season of *Serial* and the documentary series *Missing Richard Simmons*. Both were exemplary pieces of work created by top-shelf producers and talent. However, neither started with the end in mind, and so came up somewhat short. Each used the end of their production cycle as the end of the story, inserting a meditation on fame, guilt, innocence, whatever, that left a number of people disappointed because they expected that these journeys should end with a clearer sense of the outcome (something, interestingly, that the producers had not explicitly or implicitly promised at the beginning of the series).

Like most things that have potential payoff, finding the ending while you are still in the pitch stage is definitely more work. But it will build confidence in you and the story, and is more likely to result in a positive outcome for you. Knowing the end, or that there is an end, will encourage a gatekeeper to take a risk on you or a story. And the best part is that you don't even have to stick to the ending you pitched. No editor or commissioner is going to hold you to a specific outcome if a better option emerges. To be clear, if you pitch that you will solve a mystery, you better solve it. But if while working on your project, you find things you didn't expect that lead the audience to a more delightful, surprising, or satisfying conclusion, who cares what the original pitch was. Go for it!!

A FEW OTHER THINGS TO KEEP IN MIND

While pitching skills are applicable in many ways, there are three other pieces of advice that apply specifically to pitching podcasts to networks that merit some ink.

First, if you are lucky enough to catch some time with a network exec to pitch your project to remember that a successful pitch is much more than permission to create. Those execs aren't just looking for a great idea; they want to know you know what it will take to make it. "You're pitching a story and idea, a team, talent, budget, and a way to connect to an audience," Andy Bowers told me. "All of it is included in the package."

You don't have to have a degree in accounting, but if a pitch receiver's first question is "How much do you need to do it?" that's an indication that they are at least interested enough to move forward in the conversation. So you need to be able to answer that question.

The advice I give to spreadsheet-averse creators facing a need to define a budget is to start by writing down everything you'll need to spend money on. Then find someone who doesn't share your aversions to help you figure out how much each item will cost. And don't forget the trickiest, and probably most expensive, part of your budget: proper compensation for your own time. For a pitch, it doesn't need to be exact; it just needs to be reasonably complete.

Second irksome thing: Don't be one of the pitchers who ignores everything in this section, and instead spends their time producing a beautiful color PowerPoint presentation deck on glossy paper. Presentation does matter, but not at the expense of substance.

"So one of the things that drive me crazy in pitches," NPR's N'Jeri Eaton says, "[is when] I get really elaborate decks that are all visuals and no real information. They think we'll be seduced by the mood of it, or your graphics, or the cool logo you have designed, without recording a single second of audio."

And the third irksome item that is critical to remember: cold pitches. Gather any group of development execs, editors, and commissioners together, and they will start sharing stories about weird pitches they've received, or weird places they've been pitched.

I, myself, have been pitched in bathrooms (on many occasions, including more than once when someone followed me in and tried to pitch their story while I relieved myself). I have been pitched in elevators. I've had people send pitches to my house. I've been pitched at a playground. People have pitched my wife in hopes that she'd be so blown away that she'll tell me to commission it. I was even pitched once at a funeral. Please, don't be one of these people.

I understand why people do this. Having an audience with gatekeepers can seem challenging, and some producers mistakenly feel that I'll be impressed by their moxie and skill at finding me. It doesn't come off as skilled; it comes off as creepy. Not only will your pitch not get picked up; it will really make me question if I'd ever want you representing me or my company doing reporting and production.

All that said, I understand that for many new producers, it's hard to figure out how to get access to decision-makers. Many people who take in pitches offer some publicly accessible pitch policy, a portal for submissions, or other guidelines that usually take a few minutes of searching to find. It's less effort, more likely to result in a green light, and you'll never be the subject of a barroom discussion. A win for all! In any of these circumstances, if the person held back the pitch and instead simply asked, "When is a good time to pitch you a project?" now *that*, I respect. When someone asks, I make sure they have a pathway for them to pitch their idea.

CONSTRUCTING A PITCH

So how do you figure out how to make your pitch sizzle and cut through the noise? I have an exercise I've taught student groups before. It's a truncated version of The Six-Lunch Test Drive from Chapter 5, but here in a far more compressed timeline, with none of the expense and high calorie count of the six lunches.

It's worth noting that this exercise may seem bent toward narrative storytelling. That's a fair observation, but I'd argue that almost any style of podcast or radio production has many of the elements below, so it won't take much effort to shape your panel discussion or interview show using the suggestions below. First, a few principles to embrace:

- You need to fight for attention. Even someone whose job is taking pitches has something else they'd rather do than listen to a bunch of pitches. Pitch as if you are converting a skeptic, because you probably are.

- The purpose of your pitch is to advance to the next stage of the approval process. That's it. You have to grab the pitchee's attention and hook them, right up front. So therefore, don't pack your pitch with detail. You'll identify plenty of other things to talk about instead, which I outline below.

- As we've discussed elsewhere in the book, a story's "importance" is irrelevant, so make sure you don't focus on that in your pitch, Instead, let the story itself make the case for importance: show, don't tell. Few people listen to something because they "should" listen to it. They have to care, and it's your job to make them care, even in your pitch.

Here is how the exercise works.

First off, find a buddy. It's best if you can find someone else who is preparing a new project to pitch so you can help each other. Absent that, any friend with a spare fifteen to twenty minutes will do. For these instructions, we'll assume that you have another pitch-refining partner to work with. Once you sit down to work on your pitch, do the following:

- Tell each other your idea in one minute or less.

- Afterward, each partner lists the three most interesting elements of the other person's pitch. It can be a fact, a character, or a component of the story.

THE TWIST

As I mentioned in the chapter about storytelling, every great story has a twist: something surprising and unexpected. A twist is what moves a story or idea from black-and-white to technicolor. Your twist shows that you have a bigger, multidimensional story and reveals what your idea is really about:

- Spend a few minutes revising your pitch to focus more on the two or three interesting points identified by your partner, and include your twist. Lose whatever doesn't address those core elements.

- Each of you should pitch your idea in forty-five seconds this time.

- Give each other feedback on the pitch.

CHARACTER

Every story and show idea has a protagonist, central character, or thematic avatar (think of our discussion of character in Chapters 1 and 6). They represent the core idea of your project. How can you add elements to a pitch that highlight character without sacrificing story? Also, people (including gatekeepers) relate to and emotionally connect with other people. So with that in mind, how do you revise your pitch to focus on its characters?

- Revise your pitch to center attention on your most compelling character.

- Share your pitches with each other in forty seconds.

- Give each other feedback.

EMOTION

What is the emotional highlight for the listener? Not the emotional highlight for the characters, but for the person listening. Whenever you pitch a story, the pitch receiver is asking themselves, covertly, if this is a story that listeners will enjoy. Help by thinking through what will resonate emotionally with the listener:

- Revise your pitch again to include the emotional highlight.

- Share your pitches with each other in thirty seconds.

Now take a look back at what you had to start. The difference will surprise you, I'm sure. That wasn't so hard, was it? Now you are ready to schedule that meeting or phone call and blow that receiver/gate-keeper/pitchee's socks off.

BONUS EPISODE: Jesse Thorn, on How to Build Community

When Marc Maron interviewed President Obama on his podcast, *WTF*, in June 2015, it was a milestone in podcast history. A sitting president of the United States came to record a podcast interview in the garage of Marc's house (accompanied by a full Secret Service detail, who had to sweep Marc's house with bomb-sniffing dogs, much to the chagrin of Marc's cats). While podcasting had been on the transcendence for the past few years, nothing like that had ever happened. It was a breakthrough moment that was lost on no one. At the end of the episode with Obama, Marc thanked a group of people, including Jesse Thorn, owner and founder of Maximum Fun, arguably one of the original podcast networks. Why? Because when Marc first expressed interest in trying podcasting, Jesse helped him get his start, literally coming over to Marc's house to help set up his microphones and teaching Marc how to record in GarageBand on his Mac.

"I'm sure he would have figured that out himself. He's a very smart man," says Jesse. "He thanked me, I think, because he understands how much I appreciate his work, and we have a real relationship, and he has been helpful to me and I have been helpful to him, and he's a considerate guy. That kind of thing happens when you actually work to be a useful member of a creative community."

Jesse Thorn didn't start off as a podcast host, or even a podcast enthusiast. He hosted a radio show called *The Sound of Young America* on the campus radio station at UC Santa Cruz. In 2004, Jesse started to hear about this new technology to distribute audio shows, called podcasting, and started to play around with using it to distribute his radio show. After college, Jesse continued the show as a podcast,[48] as well as starting a few other podcast shows featuring Jesse and his friends. Things continued to evolve, and Jesse now runs an influential network of more than forty podcasts, mostly focused on writers and performers in the L.A. comedy scene. Every show that's part of the Maximum Fun network ends with the tagline "Listener Supported. Artist Owned." Those four words sum up Maximum Fun and the community around it quite succinctly.

The son of a community organizer, Jesse understood from an early age the power of organizing people behind shared values and interests. While this is the DNA of his network, Maximum Fun, it wasn't the reason Jesse was such an early and strong advocate for the importance of building community around podcasting. Back when Jesse started, it was a financial necessity.

"In the early days of podcasting, particularly, there was no revenue to speak of from advertising unless you were doing a show about tech," he says. "And when I say the early days, I'm talking about the first seven years or something. So I very quickly had an audience-supported model."

---

[48] Eventually changing the show's name to *Bullseye*.

As Maximum Fun started to take shape and grow, Jesse leaned into one of his inspirations, the site Okayplayer. Okayplayer was founded by Ahmir "Questlove" Thompson of The Roots.

"I had seen how quickly this thing, that had started with the idea *this is the website of The Roots*, became a group of people with shared values who have a certain way of looking at the world," Jesse says. "I knew how important that was to me because I was one of those people, and my relationship with that site and that community went far beyond being a fan of The Roots. So my goal was always to create an experience like that in any way I could around Maximum Fun. Part of that was trying to create virtual community and part of that was trying to give people an opportunity to have that in real life. Also, in having that in real life, to have an experience that was more multilateral than bilateral."

Jesse knew that for someone to take the steps of voluntarily giving him money, it would require that the listeners feel a sense of ownership and belonging that was much deeper than the traditional relationship between a listener and show. In creating Maximum Fun, he was years ahead of others in understanding the relationship between podcasting and community.

"So pretty much from the beginning the goal was to make something that was sort of like Harley-Davidson in that it represents a kind of person you can be in the world, in addition to just a product," Jesse says. The values of Maximum Fun were basically just built on what Jesse thought was important to him, personally. It goes beyond sense of humor, and includes respect and acceptance of others, a kind of shared enthusiasm for praiseworthy work, and more than a dab of love for quirk. Maximum Fun even hosts annual gatherings, called MaxFunCon, which are kind of like summer camp for comedy nerds. MaxFunCon is focused on connecting the conference-goers so they gain as much satisfaction and enjoyment from other attendees as they do from the comedy acts. It's a gathering where attendees enter as strangers and leave as friends. Its main purpose is to let the community of fans actually be a real community. I attended one of these gatherings several years ago, and knew I was in for an interesting weekend when I noticed that the registration pack included condoms.

"So I think my big feeling about it is that if you start from a point of view like, 'I am going to be helpful to others, especially others who are in a similar situation to mine; I am going to celebrate the work of others that I like and care about; I'm going to build meaningful relationships that are based on actual real interest in others and their work, an actual interchange of creativity,' that is ultimately very beneficial.

"There's this joke about how every L.A. comedy podcast is just everybody from every other L.A. comedy podcast," Jesse says. "But the other way of characterizing that is: These are people with actual relationships that are reflected on the air and actual talent that's reflected on air. They know each other, and they know each other's talent, and that's why L.A. has comedy podcasts and New York doesn't, even though there are plenty of great talented and wonderful comics in New York."

Chapter 7
LEADING CREATIVE TEAMS

Y ou may think that running teams or managing people isn't for you, but if you are any good at what you do, being a leader of a group of people is almost inevitably part of your future. And this isn't just relevant to those who work for big companies or established podcasts. Even for the solo podcasters, this may be more applicable to you than you think. You may decide to collaborate with a friend, team up with others, bring in helpers to assist with a live event or other special project, or—who knows—you may do really well and grow your small podcast into something that requires the support of more people.

Before we start talking about how to be a great leader of creative people, there is one thing we need to make clear: Creative people are a total pain in the ass.

They are needy. They are demanding. They need drama more than oxygen. They never listen. Then, when they do listen, they get it all backward. They don't think strategically (they are creators and doers). They could care less about the big picture, let alone "get it." They expect to be the center of your attention and your favorite, always and at all times.

However, they also bring your shared ideas and vision to life. Despite all the heartaches and occasional childish behavior, you need them. I know this because I am one. (If you are reading this book, you probably are, too.) I've also led hundreds of them into battle and created great things together that we couldn't have done without each other.

So if you find yourself suddenly a leader, collaborator, or a manager, I have seven tips to help your audio partners be the best version of themselves, perhaps even better than they (or you) thought were possible.

TIP 1: THE STRATEGY MANTRA

Let me begin explaining the power of the strategy mantra with a cautionary tale.

One day I ran into a young woman I knew in the audio industry who'd recently started a new job. She had previously worked for an audio production company that created very successful radio and podcast segments. Over the past decade, that company had grown from a handful of sound designers, producers, and story editors to almost 100 people. The company had taken on a ton of new initiatives and was expanding what they produced and how they distributed their work.

I asked her why she left her old job.

Her response: "We had no idea what we were doing."

To be clear: The editors knew how to edit, the producers knew how to find and frame stories. Pretty much all the employees knew their individual job roles. That wasn't in question. The problem was that none of them really understood *why* they were doing it.

In growing so much, so fast, the organization had lost itself. With all its new initiatives and projects, it was doing so many things that it had lost its sense of direction. When it was small, things felt simple. But with all the new people, roles, and ideas piled up, no one knew what their "true north" was anymore. Even worse, the company wasn't prepared for growth. Employees learned about new projects by reading about them in the press. They saw new people walking around the office and had no idea who they were or what they did. They'd sit in staff meetings and felt that management was speaking in code that they didn't understand. Directions changed, projects came and went. It was like the company had developed ADD as it grew.

So they all just kept their heads down and did their job, but grew frustrated and upset because they didn't know what the company was trying to achieve or how they fit into that vision. In short, they wanted to know their work mattered.

The true crime in this story is how avoidable it was. All of it. The spiraling initiatives. The pervasive confusion and lack of direction. The dissatisfaction and low morale of the staff. All it would take is a few simple words.

This will harken back to our Ten-Word Descriptions and the need to create a strong focus for the project. In short, imagine generating something similar for an entire company or working group. By simply answering the question, "What do we do?" you can make your work much simpler, and also more productive and satisfying for both the business and its staff. Unlike the Ten-Word Description for your next show, we won't require a specific word count, but it should use specific, unambiguous language that a stranger could read and understand with no additional context or explanation.

This is similar to the "onliness statement" that author Marty Neumeier advocates in his iconic branding book *Zag*, where he challenges brand-definers to finish this sentence: "Our brand is the ONLY _____ that _____." An example being "Our brand is the ONLY **wheat distributor** that **sells grind-it-yourself wheat for the serious home baker**." It's clear. It's unique. It sets the boundary markers.

It seems so simple, yet it's a hard exercise. Creating a strategy mantra is simply answering "What do we do?"

Another way to look at it is finding what you do in the answers to two questions:

- **What does the audience want?**
- **What can we provide?**

Like any other definitional exercise, you will be tempted to paint in broad strokes and use the most inclusive, easy-to-navigate language possible. But inclusive language is vague language. And vague language is a waste of everyone's time. It serves no point.[49] Give it a try:

What do we do?
We come to work every day to _____.

If I were a betting man, I'd put a dollar down to say that you skipped right over that, thinking that you could come back to it later. But be honest; you skipped over it because it's hard. And don't be a smartass literalist either. If you produce a podcast called *The Liver and Onions Show*, don't answer by saying, "We come to work every day to produce *The Liver and Onions Show*." That fails the "read by a stranger" test (because the stranger may not have any idea what *The Liver and Onions Show* is). Drill down a layer. Try something more complete, like "We come to work every day to create insightful recorded conversations, share recipes, and tout the nutritional benefits of the most delicious and versatile foodstuff in the world, namely, of course, liver and onions."

Let's try again. When you think of the group you lead, what do you do?

We come to work every day to _____.

Once you fill in that blank, the hard part is done. Well, at least it should be. Ideally, once you have a clear definition of what you do, then decision-making gets pretty easy. Or at least it should.

When you say "We do X," that also says that you *don't* do anything else or *won't* do it or at least *shouldn't* do it. That means that when a staffer comes running down the hall saying, "I have a terrific idea—we

---

[49] Neumeier also has a great line that I love about the need for definition: "A specialty store in a big city and a general store in a small town must adhere to the same principle: The wider the competition, the narrower the focus—and vice versa."

should do Y!" that means you, as the leader, say no. You say no because Y is not X.

Your strategy mantra becomes a filtering system. No longer do you pursue the most exciting ideas, nor the most supposedly profitable ideas, nor the newest ideas, nor the ideas that only the boss wants to do. You also don't have to be confined to giving subjective feedback like it's a "good" or "bad" idea. It's either X or it's not. If it's not, then you, as the leader, say no. It really is that simple: State a mantra and have the discipline to stick to it.

Great inspiration for this approach comes from the basic cable industry, of all places. In a world of hundreds of channels, how to you differentiate yourself? Especially in an instant-gratification world where viewing choices border on instinctual and are made in fractions of a second? By having a mantra and sticking to it.

Some channels have their focus built into their title, like Comedy Central, Cartoon Network, or DogTV. Others use positioning statements to not only provide a foothold for marketing but a clean and clear take on their programming. It's their mantra.

The classic example of this was the originally rather bland and forgettable USA Network, with its logo featuring a prominent flag as well as a rather generic and conservative serif font. It had a very "American" feel to it, and one might assume that the channel would feature something equally "American": patriotic, heartwarming, and/or values-driven. But in truth, the network and its branding stood for nothing in particular. Their programming was as uninspiring as their brand: talk shows, low-budget movies, and some kids programming sprinkled in between sports (it was originally a sports network). The network meandered on this way for almost twenty-five years.

Then USA Network kinda walked backward into their unifying theme (which, for the record, is a totally okay way to go about it). They were experiencing some success with a number of original dramatic series and decided to build their vision for the channel around that. To them, the glue that held together their series was their vivid, charming, and endearing characters on shows like *Monk*, *Suits*, and

Psych. These shows featured fun yet troubled characters in quirky and unusual, yet optimistic, situations and circumstances. The branding they came up with to frame all this: "Characters Welcome."

"Characters Welcome" was a ubiquitous brand statement for them, but they also used it to define their next generation of programming choices: literally green-lighting projects that also featured vivid, charming, and endearing characters in quirky and unusual, yet optimistic, situations and circumstances.

In an interview included in the book *The TV Brand Builders* by Andy Bryant and Charlie Mawer, USA Network's EVP of Marketing and Digital, Alexandra Shapiro, said, "The key was it wasn't just a tagline, it was a philosophy that informed both the way we operate internally and with our partners. It informed our on-air environment, our programming strategy, and our development."

The framework proved so powerful and effective for them that USA Network stuck with it for eleven years (a lifetime, if not several lifetimes, in cable programming) until they dumped it for "We the Bold" in 2016.

The branding was so intentional, consistent, and intense that it was even applied to show production, with the network instructing producers to include a fruit bowl or another bold splash of color whenever they framed a scene that lacked visual pop.

Another great example is the network FX. The name started out as Fox Extended, which originally pretty much meant that it was all the stuff that Fox owned or had rights to, but didn't have anywhere else to put, like old TV series from the 1970s and 1980s such as *Eight Is Enough*, *M*A*S*H*, and *Wonder Woman*. It was the leftover channel.

In the late 1990s, it started to invest more heavily in original programming, focusing on slightly different characters and situations than the charming and endearing variety at USA Network. FX wanted to feature characters who were rebels, placed inside stories and series that had an edge to them. When FX first started to define their brand under a unifying theme, they started with "There Is No Box" (alluding to "thinking outside the box"). But that branding and philosophy didn't land well. (Most attempts to define yourself in the negative end up that way.) So they decided to make it even more simple: one word. "Fearless." FX saw the "Fearless" moniker applying equally to its programs, the characters in those shows, and the network as a whole. That idea has held together their positioning, marketing, and programming philosophy for the better part of a decade.

In television, these taglines, mantras, brand filters—or whatever you want to call them—end up creating an expectation among viewers, so that the channel's brand itself can color the viewers expectations of what the show is about. In an interesting survey in the UK,[50] TV viewers were shown only the title of a new program, called *The Unknown Prince Charles*, then were asked what they thought the show was about. When told it would air on the BBC, viewers expected it would be a documentary about his lesser known accomplishments and achievements. When other survey respondents were told the same title would air on the slightly spicier ITV1 channel, those viewers expected it would be a "tell all" featuring former girlfriends and servants. Same title and subject, but very different programs, based solely on the viewers' understanding of the network providing it.

So how can this apply to leading a creative group of audio makers?

During my tenure at NPR, I set a goal for myself. I wanted you to be able to go up to anyone who worked for me, at any level, from on-air hosts down to interns, and ask them, "What do we do?" and have them all give the same answer.

First step? Come up with the answer.

My job at NPR was running the Programming division, which contained all the programs and shows that weren't daily news programs. While the first order of business at NPR was to produce radio journalism, when looking at where its news listeners came from (and how they discovered NPR News), they learned something interesting: More than a third of the audience first connected to NPR through

---

[50] Also discussed in Bryant and Mawer's *The TV Brand Builders*.

non-news programs and podcasts. Those non-news programs were one of the primary ways that people discovered NPR, before eventually moving on to news programs. For many new listeners, NPR's non-news programs were the gateway drug for NPR. Someone discovers *Invisibilia, Wait Wait . . . Don't Tell Me!*, or *Pop Culture Happy Hour* and then eventually tries out *Morning Edition*. Given this was such an important audience development tool, I digested down a lot of research, data, and analysis to give my staff a strategy mantra.

What do we do?
We come to work every day to create the next generation of NPR listeners.

If someone on the team wanted to know all the details and data, I was happy to share it with them. But most people didn't; they just wanted a simple marching order to let them know why we do what we do, and why it matters. Something that anyone on the team can understand. Something you could explain to a new hire or intern in a matter of minutes. Something clear, direct, and true.

Once you have a strong strategy mantra, like any good mantra, you repeat it over and over again. Which is exactly what I did.

I opened most staff meetings by saying the mantra. When we discussed something new we were undertaking, I'd tie it to the mantra. When we debated whether to take on a new initiative, we'd ask, "Is this going to help us create the next generation of NPR listeners?" The answer to that question usually was our decision. I'd include it in board presentations, budget documents, any chance I'd get to remind my team and those we work with what we do and why.

Eventually, I came pretty close to fulfilling my goal, if not actually getting there. Every member of my team, all the way up and down (and often with an eye roll) would be able to answer why we came to work that day.

We did the same thing at Audible, too.

Very early in my tenure, we wanted to create a new vertical among our original offerings. After doing some research on people interested in listening to the spoken word, we saw a huge opportunity for new programs focused on mindfulness and wellness. If you've spent any time browsing around different types of audio offerings, that might surprise you. You might notice a ton of wellness offerings, and you'd be right. There are tens of thousands of podcasts and audio offerings targeted at those interested in improving their life, meditating, lowering stress, sleeping better, and getting nutrition guidance and exercise advice.

So with so much available, why make more? Simple. True, there was a ton of stuff, but almost all of it sucked. There was a glut of material, yet few people were actually using it. Those who were curious about the genre wanted something else that they could hear themselves in: reflecting their interests, goals, and worldview.

That created a challenge to our team. How do we avoid the pitfalls that have caused so many other offerings to falter? Even though every business book will advise against defining in the negative, we started by making a list of everything that turns people off about traditional mindfulness content. The list included things like crappy new age music, a speaking style that was the sonic equivalent of a wet sock, and what we called "hippie lingo" (constant references to peace, floating, and rainbows). After finishing the list, we thought to ourselves, "Why not just take away all that?" These largely aesthetic distinctions appealed to a narrow niche. By avoiding them, we could create something that was for everyone else. So we came up with the strategic mantra:

What do we do?
We come to work every day to create evidence-based life-improvement guides specifically aimed at people who don't do wellness.

That seemingly simple statement has a lot packed into it. "Evidence-based" meant we'd focus on tactics and ideas that actually work. Proven. That eliminates more than 99 percent of the competition right there. "People who don't do wellness" refers to those who look at the glut of crap already available and realize it isn't for them. In every decision we made, about what projects to pursue, what position to take, what aesthetic choices to follow, we used our mantra.

We said it to each other so often that one time my partner in this initiative took a two-week break. When he came back, we exchanged post-vacation pleasantries, then looked at each other and repeated it again.

Make a mantra, then repeat it every chance you have.

There's an easy way to know when your group gets and has internalized it. When they start making jokes about it. Seriously, comedy comes from shared experiences and understanding. When a group has internalized your strategy mantra enough to tease you or others about it, you know it's in deep.

TIP 2: TEACH HOW TO MAKE MISTAKES
Good leaders destigmatize failure and mistakes.

It's kind of ironic, because if you are in fact a good leader, your team will really fight against failing. They look up to you and don't want to let you down. That's where your leadership comes in. You need to be very clear with them that what really disappoints you is when they *don't* swing for the fences. It's a well-worn analogy, but a Hall of Fame hitter will still fail two out of three times they go up to bat. In a crowded marketplace like podcasting, being satisfied with small, safe plays won't get you anywhere.

Good leaders *plan* for failure and anticipate it. They frame it as a learning opportunity about how to do better in the next iteration. When they lay out a plan and timeline for a new project, they build in plenty of time to retreat, rethink, and reiterate. And that starts with making it okay for a failure to happen.

And the best way to do that is by being your team's role model for how to fail. Groups of people, even doing entrepreneurial work, don't naturally embrace failure and risk. It's a particular scenario I've seen played out thousands of times at staff meetings, brainstorms, and happy hours: One person proposes an idea, then others come up with reasons why it might fail, slowly pecking it to death. An idea suffocated by an avalanche of "yeah, but." Often these reasons have (at best) a 2 percent likelihood of actually happening. This banter goes on until the originator gets exhausted or deflated, or the group concludes that there's no way to make the idea completely risk-free, or at least no way to do so before prices go up at the end of happy hour.

The unspoken groupthink at work in these situations is that an idea cannot have both merit and risk at the same time. Resources are precious. Time is limited. It is imperative that decision-makers invest in winners. Every time.

This scenario isn't an occasional happening. During my career I've probably seen variations of it occur every single day. By trying to eliminate all risk from every promising idea, and stigmatizing the failure that could teach success, decision-makers dramatically diminish the potential impact of new work. The idea that does make it past these thrashings may not fail, but it will not significantly move the needle against the problem it was designed to solve either. The solution everyone agrees on is often the one that will fail to solve the problem.

This philosophy is a petri dish for failure. And not the good kind of failure. And, yes, there is a good kind of failure. Not every industry can embrace failure. I wouldn't want to accept a high rate of screwing up by a heart surgeon or food safety inspector. But for a creative person working in audio, with its daily ability to reinvent, tweak, and adjust, podcasters certainly can.

Good groups and companies learn from failure. Weak ones don't.

Take, for example, the inventors of the app Burbn, a social media platform for whiskey lovers. Their users could "check in" at bars, distilleries, and restaurants; rate different whiskeys; post reviews and photos; and comment on each other's posts. It tanked almost immediately. However, in looking over the charred embers of their massive fail, the team noticed that users really loved to post photos and comment. They dumped the focus on whiskey and renamed the app Instagram.

There are plenty of examples of failures in podcasting's history—thousands of flopped new programs, apps, revenue strategies, and distribution opportunities that didn't work out for one reason or another. Yet consider how failure-avoiders respond after something doesn't go as planned. You will hear comments such as "I knew this would happen," or some involved will reveal how they had been quietly advocating for another tactic all along. Or there is the person who won't acknowledge failure but instead invents a metric to demonstrate that their flopped project was, in fact, a success. As in, "Our show may not have had any listeners, but we did innovate in how we schedule studio time."

Worst of all is the corrosive amount of gossip and whispering that goes on after someone experiences a setback, insinuating blame on the person who was willing to take a risk. But that is the person we should be applauding.

The reason there is such an allergic reaction to failure is an aversion to risk-taking. Risk is something to be avoided at all costs, rather than identified, mitigated against, and managed. Why embrace risk? Because nothing worth having ever came without a significant amount of it.

There is a basic equation to understanding the power of failure:

Risk aversion = Success aversion

Smart leaders build risk tolerance among their hosts, producers, and staff. Risk (and resulting failure) is expected, built into processes, and often welcomed as the pathway to better understanding and future success. Risk and risk tolerance work a lot like allergies. Most allergic reactions can be managed with medication. Allergy meds don't make the allergy go away; they just suppress the reaction. The meds create tolerance. You can do that with risk, too.

I've been fortunate enough to have had some big successes in my career, but there's a much larger number of things that have gone completely backward. Whenever someone compliments me on a success, I always have the same response: "Thank you, but you didn't notice the fifty failures it took to learn how to do that one thing right." That may be a bit of an exaggerated ratio, but in saying that I'm not ashamed of my failure, and I want to acknowledge its role in the success.

When I screw up something royally, which I do regularly, I have a routine. I sit down alone with a cup of hot chocolate, stare out the window, and think. I have a set list of five questions that I ask myself:

- What really went wrong here? [51]

- Were there any cues/signals that I missed along the way that could have changed the outcome?

- What other projects do I have going on that could immediately benefit from this experience?

- How do I share what I've learned?

- How did the failure make me feel?

That final question was a suggestion from David Cox, one of my former team members at Audible. He persuaded me to add it by saying, "Failure doesn't feel good. And people usually try to avoid not feeling good. But in order to learn from the failure, first you have to be open to feeling those feelings."

Like the response to that last question, this exercise should be all about you. You should not only answer the question, but answer each question in a way that identifies your specific role in the failure. In short, frame every error from how you touched and influenced what happened, as if you are the only one responsible. You can't say, "It was marketing's fault for not doing a solid PR campaign." You can say, "I did not set expectations and outline the necessary work with marketing to launch a successful PR campaign."

After I've answered these five questions, I mentally file this information away. Sometimes I even write a letter, giving feedback to myself.

---

[51] Not the Blame Game. Not the frustration/anger/disappointment. But what is the honest root cause of the failure?

That's where being a role model can come in. As a leader of your creative group, the best way to make failure (and smart risk-taking) okay is to share your own experiences. Share your failures, past and present, with your team. Teach them by your own mistakes. During meetings, brainstorming sessions, or just through the course of work, share your experience as well as the five answers. Never wince, grimace, or apologize, just share the story.

There is an undertone to this: The best way to fail is to own the failure—demonstrate how to channel the experience into learning for other projects. Actually, the real key to learning from failure is being honest. When something isn't working, just say so. The key to understanding failure and embracing risk is often a very subtle change in approach.

When I talk to aspiring podcasters who are part of media companies, radio stations, or small companies trying to establish a space in podcasting, they often bring the groupthink mentality to it. "We are investing seed money toward the podcast. It has to be a winner and generate impressive audience and return." That's a recipe for disaster. When you start one podcast to get one hit podcast, your chances of success are incredibly small. Like, lottery-winning-odds kind of small.

What if these organizations started their process by saying: "We want to end up with one successful podcast"? Then, instead of funding one podcast, you are funding a process. By reverse engineering success, you set the expectation that not every step needs to go 100 percent according to plan to meet the goal. Following this logic, you may start with six podcast ideas, instead of one, then slowly shut down the ideas that aren't going to pan out. The one remaining podcast has a much higher potential to break through.

Whenever I discuss this approach with companies, I hear a common refrain to the responses: "We don't have the money for that." In other words, since you don't have funds to start six podcasts, you are going to bet the farm on one idea up front. I think that's a false barrier. Wouldn't it be prudent to invest a small amount to help ensure that the rest of the funds for the initiative are spent effectively?

Risk-tolerance becomes easier with velocity, and from my perspective speed isn't just desirable, it's necessary. Many leaders of other podcasts and podcast networks use this thinking to disrupt and grow fast. If you don't fail and learn from the experience to improve your project, get used to seeing it pass you by.

TIP 3: FOCUS ON WHAT DOESN'T CHANGE

During my time as part of the Amazon ecosystem, I was exposed to a lot of the company's business philosophies and principles. It was a fascinating and illuminating time in my career (I've often referred to those years as getting paid to get an MBA). I found a lot of the "Amazon Way" to be really useful to my understanding of business, but very few of those principles make a lot of sense in a creative culture. That said, there is one bit of Bezos-wisdom that can be really useful, especially if you've gone through the effort to define a mantra or Ten-Word Description for your project or organization. His big suggestion for winning is: Focus on what doesn't change.

Jeff Bezos, famous for his focus on creating long-term value, once said, "I very frequently get the question: 'What's going to change in the next ten years?' And that is a very interesting question; it's a very common one. I almost never get the question: 'What's not going to change in the next ten years?' And I submit to you that that second question is actually the more important of the two—because you can build a business strategy around the things that are stable in time."

Bezos went on to say that customers want three basic things from Amazon: great selection, great prices, and great customer service (which includes fast shipping). So as the world has changed over the past twenty years, Amazon has kept its attention on how to advance those three things. As technology and opportunities present themselves, Amazon leaned toward those that advanced improving selection, price, and service. It's a great guiding principle and can help someone vet and process everything that presents itself.

As much as people have enjoyed making fun of Amazon's experiments with drone delivery, it makes perfect sense as an investment for Amazon, which spends a huge amount of time and resource trying to identify and reduce friction points in the delivery of packages. Though the drone tech has a long way to go, it could end up being an important component to near-instant access to your future orders. Other Amazon delivery technologies, from lockers to placing packages inside houses and cars, all get an odd bit of attention when they debut (though nothing like the delivery drones), yet each is trying to eliminate friction points to help deliver the things you want, when you want, at a price you find attractive.

You may be wondering how all this can apply to a creative enterprise. As far as I can imagine, there is little use for drones in audio production. However, the underlying thought is a perfect match for audio: From the evolution of radio through to the current podcast revolution, the winners focus on what doesn't change.

When it comes to great storytelling, *regardless of the platform used to deliver it*, listeners want some consistent, basic things— and those have remained unchanged for more than a century. You've seen me discuss them repeatedly throughout this entire book. They want:

- Great stories.
- Great voices.
- Great ideas.

And it certainly doesn't hurt if those are delivered in an entertaining way filled with delight and surprise.

The emphasis on the "platform used to deliver it" is key to understanding this. Platforms like radio, podcasting, smart speakers, and car dashboards are ways to deliver great stories. But they don't make bad stories good and usually don't make good stories bad.

I've found that when creative teams learn of a new emerging device, distribution platform, or technology, someone on the team starts running around the office insisting that we *must* pursue this opportunity immediately. If the opportunity is not activated ASAP, then everything will be lost, as the audience abandons their current options to pursue the new one (remember what I said at the beginning of the chapter about drama?).

A few years ago, when smart speakers started to become a thing—when there was only one smart speaker (the Amazon Echo) and we didn't even call them that yet—I remember members of my teams fully freaking out. "This will change everything," I heard repeatedly. "We have to get in on this *now!*"

I reminded them, as I do in many of these situations, that listeners do not change habits easily or quickly, so rarely does a change, new opportunity, or emerging tech or platform cause an immediate disruption. And even in the case of smart speakers, it took almost two years for them to even emerge as a *contender* to be a disruptor, let alone do any serious disruption. Now, I do believe that smart speakers are going to be a major factor in the future of digital audio, and their influence and ubiquity will only grow and become stronger, but I also believe that mapping that terrain shouldn't be the focal concern of a creative team. Let's keep our heads pointed in the right direction. Rather than freak out at every new invention or idea, let's focus our effort on the things that don't change: great stories, great voices, and great ideas. We creative people should think about stories that are adaptable across many platforms and that audiences can enjoy where they want to. Today, we need to focus on doing that.

In short, the ideas of "focus on what doesn't change" can be summed up in two words: calm down.

TIP 4: AVOID THE BINARY

We all like to be economical when we convey the most important information.

"Look both ways before you cross."

"Don't touch that."

"Mind the gap."

And even "I love you."

Sometimes we use short, declarative binary statements to convey ideas, danger, emotion, or simply the best way to do something.

It is THIS WAY or it is wrong, could kill you, or won't get you what you want.

And there are a lot of times when we, as recipients of information, also want something binary and simple.

"Yes."

"No."

Or "I love you, too."

But there are many times when context matters a lot.

When it comes to creative teams, I try to avoid binary statements like "Do this" or "Don't do that." Instead of trying to teach my teams to be obedient to instructions, I try to teach them how to think. Learning to think involves looking for opportunities to *not* make binary statements. Instead, I give them the context and information, then try to coach them through making the call themselves. Or, at the very least, they walk away with a decision from me that makes sense and they understand how the issue impacts our strategy, best practices, and ways of working.

Fred Jacobs, the founder and president of the commercial radio consulting firm Jacobs Media, wrote a fantastic blog post about this in 2017 that called out "6 Pieces of Bad Advice We Give Air Talent." In it, he provides examples of things radio managers tell DJs, such as "Don't talk about yourself," when what we really want to tell them (and teach them to do) is to "use relatable, interesting life experiences to create content and build your brand." Some station manager, at some point, read in an article, saw at a conference panel discussion, or heard from another manager that "DJs talk too much about themselves," and they never stopped to think about what it meant, or why it is a problem. DJ talking is bad, so don't do it. Period. In truth, there are lots of ways to make a DJ's personal anecdotes *relevant* to an audience, and that is where the effort and attention should go, not into enforcing an arbitrary and dumb binary rule.

And worse, many rules and instructions that qualify as binary statements aren't always true. There are exceptions. There are times when you would need to do something differently.

I find that so many of these binary statements took root long ago, and are followed like religious doctrine. Yet whenever you ask, no one is quite sure how it originated, from whom, or why.

I'll give you an example. For many years, many years ago, there was a rule at NPR that reporters could not write about first-person experiences. They were instructed to write that there was a smell of cinnamon in the area in a marketplace, but they couldn't say that *they* smelled the aroma. If the reporter was in a war zone and a bomb when off right next to them, they couldn't say, "A bomb when off next to me as I stood in the market square." Instead, they were instructed to write "A bomb went off in the market square," with no indication that they were standing *right there.*

This was an unquestioned rule. You just didn't write about your-self and your feelings/opinions/experiences in a reported piece of journalism. Whenever anyone asked why, often the answers from editors felt improvised and loosely moored. There was often more discussion about how important the rule was, as opposed to any clear understanding of why it existed, or where the rule came from, or to whom you would speak if you felt circumstances required you to write in first person. Many theorized that it originated in another radio news organization, like the BBC or CBS Radio News, and it was just ported over to NPR.

Then one of my mentors and former bosses, Jay Kernis, led a look at newsroom practices in an effort to evolve NPR's sound and cast off a lot of the old rules that didn't serve the organization well in the modern era. This was one of several rules (along with an equally weird rule about reporters not airing questions asked on tape) that made no sense, and were gently let go as part of Jay's efforts. This single small change resulted in NPR's reporters creating some of the most engaging and arresting reporting that audiences have ever heard. One that comes to mind is Jason Beaubien and David Gilkey's reporting about finding a young boy dying from Ebola on a beach, just lying there, everyone afraid to touch or help. If Jason and David were unable to discuss their own truth about seeing that boy, it would have felt antiseptic and odd, as well as a bizarre choice considering the situation.

The rule was binary, and in its brevity and lack of context, it served no one.

TIP 5: PLAN FOR 50 PERCENT

Of all my ideas, notions, and wild hares I've pursued and advocated for as a leader, this is, by far, the most troublesome to other executives and managers. In short, when scoping out work or a project, I only plan to use half of a person's time. I budget and schedule them for no more than twenty hours of heads-down work per week. If we need more employee time, we should hire another person.

That may seem like a luxury, but in reality it's a practical necessity. I once knew a young woman who worked for a radio station. The station decided to let her work on a new podcast full-time. It was at least forty hours of work a week, often more. Unlike many of the examples I use in this book, the project didn't go poorly. In fact, the podcast was an almost immediate and huge success. It shot to the top of the podcast charts, had a ton of downloads, and was generating buzz in its first weeks. That's when the problems began.

After a few weeks, the station asked if she could produce more episodes. She'd planned on releasing one every other week; now her bosses wanted to go weekly. Immediately. She was already working more than full-time extra hours and giving up time on most weekends to churn out two a month. By some miracle, she managed to make the space to crank out four a month.

A few weeks later she received a request to appear on a TV show. A few weeks after that she got a book offer. A few weeks after that, an offer to do a paid speech. She had no room for any of these offers, and turned most down, even though they were arguably worth more to the long-term success and viability for her and her podcast than the extra rushed episodes. Also, and most unfortunately, the quality and originality of her work started to slip. In less than eighteen months, she was completely burned out. She quit her podcast.

Hers was an uncharacteristically quick rise in popularity and opportunity. But with successful projects, the basic problem is very common. Forged in something between a puritan and monastic work ethic, the startup podcast was created on a razor-thin shoestring, with no capacity to pivot, expand, exploit, or even step back for a moment to breathe. Variations on this story happen all the time, and not just with new ventures. It even happens with established work.

Let's face it, when it comes to planning, almost everyone is terrible at estimating time. We are almost at our most terrible when we are estimating (and thus valuing) our own time. We hit peak terrible when we are trying to make the case for something we *really* want to do, kidding ourselves, our supporters, and colleagues that we can accomplish what we promise in the economical period of time we're willing to assign to it.

So to remedy this, I often book people resources with the assumption they will have only 50 percent of their time available to actually work. Before you write me off and skip to the next point, hear me out. Theoretically, let's imagine an employee named Dottie. She has forty hours a week to work. When we schedule, we want to fill up all forty hours of Dottie's hours.

But as the manager, you need to factor in Dottie's vacation and sick time, as well as having Dottie cover for other people's vacation and sick time. Add on top of that the weekly staff meetings and the monthly all-staff meetings, as well as other time-sucking obligations. When you add all this together, it can *easily* eat up as much as 20 percent of Dottie's hours.

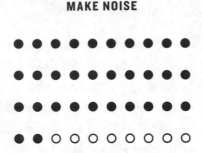

Leaders and managers spend so much time worrying about failure that they never plan for success. That's where the 50 percent idea comes in. When planning the work to do a project, you have to assume that Dottie has only twenty hours available to you.

So what about the other twenty hours a week? That covers the 20 percent of flex you need to cover basic needs like meetings, vacations, and sick time, as well as "plan for success" items like planning and executing special projects; interacting and building relationships with their audience; working on extra material; solving problems; and even courting sponsors, grant makers, and advertisers. They could also use some of this time to just sit and stare out the window to dream up an idea of how to grow/improve/change the project that neither of you would be able to think about when you are rush, rush, rushing all day.

During my tenure at NPR I came up with a concept to coordinate the promotion of the network programs across all NPR radio stations. The "Spark" Project was a huge success and was a big contributing factor in NPR's growth over the past decade. What spawned this effort? A canceled two-day executive retreat.

There was an off-site executive retreat on my calendar, sucking up two full days of my time. For some reason I can't remember, it was canceled at the last minute, leaving me with two completely open days. The first morning of the first day, I came in and sat in my office, replied to some emails, answered some questions, but generally started to feel really bored. For some reason, while staring at a blank whiteboard, I started to think about program promotion. I got up and started writing out a process flow. By midafternoon and many erased and rewritten whiteboard renderings later, I had the basic formulas worked out. I spent the rest of that day and my second free day working out details, inviting feedback, and revising.

Boom. Done. A problem solved with a solution I never would have come up with if I wasn't sitting there with some unspoken-for time on my hands. And which do you think was a better use of my time over those two days: solving a system-wide issue with promotions, or fighting to stay awake for two days of blah-blah-blah in an off-site retreat?

To share my bias, I'm generally a huge fan of boredom. When we are bored, that's one of the few times we allow ourselves permission to let our minds roam freely. I cherish that and often find that when I'm stuck on something, I make myself bored. I turn off the music/radio/TV. I put down the magazine or book. I stop distracting myself with interesting things and I just sit.

Boredom is a great friend to a creative process and a creative endeavor like a podcast or radio program. But, despite everything I've just shared over the last few pages, boredom really isn't the goal of creating this space. The goal is to create some elbow room to breathe, metaphorically and literally.

Look at mathematicians, writers, and others whose currency is original thinking. Most will tell you that, even when working on their pursuit full-time, they have about two-to-four hours of high productivity in them before they are mentally spent and need to rest and recharge. Numerous studies back this up, finding that trying to devote more time to intellectual pursuits actually produces no real additional output. More time in, no more ideas come out. Coincidentally, this applies across a lot of work. You know those folks who work twelve-hour days, burning the late-night oil? Rarely are they more productive than someone who puts in a solid eight hours of work, and leaves the remaining time for rest and leisure.

To be clear, I am not advocating for twenty-hour workweeks. I'm advocating for leaving room in an employee's work schedule so they have a work/life balance that contributes to their success; have time to pursue opportunities that advance the project and enterprise; and time to be thoughtful, insightful, and imaginative about their work. I think it is just as important to schedule that downtime as it is to schedule in time for sick leave, meals, and attending staff meetings. And while I'm at it, I could write an additional section to this chapter discussing my belief in the essential nature of vacations and downtime on weekends. After almost two decades of myself being one of the worst work/life balance violators I know, I've come to appreciate and value how important this time is. Over the past two years I've literally changed my life and the way I work. I put boundaries on work hours and activity, I allow work to consume far less of my time (and self) than I used to, and I've seen zero decrease in my work output. So please consider this idea for yourself and your teams as well. But you can't schedule that downtime if you are filling a forty-hour week with forty hours of work tasks. Since I've started advocating for this, I've had a number of people try it, and never heard a single complaint (except from finance people eager to amortize employee time). All that is required is a small amount of communication of expectations and trust in your team. They will reward that trust by making good use of the time.

So bringing it back to Dottie and the allocation of her time: If it takes forty hours of work to produce Dottie's podcast, then the staffing need is not one head but two.

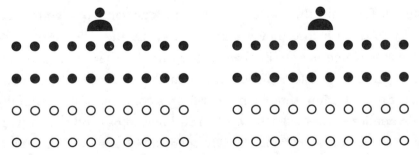

Now, let's jump back to that story I shared earlier: the woman who had a successful podcast with opportunities to expand into other platforms, like books and TV and live events. She already was working from a 20 percent deficit, made up with evenings and weekends (and then some). Would planning to use only 50 percent of her time at the start of a project help her? Almost certainly. It may not have solved all her problems, but it certainly would have decreased risk and increased the likelihood that it could work out.

And for those pessimists who insist on looking on the down side: What's the worst thing that could happen by using this idea? Your employees end up with some extra time they can then devote to other ideas and projects in your organization.

TIP 6: PROBLEMS ARE POSSIBILITIES

When confronted with bad news or an unwelcome development in the workplace, I often say to my teams, "How do we turn this problem into a possibility?" To illustrate, I'm going to share a story that I've been dying to tell, which is related to this idea.

In 2017, I worked on a series with author Jon Ronson called *The Butterfly Effect*. It was about all the unintended consequences of what happened when porn became ubiquitous and free on the Internet. The title came from the notion of a butterfly effect: where one event causes a series of otherwise unrelated events. So a flap of a butterfly's wings causes a small rush of wind that eventually cascades and grows into a hurricane.

One of those unintended flaps of the butterfly wings in our series was the evolution of bespoke pornography. Since so many of the traditional ways to make money dried up when porn became available free online, the producers and stars looked for other ways to use their talent and skill to make money. One way was to take requests and charge the customers to produce porn just for them. As you can imagine, the custom porn could get a bit freaky sometimes, with customers requesting all kinds of activities (and some didn't even involve sex: women sitting in a room swatting flies, others being covered in condiments, and another featuring two naked women burning the customer's stamp collection).

When the series was completed, we had a scene involving bespoke porn that we couldn't put into the show, the story of Mike and his commissioned porn. Mike fetishized a scene from *The Dick Van Dyke Show*, where Mary Tyler Moore's character gets her foot caught in the bathtub and she can't get out of the tub or open the locked door for help. The entire scene takes place in the hallway outside the bathroom, with the audience hearing Mary Tyler Moore shouting from inside the tub. Mike paid for a bespoke porn team to create an alternative version of the scene, with the same dialogue but from *inside* the bathroom.

So, as we were producing the series and knowing that we wanted to share Mike's story and love for this scene, we knew we'd need to include some audio from the original TV episode. That meant getting the rights to the audio from the TV episode. Surprisingly, we asked CBS, and even after we revealed what we were up to, they agreed to license the clip to us. Then our lawyer told us that we also needed to get consent from Dick Van Dyke and the estate of Mary Tyler Moore. And, in what probably surprises no one, they declined to approve it.

That should have killed the idea dead. And that's the point of the story and why it's important here. It didn't kill it.

I try to train my staff and talent to be tenacious. When it comes to getting a story, interview, or permission; breaking the rules; doing something new, or similar things, I tell them that they should never take "no" for an answer. Keep pushing, find a new angle, bust down resistance, realize that nothing worth having comes without a relative amount of work.

This leads to that question I often pose to creative teams when they are stuck: "How do we turn this problem into a possibility?" It isn't about needing an attitude adjustment, being Pollyannaish, or looking on the sunny side. As I've mentioned, I firmly believe that creativity thrives when there are boundaries. So how do we learn to turn this roadblock (the problem) into something that doesn't stop creativity, but rather forms the boundary marker for new creativity?

After learning that we couldn't use the audio of the original scene, Jon and his producer, Lina Misitzis, were both upset and a bit angry that we couldn't include the story. So one afternoon I sat down with Lina and said, "How do we turn this to our advantage?" Within ten minutes, we had an idea. We had the rights to use the scene, but not the actors' voices. So why don't we re-create the scene with other actors? In essence, create a short audio drama that conveys the scene without actually using the archival tape. We wanted to produce it well, but also wanted it to be obvious that it wasn't the real thing (not to confuse the listener).

As a leader of a creative team, *you* are the one who sets the tone on values, standards, work ethic, and the definition of excellence. Even in the worst scenarios, there is almost always a way around or through a problem. Of course there will be times when a roadblock really is a roadblock—a story will go cold, facts don't add up, the story changes (and the story/conversation needs to change, too). It happens. But, honestly, it is rare. There is often something to salvage or take away. Be the example for your staff, and as soon as the shock of bad news passes (and perhaps even before), start the conversation on how to turn a problem into something you can use to surprise and delight your listeners.

TIP 7: OFFER OPPORTUNITIES

Whenever someone visits or spends time in one of my shops, there is one consistent thing people point out, repeatedly, that always surprises me: The young staffers seem happy, engaged, deeply committed to their work, and loyal to the team. They cite the bromides about millennials in the workplace and react as if I have pulled off some kind of miracle or something. Honestly, I rarely give that any thought. First off, I really hate labels and stereotypes. I often find that the attributes that others quickly lay on any group often fail to be true. If anyone on any of my teams has been happy, it's because I often focus less on who they are and more on creating an environment that fosters opportunity for everyone on the team.

The single most important role of any leader of a creative team is to create opportunity.

Period.

Instead of worrying about how to please millennials, or the women on my team, or others, I focus on opportunity for everyone. And I acknowledge that "opportunity" means different things to different people at different stages of their careers.

To some, especially more experienced workers, "opportunity" equates with autonomy. They want to do it their way and, largely, want you to stay out of it. Fine by me. We spend a large amount of time defining projects and work *up front* (using many of the methods in this book), and then I let them go off to execute largely on their own. They know what I want. They have the experience and wisdom to do it.

They also know that I expect they will come to me when they have problems, need advice, want a sympathetic or critical ear, or just need to complain for a bit. It takes a lot of trust between you and the employee, but you end up with a creator who is eager to show how well placed that trust is and desperately doesn't want to disappoint.

For less experienced employees, I often make sure opportunity is a chance to stretch, experiment, and prove themselves. It starts when they first walk in the door.

New employees who come to work for me are often shocked when I sit them down, usually in their first few days on the job, and start the conversation by asking about their *next* job.

"Let's talk about the job you do when you leave here," I say. They often look stunned.

Then I explain that we, together, have two tasks during their tenure. The first is to help them do their new job as well as they possibly can. The second task is to prepare them for their next job. We do so by providing opportunity—select opportunity—to them during the (hopefully many) years we work together. If someone comes in as an assistant producer but wants to become a reporter someday, we look for opportunities for them to build the skills they will need, learn more about that work, and try those shoes on for a bit and walk around. I've even had people say they don't want to leave, but they want their next job to be a promotion, so we start the process—in their first week of work—of getting them ready.

I'm also a fan and practitioner of offering outsized opportunities to fairly junior employees. I often remind others that Kurt Cobain and Jimi Hendrix were both twenty-seven when they died. Martin Luther King Jr. was thirty-six. Jesus was thirty-three. The point isn't that they all died young; it's that they *achieved* young. They all failed along the way, but through a combination of circumstances, they were given the opportunity to prove themselves and did.

Remember Lina, the producer on *The Butterfly Effect* who I mentioned in the section on turning problems into possibilities? When she came to work with me on that show, she was twenty-seven and had been a junior-level producer for a few projects and networks. But that was about the extent of her audio résumé. She'd really impressed me with her tenacity, brightness, and ability to handle almost anything we threw at her. So when Jon Ronson and I realized we needed to add a producer to the show, almost on a whim I asked Lina, "Have you ever heard of the writer Jon Ronson?"

She had read and loved his work.

"So how comfortable—or not—would you be working on something about porn?"

Two days later she was basically in charge of one of the largest projects in our portfolio. I bypassed half a dozen more senior people to give the opportunity to her. And, for what it's worth, she nailed it.

So weren't those more senior people upset? Not really, because I was also trying to provide different opportunities for them, too.

Right before I offered *The Butterfly Effect* to Lina, I had read about the Slow Hiker Theory. It's floated around business literature for some time, and I'm afraid I can't really nail down where it originated. The Slow Hiker Theory tells the story of a group of hikers hiking through the forest on a long trail. If you are their leader and you need to make sure that the group all stays together, how do you organize your group? Without a deliberate plan, most groups of hikers will see the fastest hikers end up in the front, way in front of most others, and the slowest hiker taking up the rear. As the hike goes on, the group will get more and more spread out.

The Slow Hiker Theory suggests the best formulation of the group is to put the slowest hiker in front. "That's crazy," you might think. "They will slow *everyone* down." Not necessarily, especially if you see if the rest of the group can do things to help the slowest hiker go faster. Can someone carry their water? Sure thing. Can another hiker take some weight from the slow hiker's pack and move it into theirs? Yes. Can another hiker loan the slow hiker some walking poles? Yup. Each act helps make the slow hiker faster and, thus, moves the pace of the entire group forward faster, finishing as a group. By focusing your group's energy on making the slowest person faster, you raise the average of the entire group.

I strongly suggest the same applies to creative teams. Without a Slow Hiker strategy, you will let your most experienced and creative staff have all the opportunity, thus leaving the rest of the group stuck and creating a growing "opportunity gap" between your high performers and the rest of the team. Instead, the group needs to think like a team. How can we make a new or less experienced team function more like front-runners? Opportunity. Opportunity. Opportunity.

I saved this tip for last because opportunity is like a magic potion. You may not be able to pay everyone what they are worth, you may not be able to give someone every assignment they want, you may need to ask them to work extra hours or extra hard or do crap jobs that make them (and you) cringe. But all associated grumbling goes away when accompanied by a little bit of opportunity.

So I hope this has been helpful to you. It was, by far, the most difficult chapter of this book for me to write, and the one I was most committed to including. That's because how you treat people is more important than almost anything else you do in a creative environment (or, arguably, in *any* environment). It's possible to be an asshole and treat people poorly yet still get good work out of them. But using these ideas, or ideas like them, will prove to be easier, less risky, and will create an environment where better work is likely to happen more often.

But wait, we aren't done yet. There's more!

BONUS EPISODE: Anna Sale on Sacred Time

This piece is the eighth bit of advice on leading teams, from Anna Sale, host of WNYC's *Death, Sex & Money*.

Even when you hear a podcast with a singular host presence, that doesn't mean there isn't a team behind it. And that team needs to understand the "how" and "why" of what makes that podcast work. But how do you do that? And how to you make sure that communication keeps working as you go forward? One important component for Anna Sale is the idea of weekly Sacred Time.

Anna Sale was a local politics reporter for WNYC in 2013 when a callout went around asking for new show ideas. "It wasn't even specific to podcasts," she says. "I was like, 'Oh. I have a homework assignment. Let me think about this and come up with my dream show.'"

Anna wasn't even sure that the show that emerged from that process, *Death, Sex & Money*, was even supposed to be a podcast. "I thought, 'I just got picked for the JV team,'" she says. "I thought maybe I was pitching a radio show that was going to start as a podcast as a proof of concept."

Listening to *Death, Sex & Money* can be really deceptive. As a listener you feel the listening experience is so personal and intimate. It gives you the illusion that it's just Anna, her guest, and you. In truth, there is an entire team of people behind the show, even when she was working on the early pilot episodes.

"It was never a one-man-band situation," she says. While she came up with the concept herself, she had an editor and the help of sound designers and some freelance producers. Today, the team has grown to three full-time staff plus a few others devoting part of their work time to *Death, Sex & Money*. It's a small team, but there's one twist: Anna, the host and founder, lives on the West Coast, 3,000 miles away from the rest of her team.

And even though there is a team producing the show, it is still very much Anna's show: "I am a host who feels a ton of ownership over the tone of the show, the voice of the show, the spirit of the show, the way we situate ourselves politically in this charged time."

A lot of what makes *Death, Sex & Money* sound like *Death, Sex & Money* is passed on to employees through group edits and editorial meetings. I remarked to her, "It sounds like it's an oral tradition. You teach and learn by experience. You all are hearing things and participate in conversations about whether it fits the show or not. As a result of being present, staff pick up on all those little parts that make the show, the show."

Anna agrees, adding, "The teaching aspect of podcasting is shifting from being the person who has the kind of hazy idea of 'I want the listener to feel this certain way after they listen' and it's hard to put words to—to now it's something you have to share with a group of people. In the beginning, I knew what I wanted the show to do; I didn't know how to do it. And then you sort of learn tricks that you first don't know how to put to words, and then you have to learn how to say these things to someone else. So it's also a process of learning for you, too . . . about how to communicate what you're trying to achieve."

Anna then added that there is one other component that she advocates for, though she came to it reluctantly: a meeting they have every week that they call "Sacred Time."

"'Sacred Time' is the meeting you don't move," Anna says. "You don't schedule anything else during it. It's sacred. It's our time to just talk about everything from, like, whatever: the big-picture things, longer-term things, and strategy, but also if there's a communication lapse about something or how to just make sure we're taking care of what we're all working toward as a team. Sometimes we really need to think beyond the story meeting. We need to nail down some new creative ideas.

"I find it extremely helpful because I have trouble toggling between the short term and the long term," she says. "During the week we're all crashing on things and busy. We wanted a space where we could talk about things we're concerned about. Things we are excited about. We just put everything aside for this time every week and we just talk."

In her book *The Art of Gathering*, Priya Parker shares a ritual that writer and director Jill Soloway calls "Box." The Box ritual shares a lot of DNA with "Sacred Time." On the set of Soloway's show *Transparent*, after breakfast and the sets and equipment have all been arranged, right before production begins, Soloway announces it is time for Box. They place a small wooden box in the middle of the set and people gather around. Anyone—cast, crew, whoever—can then jump up on the box and have the room's attention. They share whatever's on their minds. It can be about the work or it can be personal. Then they get down and someone else gets up. The whole thing lasts about a half hour.

As Parker observes, "Box is an opening ritual that connects a large team to one another, clears people's minds, and creates a passageway of sorts into rehearsal. Box also creates a sense of authenticity—part of the secret sauce of making the show, and one of the values that its storylines explore—among the team."

Chapter 8

TIME TO GO FORWARD

So here we are. The end.

Maybe.

Maybe it is actually the beginning.

There is an existential barroom conversation that people in podcasting like to have, pondering if we are in the beginning, middle, or end of podcasting's lifespan. Even though I've been part of these conversations for more than fourteen years, I have always had the same answer: "We are at the beginning of the beginning. In fact, we are so at the beginning we don't even realize how early it is." I believe that even the most pessimistic read of where podcasting is in its lifecycle places us somewhere at the end of the beginning, or perhaps the beginning of the middle. Regardless, someday we'll look back and laugh at how naive we were.

That's another way of saying that the future is bright, full of possibility, moments of wonder and joy, and innovation that will carry digital audio so far that we won't even recognize it as "podcasting." That's great. I can't wait.

There are phrases that I often say around my staff. I think they are profound, yet my teams often greet them with patience, at best, and usually with an eye roll. They hear it so much that it becomes like listening to an elderly grandparent or something.

Phrases like:

"Never wrestle with a pig. You get dirty and the pig likes it." (My friend Sheila told me that one about twenty-five years ago and I say it to just about every person I've worked with.)

"You are a victim of the rules you live by" (which I, for years, incorrectly attributed to the movie *Thelma & Louise*. But the phrase comes from an installation by the artist Jenny Holzer).

Whenever my teams encounter an obstacle, are stuck, or don't know how to handle something, I often say, "Well, if it was easy, someone else would have figured it out by now."

Which is usually followed by me saying, "Let other people do what's easy. We are here to do what's hard."

I think this is my attempt to rally my troops. What I am saying to them is, "Look, you are the best at what you do. We can figure it out. I trust you. You can do it."

But, instead, what pops out sounds more like I'm mangling a John F. Kennedy line from his "We Choose to Go to the Moon" speech.

But what I want my staff to understand—and I share this with you now, too—is that there is a satisfaction in doing hard things. Doing distinct things. Doing things that others can't or won't do. It's worth it.

In the summer of 2015, *Ask Me Another* was invited to do a live recording at SummerStage in Central Park. It was a huge outdoor venue, capable of holding several thousand people. At that time, *Ask Me Another* had only been on the radio weekly for less than two years. To put it mildly, we were worried about whether this was a good idea or not. *Ask Me Another* recorded its episodes at The Bell House in Brooklyn in front of an audience of 250 to 300 people—and sometimes less. It was hard to imagine that people would choose to trek out to the middle of Central Park to see a recording of a radio program and podcast that they could hear that weekend, in the comfort of their homes, for free. Let alone thousands of them.

The day of the show came and I had traveled up from Washington to New York to help out and offer support. Starting in the late morning, it began to rain.

The Park Service informed us that unless there was lightning, the show needed to go on. If there was rain—there still was going to be a show. Even if there was no one sitting in the audience, there was still a show. By the time I got to SummerStage, around 2 p.m., it was pouring rain. I came to the stage to see the entire staff, performers, and crew huddled together under the canopy, trying to stay away from the blowing wind and rain. As soon as I walked up, I locked eyes with host Ophira Eisenberg. She didn't have to say a word, her eyes said it clearly: "This is a fucking disaster."

We kept trying to set up and rehearse, despite the chilly temperatures and deluge of rain. The show was slated to start at 7 p.m. In addition to being wet and cold, everyone was very nervous and worried. How humiliating it would be to have to record a show, in the rain, with no audience, and waste everyone's time.

I saw my primary job was to keep people focused and in the best possible spirits. I told everyone gathered around, "Look, it's hard to believe, but we've been in crazier situations with this on this show, and we've always pulled it off. As you can see, it's raining. It's raining really hard. But you know what I believe? I believe it will stop raining. I believe it will stop raining and we will put on a show and people will come and laugh and have a great time.

"So what we need to do is prepare for that to happen," I continued. "Even though it is miserable now, let's be ready for the moment it isn't miserable."

To say they looked doubtful would be an understatement.

They continued on with the rehearsal, periodically moving the staging and equipment around so that it would be out of the course of the shifting wind and rain.

Then, as they wrapped up the rehearsal around 4 p.m., literally at the moment they finished, we looked out from the stage . . . and it stopped raining. Not only did it stop raining, but the clouds parted and the bright sun came beaming through. Within twenty minutes, it was bright, and warm, with blue skies above.

While it would be quite convenient to end the story there, we still had one huge problem. Even though it had stopped raining, and even though the Park Service employees were dizzily drying off chairs and bleachers, I was really worried whether anyone would come. It had been raining all day. I'm sure many people would bail, simply assuming that there was no way the show was still on, or not wanting to log through the squishy park to sit in a puddle and be miserable.

The doors were to open at 6 p.m. and I was so worried that only a dozen people would show up for this that I kept myself away from the staff and performers, fearing they'd read the concern on my face. About 5:30 p.m., I decided to go for a walk. As I left the field and went toward the gate, I turned and saw something I couldn't believe.

A massive line of people.

There was a line of people so long I couldn't see the end of it. It just rolled along the pathway deeper into the park. These people were carrying blankets and coolers. They were all lined up waiting to get in to see *Ask Me Another*. Every reason I had thought of for why no one would come simply didn't matter to them. The fact that the show was young, the fact that it had so much trouble finding its footing in the world, the rain, the yuck. Everything. They didn't care.

They loved the show. They were excited to see the show. There was an energy outside that gate that I not only wasn't expecting, but I couldn't fathom that it could exist at all.

I ran back inside and told everyone, "They came. They are here. It is all going to be fine."

And boy, was it fine. The show was stellar. It was packed with people watching the crew record the show. There was laughter and energy. It was joyous and exciting for everyone. Everything was just perfect.

Partway through the show, I took my wife (who had traveled along with me) and we stood about halfway back in the audience, right about where this picture was taken.

I leaned over to her and said, "No one can ever take this moment away from me."

I had worked so hard to make this show. The people involved had all worked so hard to make this show. We had encountered strife and barriers and complications, but the way we powered through it all was by having a vision, defining that vision, and sticking to it.

It was the power of that clarity and vision that broke through all that resistance. And as I've said elsewhere in this book, resistance isn't a bad thing, if you are a protagonist or a podcast maker—or many other things. The resistance makes you stronger.

And now, on that beautiful summer evening in 2013, I was standing in the middle of a few thousand people in Central Park, all laughing and having a great time. Having a great time with something I made. A great time made possible by the power of focus and determination.

But there was one other thing present that evening, and throughout the development and production of *Ask Me Another*, and with a lot of the other projects I've been fortunate enough to work on and create.

Passion.

You may remember that when I started talking to my yoga instructor, Joe, I noticed that he had something to say and was passionate about saying it. That is my last piece of advice to you in this book. Be passionate.

If something is worth doing, it is worth putting your all into. If you are going to go through the effort and time and frustration to follow the advice I've given you over the time we've spent together, don't go meekly into it. Give it your all.

Something I've never admitted to anyone: I always treat projects like they are the last thing I'll ever do. If I bounce the tracks on a new project and post them to an RSS feed, then I walk out onto 8th Avenue and get run over by an MTA bus, I want to be fine with that last project being the last thing I ever say or do. I treat everything like it is my swan song. I treat everything like it matters. I treat everything like it is that last contribution I'll ever make to the world—and you should, too.

Be passionate. Be crazy. Take the unbeaten path. Make wild choices. Screw things up. Be delighted when it works. Work closely with others. Share credit generously. And leave it all on the floor. But do it all with a sense of purpose. That is my advice to you.

Regardless of where podcasting and digital audio are as an industry, I know that you, regardless of who or where you are, are at the beginning of your journey. Whether you are new to audio making or have been doing this longer than I have, you are still just getting started on your creative journey to make terrific audio.

I'd wish you luck, but you don't need it. You just need your passion.

Now, take all this and go out there and make some noise. Make some big, massive, bold, impossible-to-ignore passionate noise.

I'll be listening.

Bonus Episode

FOUR PIVOTAL MOMENTS IN THE HISTORY OF PODCASTING

Before you go into the future, let's take an extra few moments to talk about the past.

You may be wondering why a book about the principles of podcasting would have an extra chapter about the history of podcasting. In short, after a lot of thought, it felt weird not to have it. To be part of something's future, you have to understand its past. If you wish to innovate and build new ideas into a medium, it helps to understand how it originated and what its creators intended for it to do.

If you suddenly told a group of people to go outside and look north, some of them would go outside and figure out the direction quickly; others would stagger around in circles and try to determine the direction, possibly never settling on a direction to face. Those who find it quickly probably had some reference point to base their decision. I, for example, have spent a lot of my adult life coming up out of subterranean train and subway stations, and have gotten pretty good at using time of day, position of the sun, and shadows as my quick way to get oriented. If I was told to go outside and face north, I'd seek out some shadows (and hope that it wasn't a cloudy day).

History has the same effect: It is like a set of GPS coordinates; it tells you where you are standing.

With that in mind, there are four pivotal moments in podcast history. If they hadn't happened, podcasting as we know it wouldn't exist.

PIVOTAL MOMENT I: HACKING CODE IN A HOTEL ROOM
(aka how podcasting became free, easy, and open to all—or at least, it was supposed to be)

Podcasting came into reality in a New York City hotel room in October of 2000. No one can remember which hotel it was, though Dave Winer recalls it was a "fancy rock star–type hotel." He remembers that because he was meeting with Adam Curry, a former VJ from MTV, who Dave said was "something of a rock star himself." Adam was visiting from Belgium, where he was living at the time, and wanted to meet up with Dave to share an idea he'd had.

Dave Winer had been an early pioneer in blogging, having created RSS, the technology that drove a lot of blog infrastructure and distribution technology. Dave basically invented blogging as we know it by creating the systems that made it possible. Dave Winer has actually been a pioneer in a lot of things. He doesn't like thinking of himself as a software developer, which feels like an oversimplification for him. He refers to himself as a "media hacker." He has spent a lot of his career seeking out new media types, then building software to make that new media type possible. Early in his career he developed scripting environments, online publishing tools, Outline Processor Markup Language (OPML), and a lot of other things that most people wouldn't understand but were essential in making modern digital syndication possible. If even that doesn't make sense to you, the fact that your favorite news and entertainment sites have updated articles and material from a number of other sources around the world? Thank Dave for that.

But more important than any specific technological advancement, Dave Winer thought differently about how to use the Web to deliver information. Dave believed in making systems open, democratic, and easily accessible, going against the prevailing tide to make material on the Internet as proprietary, controlled, and commercialized as possible. Winer made subscribing to content on the Internet possible, so that users could receive information from sites they wanted to follow as a "feed" of up-to-date information.

Even though he is probably best known for his seven years as a VJ for MTV, Adam Curry has had a lot of facets to his career since then, mostly as an early advocate and entrepreneur for Internet-related businesses. In 2000, he was a big fan of Dave Winer's work on RSS, and Adam had an idea. While on a trip to Manhattan, he wanted to meet up with Dave and pitch him the idea of using blogging technology to distribute digital audio files. Adam had even rewritten some of Dave's RSS code to support the idea of distributing audio instead of text: audio blogging.

When they met in Adam's hotel room, Adam made his passionate case for the idea and its potential to really leverage the Internet to revolutionize radio, or any form of shared sound. Adam was gesticulating and trying very hard to explain. Dave listened and didn't get it.

Recently, Adam had published a thought piece called "The Last Mile" that argued that "always-on" cable modems in the home (not quite robust enough to be called "broadband," but a huge step forward from dial-in modems using telephone lines) offered an opportunity to rethink how to distribute audio files, which were monstrously huge compared to text, or even pictures. At that time, there was a "click, wait" problem with audio and video media on the Internet. You would click to listen, then wait, often for a long time. The choke point was the last link in the chain, the Internet connection to the user, aka the last yard. But Adam suggested that the "always-on" cable modem wasn't being utilized all the time. At night, for example, it just sat there largely unused. What if you could find a way to use that downtime to go grab larger files so they would be ready to listen to when you woke up in the morning? In Adam's mind, RSS was the perfect method to do this. All it needed was some changes to the code to allow for audio files to replace text files.

While Dave Winer didn't really understand what Adam was talking about, or why anyone would want to do this, he decided to give it a try. In January 2001, Dave had finished the code changes to RSS to allow for the audio enclosures as Adam had outlined to him. To test it out, he created the first podcast feed (though no one called it "podcasting" back then; it really didn't have a name). The feed launched on January 20, 2001, Inauguration Day, when George W. Bush became president of the United States. The feed contained the Grateful Dead song "US Blues." Dave eventually added a few other Grateful Dead songs, but it really didn't matter.

Nobody listened. Nobody got it. Nobody cared.

"The whole idea of that was to try to bootstrap the technology, that other people would support the technology, and that even other people would do podcasts," remembers Dave. "But I couldn't see any evidence of that actually happening."

Much like Adam and Dave's conversations in that hotel room, the wider world didn't really understand why you'd want to move this file around via RSS and what its potential could be. Dave thought of audio blogging as "an interesting experiment" and pretty much moved on.

Though some other people messed around with it like Dave had with the Grateful Dead tunes, not a lot happened with RSS audio enclosures until Dave arrived for a fellowship at Harvard in 2003.

PIVOTAL MOMENT 2: AUDIO BLOGGING BECOMES PODCASTING

There is a lot of debate about what show or project can claim to be the "first podcast ever." But we already know that. It was Dave Winer's initial Grateful Dead test in early 2001. Whenever I say that, people immediately clarify what the first piece of audio specifically created to be distributed via RSS audio enclosures (aka a podcast feed) was. That is a tad bit murkier, but there is still a clear answer.

Even though, as we mentioned, broadband or "always-on" Internet access was still relatively new, and streaming technology still sucked and sounded pretty bad, a lot of people were making early moves in streaming radio, both as continuous programming (like listening to a terrestrial broadcast station) and on-demand shows as well.

For the broadcasters to have something to broadcast, they required streaming technology that was reliable, easy to use, and sounded great. Many early webcasters (as they were called), who used technologies like RealNetworks or Windows Media to send out their streams and programs, claimed to be among the first podcasters as well. But none of them went "all in" on RSS distribution (aka audio blogging, aka netcasting, and eventually aka podcasting). Instead they just toyed with it to see how it worked. You can't really blame them. Very few listeners understood the subscription concept and fewer still were seeking out shows beyond streaming.

In the two years since the creation of podcasting in early 2001, Dave Winer was busy with a number of other things, but never quite gave up on the audio enclosure for RSS. It wasn't until he was a fellow at the Berkman Klein Center for Internet & Society at Harvard University that he found the perfect guinea pig for the idea: Christopher Lydon.

Christopher Lydon came to radio after impressive stints in television and print (including a time as a political reporter for the *New York Times*), as well as an unsuccessful run to be mayor of Boston in 1993. Beginning in 1994, he hosted a local program on public station WBUR called *The Connection*. A few years later, NPR picked up the program to distribute it nationally. In 2001, at the height of its popularity and audience size, Lydon, along with his producer Mary McGrath, were unceremoniously fired by WBUR in a contract dispute over ownership of the program. Always fascinated by the potential for blogs and the Internet as a means to stimulate international connection and conversation, Lydon landed at the Berkman Center in 2003. Chris heard of another fellow coming on a few months later, Dave

Winer. "I vividly remember writing him an email," Chris remembers, "saying, 'Dear Dave Winer, yesterday I couldn't spell blog and tomorrow I want to be one.'"

Dave pitched him on the idea of audio blogging, saying, as Chris remembers, "I know the computation involved and you know radio. What the world needs is an MP3 that can be syndicated for all sorts of purposes."

But Lydon admits that even though he was an experienced radio professional and Internet enthusiast, he didn't really get it.

"Sounds good to me," Lydon remembers telling him. "I have to say, he did most of the work and had a much better notion of where we were going."

Dave even had a suggestion for the first guest: himself.

Lydon points out that there is one factor that's often overlooked in podcast history: the catalyst for that first podcast.

"The whole story of the Internet gaining traction, and of blogging and podcasting, is a piece of the story of the Iraq war," Lydon says. "That war was the blunder of blunders, but it was not significantly debated.

"It was an evil era in American journalism," he says, referring to the failings of the press to raise critical questions and debate in the lead up to the war. "The *New York Times* endorsed it. The *Washington Post* endorsed it. David Remnick of the *New Yorker* endorsed it. Nobody had ever really questioned the implications of George Bush's minority election. We were trying to start a conversation to surface the folly of the war when nobody else was. [In that first recording,] Dave and I talked about an erosion, an atrophy in public conversation. Meaning not just newspapers over the networks, but literally what people are talking about on the street. It was very much a conversation about the drift of media. When people talk about podcasting and the origin of it, they miss the politics. Blogging and podcasting flowered in the rotten atmosphere of the war."

Another member of the Berkman community, inventor Bob Doyle, documented that first recording on July 9, 2003. He blogged a

237

number of pictures and details from that day. While Bob was a regular blogger, I don't think anyone involved really understood the magnitude of what was happening that day.

For his previous efforts in broadcasting, Chris Lydon had worked in beautiful TV and radio studios, each packed with lots of incredibly expensive precision equipment, supported by top-flight engineers. The first podcast recording was not so elaborate. It was recorded on a computer (with a minidisc recorder as backup) and a small four-channel mixing board, all placed on a standard office desk. There was a headset mic for Chris and a regular microphone for the guest, plus a couple of headphones—all set up in an occupied office, arranged around the office occupant's belongings. And that's about it. It really wasn't that much different from most new podcasters might use today.

There was one big difference, though. Today, there is a ton of hardware and software purpose-built for podcasting, as well as copious guides, instructions, tips, and how-tos on recording podcasts. Recording a podcast is so easy now that you can record one off the built-in mic in your phone and then post it. It wouldn't even sound too bad (though I wouldn't advise it). Today it is possible to have little to no technical knowledge about podcasting or how to record audio and still manage to do a passable job.

But there were no such recorders in 2003. There were no guides, tips, or instructions. This was happening four years before the first smartphone. Podcasting didn't even have a name yet. It took some finagling, but Bob Doyle figured out how to capture the interview as an MP3 as part of his setup.[52] No one present, other than Bob, understood what was happening or how it was happening, but they pressed record, and it worked. That was all that mattered.

When I look at those pictures, I've often thought about how weird it must have been for Chris to find himself there, plying his craft in a homemade patchwork of equipment in someone's office. That

---

[52] Bob kept and posted meticulous notes on all the hardware, software, adapters, encoders, and equipment used for these and later recordings.

difference seems lost on Chris Lydon. He didn't see it that way. He recalls that at that time, no one other than Dave Winer fully grasped what was going to happen afterward. Chris only knew that he was going to interview Dave, and then somehow the audio was going to be distributed using blog technology. They did the recording and it was fun. Cathartic, almost.

Chris started to come up with other ideas for interviews, and even scheduled a trip to New Hampshire to talk to people about the upcoming election. In September 2003, Dave Winer set up an RSS feed for Christopher Lydon's interviews, eventually featuring fifty conversations between Chris and other Internet pioneers, futurists, political observers, and technologists. So if anyone ever asks you what the first podcast was—the first show conceived for the medium and then fed to its listeners via RSS—it was Christopher Lydon's show, which would eventually take on the name *Open Source.*

The RSS feed went up with the batch of Chris's interviews, and again, little happened. People started to understand the audio blogging concept and idea, and many others started to listen, but the spark didn't seem to be igniting any fires.

DAVE: *Chris actually created a problem. The problem was, Chris was too good." In terms of the editorial, it was totally NPR quality, because Chris was an NPR guy, right? And it was great stuff. But, yeah, it didn't seem to give anybody the idea that they could do it. It's also true of a lot of the popular podcasts today—they tend to be radio productions. But that wasn't really the full idea. I think my hope was that a lot of regular people would do it, that there would be a lot of podcasting going on.*

ME: *Much like blogs.*

DAVE: *Yeah. That's what I thought it was. That's the way I viewed it. Whenever you have something you feel would be better communicated verbally, you would record a podcast and put it on your blog, and that was the model I had in mind.*

A professional interview program, with a top-shelf host like Lydon, set the bar too high. The structure, questions, rhythm, quality of the guests, music, editing, were all too good. Few others saw themselves as willing and able to do that. Two notable early exceptions were Doug Kaye's early show *IT Conversations* and Steve Gillmor's *Gillmor Gang*, both focused on tech. While Chris's recording did come before these two, both shows were the first podcasts produced on a regular cadence. But there was no real widespread momentum to produce mass numbers of podcasts—yet.

Then, more out of frustration with everyone "not getting" audio blogging, Dave Winer decided to start his own. He first started an RSS feed of *Morning Coffee Notes* almost a year later, in August 2004. In these episodes, Dave basically talked into a microphone about things he was doing, thinking, reading, observing—it was very uniquely and charmingly Dave. It was kind of like a blog, but with voice. The production quality was minimal, he used few if any notes, and just recorded his thoughts and then posted them to an RSS feed.

Once he did that, people started to get it.

"I think nobody listened to Chris and thought, 'I can do that,'" Dave said. "But when people heard me they thought, 'Oh, anybody could do *that.*'"

Slowly, a number of developers and bloggers began to incorporate audio enclosures into their blog feeds, and some made the transition to only offering audio.

Adam Curry was also starting to take matters into his own hands, and very soon after *Morning Coffee Notes*, he started his own podcast, called *Daily Source Code*. It sounded much more like a professional production. Adam was a radio veteran and brought a lot of those sensibilities to the show, giving it a slick and energetic feel. Listening to *Daily Source Code* really gave a sense that exciting things were happening in the podcast space and this was where you'd go to be a part of it. While a lot of the tech community gravitated to *Morning Coffee Notes*, often for no other reason than an occasion peek into Dave Winer's brain, it was *Daily Source Code* that really started to widen the vision for what would soon be known as podcasting beyond the tech and blogging enthusiasts.

By the time *Morning Coffee Notes* and *Daily Source Code* were up and running, podcasting was then known as "podcasting."

The first reference of the name "podcasting" came in an article by Ben Hammersley in January 2004, in an article in *The Guardian* about Lydon's interview series. Like many things about podcasting's early days, it really didn't pick up traction right away. People still referred to RSS-delivered audio files as "audio blogging" or "netcasting."

Later in the summer of 2004, early advocate Danny Gregoire suggested in a developer forum that they should adopt the term. This time, it seemed to stick. Podcasting was now podcasting.

By the time the name was settled in the fall 2004, things started to happen, and happen fast.

In September, Dawn Miceli and her husband, Drew Domkus, started *The Dawn and Drew Show*. Not only was it an early podcast, but Dawn and Drew truly helped pioneer the "chumcast" esthetic: two (or more) people (often friends) recording themselves being friends. They tell stories, bicker, banter on about subjects they love or have expertise in, and just generally enjoy talking to each other.

The Dawn and Drew Show pretty much invented this format, which is one of the mainstays of podcasting even now. The show was loose, funny, endearing, and sounded deliberately unproduced. It's like listening to a conversation with incredibly witty friends. Dawn and Drew got a lot of attention. Within a year, they were earning their living from the podcast.

From there, things pretty much exploded. There were so many new podcasts coming out every week that it was impossible for their chief advocates, Dave Winer and Adam Curry, to keep up with them. The four-years-in-the-making "overnight phenomenon" of podcasting had, in the course of a few months, quickly outgrown the reach and control of its inventors, exactly as it was intended to do. But even then, with all the excitement, there were harbingers of a podcasting future that wasn't as democratized and open.

"A lot of people don't understand this, but there is a reason why there's no barriers to entry in podcasting," Dave Winer says. "Why anybody can do it, and if we aren't aware of that and if we don't protect it, we are going to lose it. In my experience in talking to people, people had no idea that podcasting was ever 'created.' And they certainly had no idea [about] the gift that we are all sharing right now, the fact that there is no barrier to entry. And I believe that we will lose it eventually, probably pretty soon."

PIVOTAL MOMENT 3: LIKE *WAYNE'S WORLD* FOR RADIO

"What is podcasting?" was the rhetorical question posed by Apple cofounder and CEO Steve Jobs. "It's been described a bunch of different ways."

June 6, 2005. Steve Jobs was on stage for one of Apple's theatrical keynote speeches to announce new products at that year's Worldwide Developers Conference. It was almost two years to the day before the first iPhone was released and almost eighteen months before the iPhone was even announced.

A few days earlier, Adam Curry had a meeting with Steve Jobs during the *All Things D* conference in San Diego. Execs at Apple had reached out asking if Adam could make time to talk to Steve about podcasting. Steve was impressed with it.

"He told me, 'Listen, Adam, I wanna put podcasting on iTunes, is that okay?' And I say, 'Yeah, of course it's okay. Better yet, I'll give you the entire directory to get you started.'"

But Jobs didn't need the directory. He already had it. Unknown to Adam, or Dave Winer, or almost anyone in the burgeoning podcast community, Apple was about to wrap its arms around podcasting in a massive way.

First up for Jobs' Apple keynote on June 6, after some welcoming remarks and comments about Apple's expanding network of retail stores, were enhancements to iTunes. This keynote came just over two years after Apple evolved its iTunes media player into a store for purchasing digital music files. At the time, the big hardware innovation Apple was touting was the iPod, which, at the time, was celebrating 16 million units sold since it was introduced almost four years earlier.[53]

On the screen behind Jobs while he posed his question to introduce podcasting were the words "iPod + Broadcasting."

According to Jobs, podcasting could be described three ways. The first was "TiVo for radio." At the time, TiVo was a pioneering way to record live television in the time before DVR recording was a common feature of set-top boxes and video on demand.

"The second way to describe podcasting," Jobs continued, "is *Wayne's World* for radio."

The keynote audience laughed.

"Anyone, without much capital investment, can make a podcast, put it on a server, and get a worldwide audience for their radio show," said Jobs.

"We see it as the hottest thing going for radio," Jobs continued. "Not only can you download and listen, but you can subscribe. So that every time there is a new episode, it automatically gets downloaded to your computer and you can listen to it there or you can automatically have it synced to your iPod. So it's very, very exciting."

Jobs called out that there were now 8,000 podcasts available to browse, subscribe to, and listen to right inside of iTunes (even though the corresponding Apple press release that came out on the software's release day three weeks later put the number at 3,000).

Jobs went on to clarify that it wasn't just *Wayne's World*–like productions made in basements, but that many major organizations were producing podcasts, such as ESPN, Rush Limbaugh, *Forbes*, *Businessweek*, the *Washington Post*, Disney, Ford, and General Motors.

In all, Jobs spent more than five minutes talking about how easy and fun listening to podcasting could be, especially using Apple's software. He used Adam's *Daily Source Code* as the first example of how podcasts can work (referring to Adam as "one of the inventors of

---

[53] Apple now sells the equivalent number of iPhones in about 5 weeks.

podcasting"), playing a bit of a few episodes, and demonstrating how subscribing works.

"We think this will take podcasting mainstream," he concluded, "to where anyone can do it and find all these podcasts really easy to listen to."

Arguably, podcasting was still a bit of a pain to listen to. You had to subscribe on your computer (in the iTunes app) and then wait for it to download. You could listen to it on your computer right away (after it downloaded, though, which in 2005 could still take a while for an audio file to make that journey to your computer). But if you wanted to listen on your iPod, you had to sync the podcasts from your computer to your phone (and hoped it actually worked), then listen. And if a new episode came out five minutes after you synced your iPod, too bad. It would sit there waiting for you until you synced again. But the intention was there: to make it simple and easy.

People often forget that new technologies don't break into the mainstream until one of two things happen. Really, it's only one thing: making it easy. The Internet was a widely known buzzword for years before it became a part of mainstream life. When did that happen? When you could buy a computer with Internet access software already installed. No disks, no download, no installation, no setup parameters, no nothing. Just connect and go. That is when Internet blew up and changed the world. It wasn't when it was first available; it was when it was easy to the point of almost being no effort.

The second thing that shows a new technology is about to go mainstream? Porn. If you want to know what technologies are going to break into the mainstream, just look at the porn industry. In everything from videotapes to DVD and online streaming, porn has always been on the front lines of consumer distribution technology. You knew a new platform was about to break when you saw it being used to distribute porn. Porn is the technological canary in the coal mine.

However, moving the ball forward on mainstreaming podcasting was the only thing that made this a pivotal moment in podcast history; it was the legitimacy of Apple's embrace: Not only by including it in the iTunes software, but by making it the lead item in the company's keynote. Jobs and Apple were forecasting: Podcasting is a real thing. It isn't just a domain for nerds and techies. Podcasting is going to be for everyone.

After that keynote, a lot of media companies got very serious, very fast, about podcasting, including my employer at the time, NPR.

PIVOTAL MOMENT 4: BAKED IN

Most people are surprised that podcasting has been around, in some form, since the early 2000s. Those people think podcasting started sometime around the release of *Serial* in October 2014.

There is no doubt that *Serial* itself was a transformative project that was the platform's first full-throated worldwide mainstream hit, with its episodes being downloaded more than 350 million times. But *Serial* wouldn't have been *Serial* if something hadn't happened first. There was one event that happened just two weeks before that made *Serial* into the hit it was: the release of the iOS 8 iPhone operating system. Without iOS 8, the phenomenon of *Serial* probably would never have happened.

"Whoa, wait a minute," I imagine more than one of you readers saying. "You just skipped ahead *nearly a decade* in the history of podcasting. What happened in between?"

Fair question.

Short answer: a lot, then not a lot.

The longer answer is that the tsunami of new podcasts that started in late 2004 didn't slow down. The number of podcasts grew exponentially. It seemed that every week a new media company was launching its own podcast, or a new podcast came out with an interesting premise or engaging set of characters, hosts, and guests. Even the President of the United States became a podcaster, kinda, when the White House started a podcast feed of George W. Bush's weekly presidential addresses. This snowball continued to roll onward for the better part of a year.

Then it all seemed to fizzle out.

What happened? YouTube happened. As the video-sharing plat-form took hold, and especially after its acquisition by Google, a lot of the investment and advertising money that was flooding into podcast-ing was rechanneled into video. Where one day everyone was talking about podcasting, its potential, and all the excitement around it and its offerings, the next day everyone was having the exact same conver-sation, except this time it was about YouTube and online video.

Then, after YouTube happened, the 2008 Great Recession hap-pened. For a number of years, people's attention was focused on viral video and/or whether the world was going to fall apart. Either one seemed like it could cause the downfall of civilization as we knew it. Podcasting just felt a bit like yesterday's "next big thing."

This lack of focal attention might seem like a bad thing, but I'd argue that it wasn't. With all the new infrastructure, yet none of the crazy buzz-fueled hype and piles of investment money, podcasting finally had a chance to grow in a more organic way. People could try new things and experiment, and podcasting had enough of an audi-ence at that point that you could build enough of a following to justify making more episodes.

Most podcasts felt small and boutiquey, but that also created the fertile environment to build podcasts into the hub for communities of interest (even if they were just interested in the host). It allowed for the evolution of podcast "tribes."

Pete Seeger had a parable that helps this long era make sense. When talking about the social justice movement of the 1960s and opposition to the Vietnam War, he likened it to a seesaw.

"One end of this seesaw is on the ground with a basket half-full of big rocks in it," he said. "The other end is up in the air. It's got a basket one-quarter full of sand. And some of us got teaspoons, and we're try-ing to fill it up with sand . . .

"One of these years, you'll see that whole seesaw go *zooop* in the other direction. And people will say, 'Gee, how did it happen so sud-denly?' Us and all our little teaspoons."

The same idea applied to these "fallow middle years" in the

evolution of podcasting. Between 2006 and 2014, a lot of people launched podcasts and received just enough encouragement, attention, and compensation to make it worth continuing. It felt clubby and isolated away from most other media, but it was fertile. And the podcasts themselves contained a growing spread of subject matter, interests, and diverse perspectives. Most of the podcasts you associate as being iconic today, such as those by Adam Corolla and Joe Rogan, *99% Invisible* and *This American Life, Hardcore History* with Dan Carlin, *Radiolab*, and *How Stuff Works*, among thousands of others, all started podcasting during this era. Many enthusiasts started to realize that podcasting would be a great avenue to connect to others who shared their passions and interests. Podcasts about beekeeping, quilting, woodworking, 1950s comic books, and so on began to pop up and become centers of virtual communities.

None of these were pivotal on their own, and if *Serial* hadn't come along, they would most likely still all be going strong. But by the time *Serial* came about in 2014, these thousands of podcasts had made the ecosystem of podcasting strong and ready for its first mainstream hit.

But again, *Serial* would have never been *Serial* without the introduction of the podcast app in iOS 8.

On June 4, 2014, iOS 8 was announced at Apple's Worldwide Developers Conference almost nine years to the date after Steve Jobs first announced that podcasting was to be included in iTunes. At that time, he noted that he was so excited about the integration because it would make podcasts "really easy to listen to." It wasn't until the release of iOS 8 that the promise really was fulfilled.

After the introduction of the iPhone, podcasts, like many other audio media types, were played through the iPhone's "Music" app (known as the "iPod" app in early versions of the phone's operating system). Two years before iOS 8, Apple debuted its stand-alone podcast app. While that solved the "square peg" feeling of having the spoken-word podcasts inside of a "Music" app, it created a new problem: Anyone interested in podcasts now needed to download and install a separate app to access them. And as anyone in the app world will tell you, getting someone to download a new app, even a free app, loses most people. They simply give up. Even though the app is free, and it takes a mere handful of clicks to download, sadly and surprisingly, that is too much effort for a majority of interested potential users.

For a lot of those already listening to podcasts, downloading an app has never been a problem, because they have preferred using apps other than Apple's player, such as Outcast, BeyondPod, Overcast, iCatcher, Stitcher, Podcast Addict, and Pocket Casts along with dozens (and eventually hundreds) of others, including mainstream media apps like Pandora, Spotify, and Google Play. But Apple has always been the dominant choice for listening, accounting for 60 to 80 percent of podcast listening over the past decade, and is the way that most new users find their way into podcasting. Therefore, when Apple makes it easier (or harder) to listen to podcasts, it accelerates (or impedes) the entire podcast ecosystem.

Shortly before the time *Serial* rolled around in 2014, if someone saw a link to a podcast or podcast episode in social media, an email, or a text message, it would require nine clicks and an app download to listen. For the app-averse, effort-averse, and complexity-averse (aka almost everyone using a smartphone), this was *a lot* of effort. However, with iOS 8, all that changed.

In the weeks that *Serial* was growing from a *This American Life* spin-off into a genuine phenom, millions of iPhones around the world were quietly being equipped with the stand-alone Apple Podcast app. By now becoming part of the default operating system, the app reduced the number of clicks for a first-time listen down to two: Click the link to open the Podcast app, then click again to play. That simple change, from nine clicks and an app download to two clicks and no app download, finally fulfilled Jobs's promise to make it easy. Now when someone saw an article or post talking about this amazing new show *Serial*, most curious new listeners could get to the content without a lot of fuss. *That* was the transformative moment.

That said, let's not discount the impact of *Serial* on podcasting. Unlike any other program before or since, *Serial* would go on to completely reset expectations and interest in podcasting, bringing in tens of millions of new listeners, many of whom stuck around to discover more and more shows they loved. *Serial* also inspired literally thousands of copycat programs, each trying to tell the story and investigate a seemingly bottomless well of unsolved mysteries, to establish "true crime" as one of the pillar genres of podcasting.

At the time of *Serial*'s release, and despite the Apple podcasting app starting to show up on more and more phones, it was still generally accepted that podcasting was hard to figure out. When *Serial* was released, *This American Life* put out a video of host Ira Glass demonstrating to his octogenarian neighbor Mary Ahearn how to listen to a podcast. In the two-minute video, Ira says, "We've come to learn that many of you do not know how to get a podcast."

In the midst of the explanation on how to listen, we learn that Ira's neighbor listens to his show every week by going to the website and "pressing the little arrow."

"And congratulations," Mary said. "You are listening to a podcast."

ACKNOWLEDGMENTS

Over the past twenty-five years, I have learned, unlearned, and rethought much of what eventually landed in this book. I have learned at the feet of giants and worked with so many amazing people who have deeply influenced my work and thinking about that work.

To my crews who have followed me into battle at WKSU, NPR, Audible, and Magnificent Noise, the contents of this book will seem eye-rollingly familiar, as you have sat through many of my rants in meetings, planning sessions, edits, and "fuck it, we're done working for today" impromptu happy hours. You have all pushed back at me, which made my thinking stronger. I hope you see a bit of yourselves and your work in this.

To Jay Kernis, Margaret Low, and Kinsey Wilson, so many good things have come into my life because you let me walk in your shadows. You have been great mentors to me.

To David Giovannoni, George Bailey, and John Sutton, your clear and profound thinking about radio inspired so much of my thinking and the way I create.

To Matt Martinez. The introduction of this book focused on three critically important dates in my professional life and you were an essential part of two of them.

To Izzi Smith, we've been friends, mutual-respecters, colleagues, button pushers, and wild dreamers together for a quarter century. You are still my great sounding board and wise counsel.

To Jesse Baker, you are the kid sister I never had, and even if I had a kid sister, I'd like you more. Top that with being the best coconspirator any insurgent could ever ask for, and that's why I'm so grateful to work with you.

To my many radio and podcasting friends, colleagues I've been privileged to work with directly, as well as the many acquaintances I've made in this wonderful profession of audio making. You have taught me, listened to me, tolerated me, inspired me, and molded me. But more important, you have repeatedly demonstrated the most elevated and meticulous devotion to craft. You have also entertained, informed, enlightened, and challenged me countless times. I'm grateful for all of it.

Every professional career encounters a few assholes along the journey. To mine, thank you, your smallness inspired me to be a better thinker, leader, and maker.

To those who helped me puzzle through this book and the principles shared here, as well as those who sat down to offer all of us their wisdom.

To my talented editor, Maisie Tivnan, and the great staff at Workman—including Beth Levy, Sun Robinson-Smith, Rebecca Carlisle, Lathea Mondesir, and Becky Terhune—who have all blown me away with their excitement about this book since day one.

To my agent, Jane Dystel, for always being my defender, advocate, and the teller of truth.

Thank you to my yoga teacher, Joe Gandarillas, for immediately agreeing to be my guinea pig for a chapter in this book.

To Calvin, yes, Dad will come downstairs in just a few minutes. He just wants to finish this page first.

To Edie and Lolly, thank you for filling my office with dog farts and never letting me be lonely.

To those I've forgotten to mention and are chill enough not to be upset about it.

And Katherine, the alpha and omega of everything in my life. Nothing important in my life happens without you being a part of it. It's all because of you.

Thank you.

RECOMMENDED READING

Just to be clear, this isn't a bibliography. What follows is a list of books and articles that, if you liked this book, you'll probably enjoy reading as well. Some works are name-dropped in the book; others have been inspiring to me throughout my career.

BOOKS

Out on the Wire by Jessica Abel (Broadway Books, 2015).

About two decades ago, Ira Glass asked Jessica Abel to write a comic book on how *This American Life* made radio stories. It became a loving and instructive introduction to audio craft for many people (and even included illustrated advice from yours truly). Jessica expanded that work into a full book—and retained its graphic novel form to boot. A unique and amazing work.

Sound Reporting by Jonathan Kern (University of Chicago Press, 2008).

An insider's guide that gives a comprehensive look at NPR's editorial standards, practices, and approach to audio journalism.

Radio Diaries: DIY Handbook by Joe Richman (Radio Diaries, 2017).

A brief primer on radio interviewing, storytelling, and principles from one of the modern masters of the craft.

Selling the Invisible by Harry Beckwith (Grand Central Publishing, 2012).

I learned so much from this book. Beckwith teaches you how to talk to people about ideas—and how to frame them so they are most connecting and useful. Lessons that are essential in marketing but also in listener-centric audio storytelling.

The Writer's Journey: Mythic Structure for Writers by
Christopher Vogler (Michael Wiese Productions, 2007).

A classic on story structure and guidance. Beloved by print writers
and screenwriters—should be used by more audio makers as a source
of inspiration.

Words That Work by Frank Luntz (Hachette, 2008).

This may seem like a weird choice for this list. Luntz is a pollster
responsible for relabeling "estate tax" as "death tax," "global
warming" as "climate change," and so on. Politics aside, there
is a lot in this book to help writers (including audio makers)
understand the power of word choice in influencing an audience's
perception.

Making Waves by Mark Ramsey (iUniverse, 2008).

Ramsey has been a provocative thinker about radio and podcasting
for many years. You always learn from reading his ideas.

Listener Supported by Jack Mitchell (Praeger, 2005).

One of the founders of public radio and National Public Radio
shares history from the early days—stories that sound a lot like
these early days of podcasting.

Radio Intelligence by David Giovannoni (Corporation for Public
Broadcasting, 1991).

A collection of articles originally published in the public broadcasting
trade newspaper *Current* looking at audience data from the early days
of public radio.

253

The Elements of Style by William Strunk Jr. and E. B. White
    (Pearson, 2000).

A classic reference that any writer, regardless of medium, should review periodically for guidance and inspiration.

The Observation Deck: A Tool Kit for Writers by Naomi Epel
    (Chronicle Books, 1998).

This card set provides a great series of tools and exercises to help writers extract the elements of story as well as the story structure.

Creating Customer Evangelists by Jackie Huba and Ben McConnell
    (Kaplan Business, 2012).

Thought-provoking stories and lessons on the importance of customer-centric thinking.

Reality Radio edited by John Biewen and Alexa Dilworth
    (University of North Carolina Press, 2017).

Essays from podcasters and public radio makers on their approach to craft. They're a bit lofty and unspecific, but there is a lot of inspiration to be found in this collection.

The TV Brand Builders by Andy Bryant and Charlie Mawer
    (Kogan Page, 2016).

I just found this a fascinating read.

The Hero with a Thousand Faces by Joseph Campbell
    (Pantheon Books, 1949; New World Library, 2008).

The definitive text on the narrative arc of the hero's journey. A bit dense for today's reader, but worth the effort.

Storycraft by Jack Hart (University of Chicago Press, 2011).

I find myself applying the lessons in this book to almost every audio project I create.

Guerilla Marketing by Jay Conrad Levinson (Houghton Mifflin, 2007).

Mentioned repeatedly in this book. Whenever I'm asked about how to market podcasts, I tell people to read this book.

Story by Robert McKee (HarperCollins, 1997).

Another classic on story structure. Very inspiring.

ZAG by Marty Neumeier (New Riders, 2007).

This book was designed to be read over the course of a plane ride. It's highly digestible and extremely thought provoking.

The Art of Gathering by Priya Parker (Riverhead Books, 2018).

Mentioned in this book—and, admittedly, not totally applicable to podcasting, but an incredibly insightful and instructive read.

The Responsive Chord by Tony Schwartz (Anchor Press, 1973).

Considered sacred among public radio makers for many years, its application for podcasts is inspirational.

You Can Write a Novel Kit by James V. Smith Jr.
    (Writer's Digest Books, 2008).

Mentioned in this book—resources like this can be useful to writers in any medium.

Save the Cat! by Blake Snyder (Michael Wiese Productions, 2005).

Regarded as a classic guide for screenwriters. Contains a lot of relevant and useful tools that can be used by narrative podcasters as well.

Follow the Story by James B. Stewart (Simon & Schuster, 1998).

A great book on narrative nonfiction. Not written with audio in mind but offers a lot of insight that narrative podcasters can make good use of.

ONLINE RESOURCES

"Audience 98" by David Giovannoni, Leslie Peters, John Sutton, and others (arapublic.com, 1997).

prndg.org/docs/sample-audience-98.pdf

A compendium of articles written as part of public radio's last major audience data project. Articulated many principles and ideas that form the basis of public radio's programming and appeal. Still very relevant and many concepts are applicable to podcasting as well.

"Story Structure 101" by Dan Harmon.

channel101.fandom.com/wiki/Story_Structure_101:_Super _Basic_Shit

"6 Pieces of Bad Advice We Give Air Talent" by Fred Jacobs.

jacobsmedia.com/6-pieces-of-bad-advice-we-give-air-talent-2/

"The Schwartz Technique: How to Get Vivid Colour and Riveting Detail from Your Interview" by Jacob Kreutzfeldt.

cbc.ca/radio/docproject/blog/the-schwartz-technique-how-to-get -vivid-colour-and-riveting-detail-from-your-interview-1.3938069

"Podcast Success in One Graph" by Steve Pratt.

blog.pacific-content.com/podcast-success-in-one-graph-creative
-bravery-x-commitment-43c89ecb82df

"The Turnaround: Interviewers Interviewed" by Jesse Thorn.

maximumfun.org/shows/the-turnaround

INDEX

A

Abbott, David P., 121
action, 113, 117–118
Ahearn, Mary, 249
Allusionist, The, 174
*Amazing Adventures of Kavalier & Clay,
    The* (Chabon), 23–24
Amazon, 207–208
ambition, 73–75
"American" style, 100
Anderson, Chris, 66 (footnote 15)
Anna Faris Is Unqualified, 59–60
answering back, 166–171
Apple, 242–245, 247–249
Art of Gathering, The (Parker), 225
Ask Me Another, 13–14, 33, 168, 227–230
asking questions
    advice regarding, 103–105
    being quiet, 83–87
    editing, 92–99
    interviews, 90–92
    introduction to, 76–81
    listening, 83–87
    preparedness, 87–89
    rapport, 89–91
    Schwartz Technique, 99–103
    wondering, 81–83
attention grabber, 127
audience building
    overview of, 149–164
    pitching, 178–190
    tactics for, 163–177
audience/listeners
    asking for help from, 158–159, 169–171
    effect on, 48–49, 53, 55, 57–58
    feedback from, 166–172
    finding your, 40–49
    focus on, 49, 69

identifying, 53, 54, 56
knowing your, 181–182
taking it to, 176–177
target, 40–49, 156–157
authenticity, 25, 30
autonomy, 220–221
avatar bios, 42–47, 56
avatars, 40–49

B

Bakaya, Mohit, 179–181, 183
Baker, Jesse, 98, 168
Bannon, Chris, 179–181
Beaubien, Jason, 211
being quiet, 83–87
bespoke porn, 217–218
Bezos, Jeff, 207
binary, avoiding, 66, 209–212
blogging technology, 234–236
Bolz-Weber, Nadia, 64
boredom, 215
Bowers, Andy, 179–181, 185
Box ritual, 225
brainstorming sessions, 55–56
Branson, Richard, 17–18, 40
Bryant, Andy, 198–199
Bryant Park Project, The, 2–5, 13
budgets, 13, 26, 162, 186–187
Butterfly Effect, The, 217–222

C

Campbell, Joseph, 70, 123–124
Carter, Graydon, 35
Chabon, Michael, 23–24
characters, 23–25, 111–119, 188–189,
    197–199

Chart, The, 161–163
closed ending, 119
cold pitches, 186–187
comedy podcasts, 45–46, 49, 192
Commitment, 160–163
community, building, 190–192
companion medium, 11, 23
compelling stories and ideas, 20–23
complication, 115, 118–120, 125, 230
confidence, 2, 22, 81, 185
constraints, form and, 61, 74–75
content (term), avoidance of, 8
conversations, 61–62, 67–69, 130–131,
    154, 161
Cox, David, 205
Creative Bravery, 161–162
creative laziness, 17
creative teams, leading
    avoiding the binary, 66, 209–212
    introduction to, 194–196, 208–210,
        218–222
    mistakes, 203, 208–210
    offering opportunities, 220–224
    planning for 50 percent, 212–217
    problems as possibilities, 217–219
    Sacred Time, 223–225
    strategy mantra, 194–202
    what doesn't change, 207–209
curiosity, 25, 79, 81, 89, 104–105
Curry, Adam, 233–235, 241–243

D

Daily Source Code, 240–243
"Danish" style, 100, 109
Dawn and Drew Show, The, 241
Death, Sex & Money, 223–224
deep dives, 72–75
diagramming the story, 126–128
discovery, moment of, 22
DIY networking, 163–165
Domkus, Drew, 241
Doyle, Bob, 237–238

du Plantier, Sophie Tuscan, 126
dumb questions, 89
Dunne, Finley Peter, 48 (footnote 10)

E

Eaton, N'Jeri, 179–180, 186
"echo" bookings, 18
editing, 60–61, 92–99, 104, 133–134
    effect on listeners, 48–49, 53, 55, 57–58
Eisenberg, Ophira, 228
email, answering, 165–166
emotional anchor/highlight, 24, 189
empathy, 12, 43, 47
empty modifiers, 35
engaging characters, 20, 23–25
episodic narrative, 63, 69–70
Eric's Forbidden Word List, 34–35
Essentialism (McKeown), 32
Evans, Dixie, 111
Exotic World, 110–113

F

failure, 202–207, 214
fame economy, 171
feedback, 30, 36, 136–140, 158–160,
    166–168, 188–189, 205
field interviews, 80
50 percent, planning for, 212–217
floating ball routine, 121–122
focus, 32, 49, 53–58, 102–103, 114–115,
    127–128, 138–139, 188–189, 195,
    196 (footnote 49), 197, 207–209
focus on what doesn't change, 207–209
Folk Alley, 171–172
follow-up questions, 84–86, 105
form, 58–75, 96, 165
Four-Pointed Circle, 52–58, 63, 69–71
Fresh Air, 62, 84–85, 104–105
Full Schwartz, 99–103
function, 50–58
FX, 198–199

G

Gano, Gordon, 77
Gilkey, David, 211
Gillmor, Steve, 240
Gillmor Gang, 240
Glass, Ira, 38–39, 110–111, 122,
    140–148, 249
Godard, Jean-Luc, 122
Gregoire, Danny, 241
Gross, Terry, 79, 84–85, 103–105
guerrilla marketing, 155–160
guest, being a, 159, 173, 237

H

Half Schwartz, 102–103
Hammersley, Ben, 241
Harmon, Dan, 124, 252
hatred, 16–17
Health and Living podcasts, 46–47
help, asking audience for, 158–159,
    169–171
Hero with a Thousand Faces, The
    (Campbell), 123
hero's journey, the (Campbell), 70, 123
Herrera, Mike, 25–26, 27
high concept, 21, 33, 39–40
highbrow, 21
Hollywood ending, 119
Holmes, Linda, 28
host, you as, 54–55, 63, 173, 175, 224
*How to Lose Friends and Alienate
    People* (Young), 35
humility, 2, 55
"hunger by proxy," 25

I

ideas, 131–132
Iggy Pop, 16–17
important stories, 128–131
influencers, 159

InspiroBot, 140–148
Interviewer, role of, 78–79
interviews. *See* asking questions
intimacy, 11, 30, 47, 116, 156
Invisibilia, 4–5, 33, 63, 200
iOS 245, 247–248
Iraq War, 237
IT Conversations, 240
iTunes, 26, 242, 243–245, 247

J

Jacobs, Fred, 210
jargon, 36
Jobs, Steve, 242–245, 247
Joey Reynolds Show, 82–83
journalism, 112, 128–131, 183–184

K

Kagan, Eleanor, 175
Kaye, Doug, 240
Kernis, Jay, 211, 250
Koenig, Sarah, 125–126

L

land the ending, 180, 184–187
Lane, Nathan, 84–85
lead by serving, 6
Leadley, Rob, 161
Lee, Hae Min, 125–126
length of podcast, 60–61, 71, 95, 130
lessons, 113, 119–120
Letson, Al, 108
Levinson, Jay Conrad, 154–156
likability, 25
listener surveys, 167–172
listeners. *See* audience/listeners
live events, 29–30, 175–177
logging your tape, 96–99, 144, 147
Lore, 19, 75
Lydon, Christopher, 236–242

M

"Magic Show, The," 121–122
marketing, 149–164
Maron, Marc, 59, 62, 74, 189–191
Martinez, Matt, 3
Mawer, Charlie, 198–199
Maximum Fun, 189–192
McCarthy, Cormac, 109
McConnell, Ben, 171–173
McGrath, Mary, 236
McKee, Robert, 119
McKeown, Scott, 32
message, identifying, 53, 54–55,
    56–58
Miceli, Dawn, 241
Miller, Lulu, 5
Misitzis, Lina, 219
Missing Richard Simmons,
    184–185
mistakes, 25, 103, 105, 202–207
monomyth template, 123–124
morals, 70–71, 119–120
Morning Coffee Notes, 240–241
motivations, 113, 116–118
multiple narratives, 63

N

narratives, types of, 62–63
networks, 149 (footnote 36),
    163–165
Neumeier, Marty, 195, 196
    (footnote 49)
niche podcasts, 26–27
Nielsen consumer product study, 46–47

O

Obama, Barack, 189
"onliness statement," 195
open ending, 119
Open Source, 239

opening minutes, 127
opening the kimono, 159, 171–173
opportunities, offering, 219–223
outcome, desired, 48–49
Outside/In, 32, 34
overconfidence, 2
overpreparation, 88–89

P

Pacific Content, 161–162
Parker, Priya, 225
passion, 230–231
Penn and Teller, 121–122
people chatting, 61–62
people telling stories, 62–63
Perel, Esther, 64–66
Pistorius, Martin, 4–5
pitching, 177–189
podcasts
    defining, 8–12
    expectations of, 12
    length of, 60–61
    pivotal moments regarding, 101,
        233–249
Pop Culture Happy Hour, 28–30
Pratt, Steve, 161–163
prep work, 59
preparedness, 87–89, 104–105
problems as possibilities, 217–219
production detail, 26
protagonist, 125
provocations, 70–71

Q

questions
    and answers, 62
    dumb, 89
    follow-up, 84–86
    unanswered, 117
    "why," 35
    See also asking questions

R

Rafsanjani, Nazanin, 179–180
rants, 60–61
rapport, 77, 89–91
Raz, Guy, 49, 71–75
resistance, 113, 118–119, 230
resolution, 113, 119, 125
resources, 73–75
Reunert, Willy, 100
Reynolds, Joey, 82–83
risk tolerance, 204–207
Road, The (McCarthy), 109
Rogan, Joe, 39, 247
Ronson, Jon, 217, 221–222
RSS code, 233–236

S

Sacred Time, 223–225
Sale, Anna, 223–225
sameness, 18–19
scenes, 113, 114–115
Schwartz, Stephen, 100, 101
Schwartz Technique, 99–103
seasonal narratives, 62–63, 69
Seeger, Pete, 246
self-narrated storytelling, 100
Serial, 62–63, 125–126, 184–185, 245,
    247, 248–249
Shapiro, Alexandra, 198
Sibley, Destry, 184
Sincerely, X, 33
Six-Lunch Test Drive, 128, 134–136
Slow Hiker Theory, 221–222
Snap Judgment, 24, 27, 63, 131
social media, 154, 163–165, 171–172,
    203, 248
Soloway, Jill, 225
Song Exploder, 75
sound design, 132–134
Sound of Young America, The, 190
So-What Factor, 40

"Spark" Project, 214
specificity, 34–37
Spiegel, Alix, 5
Spirit of Hessle Road, The, 109–110
Star Wars, 110, 124
Stewart, Alison, 3
stories
    action in, 117–118
    audio format for, 132
    characters in, 115–117
    compelling, 20–23
    defining, 110–113
    elements of, 113
    feedback for, 136–140
    Glass on, 140–148
    ideas for, 131–132
    "important," 128–131
    introduction to, 106–110
    lesson of, 119–120
    motivation and, 116–118
    pitching and, 180–189
    reasons for telling, 182–184
    resistance in, 118–119
    resolution of, 119
    scenes of, 114–115
    Six-Lunch Test Drive for, 128,
        134–136
    sound with, 132–134
    structure of, 122–128, 140–142
    twists in, 120–122
Story (McKee), 119
"Story Circle" technique, 124
strategy mantra, 195–202
streaming technology, 236–237
structure
    for interviews, 90–92, 96
    story, 122–128
surveys, 167–169, 171

T

target audience, 40–49, 167, 176, 182
Tavis Smiley Show, The, 13

TED Radio Hour, 32, 35, 49, 66–69, 71–73
Teller, Penn and, 121–122
Ten-Word Description, 31–39, 50, 52, 87, 93, 118, 158, 181, 196
This American Life, 9, 24, 38–39, 100, 110, 121–123, 131, 140–149, 247, 248, 249
This Is Radio, 103–104
Thorn, Jesse, 189–192
time, as resource, 73–75
time commitment, 58–60
transcriptions, 98–99
"tribes," 27, 246
"truth speakers," 56
TV Brand Builders, The (Bryant and Mawer), 198, 199
twists, 112–113, 117, 120–122, 188

U

unique voice, 20, 25–30
USA Network, 197–198

V

Valéry, Paul, 1
Violent Femmes interview, 76–77, 80
vision, defining, 31–39
visualization, 100
voice, 20, 25–30

W

Walker-Brown, Hana, 109–110
Weekend All Things Considered, 75
weird, focus on, 25
West Cork, 33, 118, 126
what doesn't change, 207–209
Where Should We Begin? with Esther Perel, 64–66
WhiskeyCats, 20
"why" questions, 35
Winer, Dave, 233–237, 239–242
WKSU, 6, 250
wondering, 81–83
work/life balance, 216
WTF, 59–60, 62, 189–190

Y

you, as host, 53–54, 57
You Can Write a Novel Kit, 106–107
Young, Toby, 35
YouTube, 246

Z

Zaltzman, Helen, 174

ABOUT THE AUTHOR

ERIC NUZUM is a media consultant and creator of podcasts. Since 2005, he has made podcasts that routinely top the charts, appear in yearly "best of" lists, win awards, and generate hundreds of millions of downloads. He is considered a leading "go-to" creative strategist in audio, podcasting, radio, and spoken word entertainment. He has led the podcast and original programming efforts at NPR and Audible (an Amazon company) and now is the cofounder of Magnificent Noise, a podcast and creative consulting company based in New York City.

Eric has written three other books: a polemic against music censorship (*Parental Advisory: Music Censorship in America*), a cultural deep dive on vampires (*The Dead Travel Fast: Stalking Vampires from Nosferatu to Count Chocula*), and a memoir (*Giving Up the Ghost: A Story about Friendship, 80s Rock, a Lost Scrap of Paper, and What It Means to Be Haunted*).

Otherwise, Eric wastes a lot of time arguing with his friends in bars, reading, listening to music, and playing one mean game of Canasta. He and his family live in Montclair, New Jersey.